R. Gupta's®

JNU
Jawaharlal Nehru University

BA (Hons.)
3 Years

Foreign Languages Entrance Exam

Previous Years' Papers
(Solved)

Cluster-1: French, German, Russian & Spanish
Cluster-2: Japanese, Korean & Chinese
Cluster-3: Persian, Arabic & Pashto

2020 EDITION

RAMESH PUBLISHING HOUSE, NEW DELHI

Published by
O.P. Gupta *for* Ramesh Publishing House

Admin. Office
12-H, New Daryaganj Road, Opp. Officers' Mess,
New Delhi-110002 ① 23261567, 23275224, 23275124

E-mail: info@rameshpublishinghouse.com
Website: www.rameshpublishinghouse.com

Showroom
● Balaji Market, Nai Sarak, Delhi-6 ① 23253720, 23282525
● 4457, Nai Sarak, Delhi-6, ① 23918938

Book Code: R-1923

ISBN: 978-93-86845-50-4

HSN Code: 49011010

CONTENTS

———————

Jawaharlal Nehru University (JNU)
BA (Hons.) Entrance Examination, 2019*

CLUSTER-1: French, German, Russian and Spanish

1. Which of these countries does not share a border with France?
   A. Belgium
   B. Luxembourg
   C. Germany
   D. Portugal

2. Which among the following rivers is the longest?
   A. Seine
   B. Loire
   C. Garonne
   D. Rhone

3. The Nazi Party was a ....
   A. Fascist party
   B. Democratic party
   C. Socialist party
   D. Neoconservative party

4. Which colours can we see on Spanish flag?
   A. Red & White
   B. Blue & Yellow
   C. Red & Yellow
   D. Red & Blue

5. Who among the following is not a famous Spanish Painter?
   A. Francisco de Goya
   B. Pablo Picasso
   C. Salvador Dali
   D. Ana Maria Matute

6. Where is Spain located?
   A. North of Germany and West of Poland
   B. South of France and East of Portugal
   C. East of Italy and East of France
   D. Right next to Greece

7. Who was the first woman in space?
   A. Sunita Williams
   B. Valentina Tereskova
   C. Kalpana Chawla
   D. Ilya Petrova

8. Until today, France has had how many Republics?
   A. Two
   B. Three
   C. Four
   D. Five

9. Which of the following separates Spain from Africa?
   A. Strait of Malacca
   B. Strait of Magellan
   C. Strait of Gibraltar
   D. Strait of Waist

10. Which of the following colours are not there in the flag of the Russian Federation?
    A. White
    B. Blue
    C. Red
    D. Green

11. France has a coastline measuring:
    A. 5500 kms
    B. 7900 kms
    C. 2400 kms
    D. 1000 kms

12. The Blue Danube is ....
    A. A river
    B. A musical composition
    C. None of the above
    D. Both (A) and (B)

13. Which of the following countries has the largest surface area?
    A. Spain
    B. Germany
    C. France
    D. Italy

14. How many time zones are there in Russia?
    A. Nine
    B. Thirteen
    C. Eleven
    D. Seven

15. Beethoven was ....
    A. Not a labrador puppy
    B. In all likelihood not an unmusical person
    C. None of the above
    D. All of the above

16. The Brandenburg Gate is in ....
A. Brandengrub   B. Berlin
C. Bremen   D. Bockstadt

17. What is the name of the peninsula where Spain and Portugal are located?
A. Sinai Peninsula   B. Iberian Peninsula
C. Peloponnese   D. Catalonia

18. What currency was used in Spain prior to the change to the Euro?
A. Peseta   B. Dollar
C. Escudo   D. Corona

19. The "Social Contract" was written by:
A. Montesquieu
B. Jean-Jacques Rousseau
C. Voltaire
D. Diderot

20. What was the Islamic region of Spain called?
A. Magreb   B. Alcantara
C. Al-Andalus   D. Basque

21. The Kourou space centre from which the European Ariane rocket are launched are located in:
A. French Polynesia
B. French Guyana
C. Reunion Islands
D. Nouvelle Caledonte

22. Which of the following men has not been the President of France?
A. Giscard d'Estaing
B. Gérard Depardieu
C. François Mitterrand
D. Nicolas Sarkozy

23. Napolean Bonaparte belonged to:
A. Early 16th century
B. Early 17th century
C. Early 20th century
D. Early 19th century

24. The Reichstag Dome was designed by:
A. Frank Gehry   B. Norman Foster
C. Renzo Piano   D. Rem Koolhaas

25. Who is the first man in space?
A. Neil Armstrong   B. John Warner
C. Edwin Aldrin   D. Yuri Gagarin

26. Which is the national animal of Russia?
A. Bear   B. Lion
C. Tiger   D. Wolf

27. The prehistoric Frescoes in the French caves are located in:
A. Montignac (Dordogne region)
B. Rhone-Alpes region
C. Parisian Basin
D. Aquitain Basin

28. The highest mountain peak is found in which mountain range:
A. Vosges   B. Pyrénées
C. Massif Central D. Alpes

29. The Three Musketeers is a French historical adventure novel written by:
A. Jules Verne   B. Alexandre Dumas
C. Jean-Paul Sartre   D. Gustave Flaubert

30. The famous poet Octavio Paz is from:
A. Spain   B. Mexico
C. Argentina   D. USA

31. Daimler has its headquarters in ....
A. Stuttgart   B. Karlsruhe
C. Bremen   D. Mannheim

32. Who invented the periodic table?
A. John Dalton   B. Lothar Meyer
C. Dmitri Mendeleev   D. William Odling

33. The Holocaust refers to the brutal murder of millions of ....
A. Christians
B. Jews
C. Jews homosexuals, leftists, and other minorities
D. All of the above

34. The author of the famous comic strip Tintin belongs to:
A. Switzerland   B. France
C. Belgium   D. Canada

35. Nelly Sachs, Elfriede Jelinek, and Herta Muller have the following in common:
A. The Nobel Prize for Peace
B. The Nobel Prize for Chemistry
C. The George Buchner Prize
D. None of the above

36. During the Second World War, Germany did not invade ....
A. Russia   B. Poland
C. Switzerland   D. All of the above

37. The second largest religion in France is:
A. Islam   B. Buddhism
C. Christianity   D. Shintoism

38. In which city can you visit the Sagrada Familia Church?
A. Salamanca   B. Granada
C. Barcelona   D. Madrid

39. "Hundred years of Solitude" is written by:
A. Gabriel Garcia Marquez
B. Mario Varas Llosa
C. Pablo Neruda
D. Gabriela Mistral

40. "Tapas" is:
A. An appetizer or snack
B. A dance form
C. A famous mountain
D. A river in Spain

41. Which dynasty ruled Russia before the Revolution of 1917?
A. Khan   B. Tudor
C. Romanov   D. Rublov

42. Which one of the following languages is not from Spain?
A. Basque   B. Galician
C. Castilian   D. Guarani

43. Which Russian revolutionary leader was murdered in Mexico in 1940?
A. Leonld Brezhnev   B. Leon Trotsky
C. Sergei Kirov   D. Joseph Stalin

44. There are three major dynasties from which France can claim its identity. Find the odd man out:
A. Merovingian   B. Carolingian
C. Capetian   D. Napoleonian

45. Mont Blanc is the highest peak in Europe located in:
A. Italy   B. Switzerland
C. France   D. Germany

46. Which of the four novels is French?
A. Anna Karenina   B. Don Quixote
C. Ulysses   D. Germinal

47. Which is the deepest lake in the world?
A. Baikal   B. Chilka
C. Vostok   D. Tanganyika

48. Which of these is a strong wind sweeping down the Rhone valley?
A. Adrets   B. Ubacs
C. Mistral   D. Oceanic

49. Who said, "After me the deluge"?
A. Louis XIV   B. Louis XVI
C. Napoleon   D. Louis XV

50. Austria signed the Schengen Agreement in:
A. 1993   B. 1994
C. 1995   D. 1996

ANSWERS

1	2	3	4	5	6	7	8	9	10
D	B	A	C	D	B	B	D	C	D

11	12	13	14	15	16	17	18	19	20
A	B	C	C	B	B	B	A	A	C

21	22	23	24	25	26	27	28	29	30
B	B	D	B	D	A	A	D	B	B

31	32	33	34	35	36	37	38	39	40
A	C	C	C	D	C	A	C	A	A

41	42	43	44	45	46	47	48	49	50
C	D	B	D	C	D	A	C	D	C

Jawaharlal Nehru University (JNU)
BA (Hons.) Entrance Examination, 2019*

CLUSTER-2: Japanese, Korean and Chinese

SECTION-A

1. In an artificial language, Rabbonmiya means sweetheart; Gaffuniya means sugar powder; Juooniga means lime juice, then

Which word could mean 'Sweet Lime powder'?
A. Rabbnigaraboonniya B. Rabboniganiya
C. Rabbonigagaffu D. Rabbojuooniya

2. Complete the series:
2, 3, 5, 9, 17, 33, 65, ?
A. 129 B. 125
C. 164 D. 121

3. In a certain language, "sun shines brightly" is written as "ba lo sul", "houses are brightly lit" as "kadoulaariba"; and "light comes from sun" as "dopikup lo nro". What would the code for "sun" and "brightly" be?
A. Ba sul B. Sul lo
C. Lo ba D. Na nro

4. Choose the word which is different from the rest:
A. Deer B. Hippopotamus
C. Rhinoceros D. Unicorn

5. If "she goes to school" is "Qz atv x qves; and "She meets her friend" is "Qz poiz tu cvxy". What could be "She went to school to meet a frined"?
A. Qz cvxy x qves x spartv tu
B. Qz spatv x qves x poiz I cvxy
C. Qz cvxy x spatv x qves poiz
D. Qz spatv x atv x poiz tu cvxy

6. The total of the ages of A, B and C is 80 years. What was the total of their ages three years ago:
A. 71 B. 72
C. 74 D. 77

7. What is the product of all the numbers on the dial of a telephone?
A. 1,58,480 B. 1,59,450
C. 1,59,480 D. None of the above

8. If ROSE is coded as 6821; CHAIR as 73456; and PREACH as 961473, then what will be the code for SEARCH?
A. 246173 B. 214673
C. 214763 D. 216473

9. Arrange the words below in a meaningful sequence:

1. Yarn 2. Plant 3. Saree 4. Cotton 5. Cloth
A. 2, 4, 5, 1, 3 B. 2, 1, 4, 5, 3
C. 2, 4, 1, 5, 3 D. 2, 4, 5, 3, 1

10. If you write down all the numbers from 1 to 100, then how many times do you write 3?
A. 11 B. 18
C. 20 D. 21

11. Find out the missing number:

20, 19, 17, ?, 10, 5
A. 14 B. 15
C. 13 D. 11

12. If A is the brother of B; B is the sister of C; and C is the father of D, how is D related to A?
A. Brother
B. Sister
C. Nephew
D. Cannot be determined

13. Choose the word which is different from the rest:
A. Stereo
B. Radio
C. Television
D. Loudspeaker

14. Complete the series:
5, 16, 49, 104, ?
A. 171
B. 191
C. 181
D. 161

15. In a certain code, TEACHER is written as VGCEJGT. How would CHILDREN be written in that code?
A. EJKNEGTP
B. EGKNFITP
C. EJKNFGTO
D. EJKNFTGP

SECTION-B

1. The school .... quality education in a home-like environment.
A. requires
B. hires
C. suggests
D. provides

2. Complete the idiomatic expression:

As thick as ....
A. Thieves
B. Dictionary
C. Grass
D. Friends

3. Complete the idiomatic expression:
As smooth as ....
A. Skin
B. Kitten
C. Baby
D. Velvet

4. There is no exception .... this rule.
A. for
B. at
C. to
D. about

5. I am going to buy something for dinner from the Chinese take ....
A. away
B. out
C. off
D. in

6. Complete shutdown .... observed today against the new law.
A. is being
B. is been
C. can be
D. was been

7. Choose the equivalent for the expression 'at the spur of the moment'.
A. A difficult moment
B. Without delay
C. Great moment
D. Very slow

8. What is the equivalent for the word 'remote'.
A. Distant
B. Automatic
C. Extremely
D. Near

9. Choose the correctly spelt word:
A. Occassionally
B. Ocassionally
C. Occasionally
D. Occasionaly

10. A .... is a person who is very rich and powerful, especially in industry.
A. Magnate
B. Tyrant
C. Radical
D. Dictator

11. Choose the correctly spelt word from the following:
A. Itenerary
B. Itinarary
C. Itinerary
D. Itinerery

12. The committee .... decided to launch 'Green Land' Project for the commemoration of Pt. Jawaharlal Nehru's 130th birthday.
A. proposed
B. unanimously
C. strongly
D. recommended

13. Choose the equivalent for the expression 'at the drop of the hat'.
A. As soon as it was spoken
B. Done easily, without any preparation
C. Done in an instant
D. After something is done

14. Fill in the blanks with the correct word.

Warning! No authorized personnel .... this point.
A. beyond
B. about
C. from
D. on

15. I don't have .... money to buy a new house.
A. enough
B. very much
C. little
D. too much

SECTION-C

1. The river on the border of China and North Korea is:
A. Yalu
B. Imjin
C. Han
D. Naktong

2. Which capital city is divided into two parts by a main river?
A. Beijing
B. Tokyo
C. New Delhi
D. Seoul

3. The grandfather of the current President of North Korea was:
A. Kim II Sung
B. Kim Dae Jung
C. Kim Jong-Eun
D. Kim Jong-II

4. The period of rapid economic growth in Korea is also know as:
A. Magic of Hallasan Mountain
B. Miracle of Land of Morning Calm
C. Magic on Tuman River
D. Miracle on the Han River

5. The 9th BRICS Summit was held in:
A. New Delhi, India
B. Xiamen, China
C. Brasilia, Brazil
D. Yekaterinburg, Russia

6. Who is the author of the book 'Around the World in Eighty Days'?
A. William Shakespeare
B. V.S. Naipaul
C. Jules Verne
D. William Wordsworth

7. Osama Bin Laden was killed in Pakistan by the Special US forces known as:
A. MARINE
B. COBRA
C. SEAL
D. BLACKCAT

8. Which of the following is not a name of a Japanese dish?
A. Sushi
B. Sashimi
C. Bulgogi
D. Okonomiyaki

9. Which country is not the part of the Shanghai Cooperation Organization?
A. India
B. China
C. Pakistan
D. Afghanistan

10. Who is the first person to reach North Pole?
A. Robert Peary
B. Charles Hillary
C. Johan Don
D. Edmund Hillary

11. This desert is the largest desert in Asia and is the fifth largest in the world.
A. Thar desert, India
B. Tottori, Japan
C. Gobi, Mangolia
D. Mui Ne, Vietnam

12. Which is the longest river of Japan?
A. Shinano River
B. Sumida River
C. Tone River
D. Arakawa River

13. The crux of Confucian thought is:
A. Benevolence
B. Trust
C. Propriety
D. Loyalty

14. Which of the following is the largest island of Japan?
A. Hokkaido
B. Honshu
C. Kyushu
D. Shikoku

15. Who among the following Chinese nationals has been awarded Padma Bhushan by the Indian Government?
A. Tan Chung
B. Ji Xianlin
C. Zhou Enlai
D. Tan Yunshan

16. Which of the following planets is known as "Morning Star"?
A. Mercury
B. Venus
C. Mars
D. Jupiter

17. Which country has accused China of currency manipulation?
A. Russia
B. India
C. United States
D. South Korea

18. The 2010 World Cup Football tournament was held in:
A. Austria
B. Germany
C. South Africa
D. Turin

19. Who is regarded as the first patriotic poet of China?
A. Li Bai
B. Tu Fu
C. Bai Juyi
D. Qu Yuan

20. Boxers Revolution took place in:
  A. United States   B. South Africa
  C. China   D. Spain

21. The capital of which of the following means 'Red Hero'.
  A. Japan   B. Mongolia
  C. China   D. Korea

22. What is the name given to Japan's national legislature?
  A. Parliament   B. Duma
  C. Diet   D. Congress

23. Which flower represents the imperial family of Japan?
  A. Sunflower   B. Chrysanthemum
  C. Tulip   D. Orchid

24. The two countries sharing the same date of independence "15th August" are:
  A. India and China
  B. India and Korea
  C. India and Japan
  D. India and Vietnam

25. Which of the following is not a permanent member of the UN Security Council?
  A. China   B. Russia
  C. Japan   D. France

26. Which state has the largest coastline in India?
  A. Gujarat   B. Tamil Nadu
  C. Karnataka   D. Andhra Pradesh

27. In which year did Japan host its first summer Olympics?
  A. 1972   B. 1964
  C. 1948   D. 1952

28. The large woodblocks with carving of the entire Buddhist canon in Korea are known as:
  A. Tripicana   B. Tripikoryo
  C. Tripitaka   D. Tripioka

29. China's National day is celebrated on:
  A. 2nd October   B. 1st October
  C. 15th October   D. 26th January

30. The election of the South Korean Assembly is held every:
  A. 5 years
  B. Whenever a new President is elected
  C. 3 years
  D. 4 years

SECTION-D

Directions (Qs. 1-2): *Read the following passage and answer the questions:*

In the 16th century, an age of great terrestrial exploration, Ferdinand Magellan led the first expedition to sail around the world. As a young Portuguese noble, he served the king of Portugal, but he became involved in the quagmire of political intrigue at court and lost the king's favour. After he was dismissed from service by the king of Portugal, he went to Spain and offered his services to the Emperor of Spain.

1. Magellan lost the favour of the king of Portugal when he became involved in a political ....
  A. discussion   B. negotiation
  C. bargain   D. entanglement

2. The 16th century was an age of great .... exploration.
  A. land   B. cosmic
  C. mental   D. None of the above

Directions (Qs. 3-5): *Read the following passage and answer the questions:*

The world's nuclear plants have accumulated vast stocks of highly radioactive waste. Worldwide, high-level waste is currently stored above ground, and no government has a clear policy on its eventual disposal. While most experts believe that burying the waste is the safest bet in the long term, the problem is finding sites that everyone can agree are geologically stable. Decaying radioactive isotopes release heat. As a result, high-level waste must be constantly cooled; otherwise, it becomes dangerously hot. This is why many experts want to store waste above ground until it has decayed and is cool enough to be stored safely in sealed repositories several hundreds of metres below ground. According to one recent theory, however, waste should be lowered down boreholes drilled to 4 kilometres. The trick is to exploit heat generated by the waste to fuse the surrounding rock and contain any leaking radioactivity.

3. The passage describes a new method, still only a theoretical one, for the disposal of radioactive waste.
A. in which the radioactive isotopes are prevented from releasing heat
B. at a depth considerably less than the normally recommended but the chosen site must meet certain geological requirements
C. whereby the heat produced by the waste will serve to seal it safely into the rock under which it has been buried
D. which uses bore holes so that all sites are suitable

4. It is clear from the passage that the safe disposal of radioactive waste:
A. is a problem that has not attracted enough attention
B. remains a global problem of great magnitude
C. is a problem that each government must decide for its own country
D. will in all likelihood soon be resolved, and a clear policy agreed upon by concerned governments

5. As it is pointed out in the passage, many experts are of the opinion that radioactive waste:
A. should not be stored underground while the radioactive isotopes continue to let off substantial amounts of heat
B. does not require to be cooled when stored above ground
C. cannot be safely disposed of anywhere and the problem of what to do with it intensifies as the amount increases
D. should never be stored underground as it cannot then be monitored

ANSWERS

SECTION-A

1	2	3	4	5	6	7	8	9	10
D	A	C	D	B	A	D	B	C	C

11	12	13	14	15
A	D	C	C	D

SECTION-B

1	2	3	4	5	6	7	8	9	10
D	A	D	C	A	A	B	A	C	A

11	12	13	14	15
C	B	B	A	A

SECTION-C

1	2	3	4	5	6	7	8	9	10
A	D	A	D	B	C	C	C	D	A

11	12	13	14	15	16	17	18	19	20
C	A	A	B	B	B	C	C	D	C

21	22	23	24	25	26	27	28	29	30
B	C	B	B	C	A	B	C	B	D

SECTION-D

1	2	3	4	5
D	A	D	B	A

Jawaharlal Nehru University (JNU)
BA (Hons.) Entrance Examination, 2019*

CLUSTER-3: Persian, Arabic and Pashto

SECTION-A

1. Which is the third holiest city in Islam?
   A. Ajmer
   B. Medina
   C. Jerusalem
   D. Mecca

2. The northern and southern regions of which Arab Gulf country were united in 1990?
   A. UAE
   B. Oman
   C. Saudi Arabia
   D. Yemen

3. Match the country with the correct official name of the language spoken there:
   1. Iran   (*a*) Tajik
   2. Iraq   (*b*) Dari
   3. Afghanistan   (*c*) Arabic
   4. Tajikistan   (*d*) Farsi

   Choose the correct match:

	1	2	3	4
A.	(*c*)	(*d*)	(*b*)	(*a*)
B.	(*c*)	(*d*)	(*a*)	(*b*)
C.	(*d*)	(*c*)	(*b*)	(*a*)
D.	(*d*)	(*c*)	(*a*)	(*b*)

4. Which among the following is not a work of Kalidas?
   A. Abhigyan
   B. Meghdoot
   C. Shakuntalam
   D. Geetgovind

5. Iran has the world's second-largest proved gas reserves after:
   A. USA
   B. Russia
   C. Indonesia
   D. Saudi Arabia

6. Each of the following questions contains two statements followed by two conclusions numbered I and II. You have to consider the two statements to be true, even if they seem to be at variance with the commonly known facts. You have to decide which of the given conclusions definitely follows from the given statements.

   Give answer:
   A. if only I follows
   B. if only II follows
   C. if neither I nor II follows and
   D. if both I and II follow

   Statement: Some Iranians are Parsis.
   All Persians are Iranians

   Conclusions: I. Some Persions are Parsis.
   II. Some Parsis are Persians.

7. In name of the Dubai Towar *"Burj Khalifa"*, what does the word "Burj" mean?
   A. Tomb
   B. Tower
   C. Dome
   D. Tallest Building

8. If in a certain language KINDLE is coded as ELDNIK, how is EXOTIC coded in that code?
   A. EOXITC
   B. EXOTLC
   C. CITOXE
   D. COXITE

9. According to Abrahamanic tradition who is considered the first prophet?
   A. Moses
   B. Muhammad
   C. Adam
   D. Jesus

10. The second language in which the great bilingual poet Mirza Ghalib composed poetry besides Urdu was:
A. Hindi
B. Persian
C. Punjabi
D. Sindhi

11. Flexible : Rigid :: Confidence : ?
A. Indifference
B. Cowardice
C. Scare
D. Diffidence

12. Fill in the blanks with appropriate option:

Egg : Fish :: .... : Plant
A. Stem
B. Leaf
C. Seed
D. Root

13. Which Indian city was called 'the Shiraz of Hind'?
A. Kanpur
B. Jaunpur
C. Fatehpur
D. Gorakhpur

14. Afghanistan is bordered by three Central Asian countires in the north. Choose the correct combination:
A. Turkmenistan, Uzbekistan and Tajikistan
B. Kazakhstan, Uzbekistan and Tajikistan
C. Kyrgyzstan, Uzbekistan and Tajikistan
D. Turkmenistan, Uzbekistan, Kazakhstan

15. The Dead Sea, a Salt Lake lies on the:
A. Eastern borders of Jordon
B. Western borders of Jordon
C. Southern borders of Jordon
D. Northern borders of Jordon

16. The second largest language spoken in Afghanistan after Pashto is:
A. Dari
B. Tajik
C. Uzbek
D. None of the above

17. Which of the following statements are correct regarding Dead Sea?
A. It is rich in mineral
B. Anyone who steps into it dies
C. Dead bodies are thrown into it
D. Its waters have dried out

18. Omar Khayyam has primarily composed poetry in the following form:
A. Ghazliyat
B. Rubaiyat
C. Mathnaviyat
D. Marsiyat

19. Each of the following questions contains two statements followed by two conclusions numbered I and II. You have to consider the two statements to be true, even if they seem to be at variance with the commonly known facts. You have to decide which of the given conclusions definitely follows from the given statements.

Give answer:
A. if only I follows
B. if only II follows
C. if neither I nor II follows and
D. if both I and II follow

Statement: All students are girls.
No girl is dull.

Conclusions: I. There are no boys in the class.
II. No student is dull.

20. The Sasanians were rulers of:
A. Saudi Arabia
B. India
C. Persia
D. Greece

21. "Al-Rabi al-Arabi" also known as "The Arab Spring" refers to:
A. Water source in the deserts of Arab
B. Peoples uprising in the Arab World
C. Iraq-Iran war
D. Allied Forces war against Iraq

22. The part VI of constitution of India is not applicable to:
A. Arunachal Pradesh
B. Jammu & Kashmir
C. Sikkim
D. Goa

23. United Arab Emirates, a country in Western Asia is a federation of:
A. Seven emirates
B. Six emirates
C. Five emirates
D. Four emirates

24. Which of these is not an official language of the United Nations?
A. Chinese
B. Arabic
C. Spanish
D. German

25. The Chabahar Port, the only seaport of Iran is located in:
A. Southwestern Iran
B. Southeastern Iran
C. Western Iran
D. Eastern Iran

26. Victory is related to Happiness in the same way as Failure is related to:
A. Defeat
B. Anger
C. Frustration
D. Sad

27. If BAD is written as YZW and SAME as HZNV, then LOVE will be coded as:
A. ROWN
B. OJUS
C. OLEV
D. NOPL

28. The only nation in the Middle East with both a Red Sea coast and a Persian Gulf coast is:
A. Qatar
B. UAE
C. Kuwait
D. Saudi Arabia

29. Which is the chief port of Israel?
A. Eilat
B. Tel Aviv
C. Haifa
D. Aqaba

30. The currency of United Arab Emirates is:
A. Dinar
B. Dirham
C. Riyal
D. Somoni

31. Which is the English equivalent of Pahalavi language of ancient Iran?
A. Old Persian
B. New Persian
C. Modern Persian
D. Middle Persian

32. Who is currently the crown Prince of Saudi Arabia?
A. Mohammed Bin Salman
B. Faisal ibn Saud
C. Mohammad Bin Abdul Aziz
D. Abdullah ibn Saud

33. How long a person should have practiced in a High Court to be eligible to be appointed as a Judge of Supreme Court of India?
A. 10 Years
B. 12 Years
C. 15 Years
D. 20 Years

34. From which language do the words algebra, sugar, and zero come?
A. Icelandic
B. Arabic
C. French
D. German

35. Complete the series with correct option to be placed at "?".

DKY, FJW, HIU, JHS, ?
A. KGR
B. LFQ
C. KFR
D. LGQ

36. The Surgical Strike Day was observed by India on:
A. 11th September
B. 29th September
C. 20th September
D. 24th September

37. Which of the following is a correct set of two official languages of the United Nations?
A. Hindi and Chinese
B. Arabic and Chinese
C. Japanese and French
D. Arabic and Hindi

38. Find the odd one out:
A. Echo
B. Resonance
C. Ear
D. Tone

39. What is the capital of Saudi Arabia?
A. Mecca
B. Cairo
C. Jeddah
D. Riyadh

40. Which Moghal emperor is supposed to have promoted Persian studies most in India?
A. Akbar the great
B. Shahjahan
C. Aurangzeb
D. Jahangir

41. The prime minister of India cannot participate in voting on a No-confidence motion against his/her government if he/she:
A. leads a coalition government
B. has minority in Rajya Sabha
C. is a member of Rajya Sabha
D. forbidden by speaker of Lok Sabha

42. Which of the following country does not have a single operating airport?
A. Syria   B. Iraq
C. Palestine   D. Qatar

43. Prime Minsiter Narendra Modi launched the 'Swachhata Hi Seva' movement on 15 September from:
A. Baba Sahib Ambedkar Higher Secondary School in Delhi
B. Baba Sahib Ambedkar Higher Secondary School in Pune
C. Baba Sahib Ambedkar Higher Secondary School in Mumbai
D. Baba Sahib Ambedkar Higher Secondary School in Kolkata

44. Saddam Husain of Iraq invaded Kuwait in the year:
A. 1990   B. 1995
C. 1989   D. 1993

45. Pointing to a photograph, a man said, "I have no brother or sister but that man's father is my father's son." Whose photograph was it?
A. His Nephew's   B. His grandson's
C. His son's   D. His own

46. Which among the following languages is the most influenced by Arabic language?
A. Urdu   B. Hindi
C. Pashto   D. Persian

47. In which of the following cities Elephant festival is celebrated annually?
A. Jaipur   B. Jodhpur
C. Kota   D. Ajmer

48. Which among the following countries does not have a border with Iraq?
A. Syria   B. Kuwait
C. Jordan   D. UAE

49. Which among the following ethnic groups does not belong to Afghanistan?
A. Persian   B. Pashtoon
C. Tajik   D. Uzbek

50. Consider the following statements:
I. Shirin Ebadi is the first Muslim woman to receive Nobel Prize.
II. Sir C.V. Raman is th first Asian to get a Nobel prize in Science.
III. Rabindranath Tagore is the first Asian Nobel laureate.

Choose the correct statement/statements:
A. Statements I and III are correct
B. Only statement I is correct
C. Statements II and III are correct
D. All of the above statements are correct

51. Select the correct synonyms of the following words
Fostering
A. Safeguarding   B. Ignoring
C. Neglecting   D. Nurturing

52. Atul failed in examination because none of his answers were .... to the questions asked.
A. allusive   B. pertinent
C. revealing   D. referential

53. Choose the word, which is the exact OPPOSITE of the given word.
Dissect
A. Divide   B. Dismember
C. Stitch   D. Analyse

54. Find the correctly spelt words:
A. Adulation   B. Adelution
C. Adulasion   D. Adalution

55. To keep one's ....
A. temper   B. mood
C. anger   D. happiness

56. Choose the correct option to fill in the blanks:
I have been told that the two brothers have fallen ....
A. through   B. out
C. upon   D. in

57. Choose the word, which is the exact OPPOSITE of the given word.
Relinquish
A. Deny   B. Renounce
C. Abdicate   D. Possess

58. Choose the correct option to fill in the blanks:

He has a lot of affection .... me.
A. with
B. on
C. for
D. in

59. To smell ....
A. cat
B. fox
C. rat
D. mat

60. Select the correct synonyms of the following words:

Massive
A. Little
B. Lump sum
C. Huge
D. Strong

61. Every human being is .... to the Almighty for his action on earth.
A. faithful
B. approachable
C. accountable
D. responsible

62. To pick ....
A. wholes
B. nails
C. holes
D. doles

63. Choose the correct option to fill in the blanks:

He took .... his hat while greeting him.
A. of
B. out
C. off
D. in

64. Find the correctly spelt words:
A. emancepation
B. emancipation
C. emansipasion
D. emunsipasion

65. Choose the correct option to fill in the blanks:

He has not recovered fully .... the injury he sustained in an accident.
A. against
B. off
C. from
D. of

66. Although he never learnt to read, his exceptional memory and enquiring mind eventually made him a very .... man.
A. dedicated
B. erudite
C. pragmatic
D. benevolent

67. Choose the word, which is the exact OPPOSITE of the given word.

Acquitted
A. Neglected
B. Discharged
C. Arrested
D. Convicted

68. Choose the most appropriate meaning of the given idiom/phrase:

For Good
A. for a good cause
B. temporarily
C. permanently
D. seriously

69. Choose the word, which is the exact OPPOSITE of the given word.

Amnesty
A. Reward
B. Gift
C. Crowd
D. Punishment

70. Man who has committed such an .... crime must get the most severe punishment.
A. injurious
B. uncharitable
C. abominable
D. unworthy

71. Choose the most appropriate meaning of the given idiom/phrase:

Blow by Blow
A. Eruption in quick succession from a great volcano
B. Continuously raining with thunders
C. Describe an event as it occurred in every detail
D. A rapid decline of business leading to its closure

72. To cry ....
A. horse
B. cat
C. dog
D. wolf

73. Find the correctly spelt words:
A. Evolution
B. Evalution
C. Evolusion
D. Evalution

74. To .... in harness.
A. lie
B. die
C. dye
D. pie

75. Select the correct **synonyms** of the following words.

Devise
A. Revise
B. Device
C. Plan
D. Defend

ANSWERS

1	2	3	4	5	6	7	8	9	10
C	D	C	D	B	D	B	C	C	B

11	12	13	14	15	16	17	18	19	20
D	C	B	A	B	A	A	B	D	C

21	22	23	24	25	26	27	28	29	30
B	B	A	D	B	C	C	D	C	B

31	32	33	34	35	36	37	38	39	40
D	A	A	B	D	B	B	C	D	A

41	42	43	44	45	46	47	48	49	50
C	C	A	A	C	D	A	D	A	D

51	52	53	54	55	56	57	58	59	60
D	B	C	A	A	B	D	C	C	C

61	62	63	64	65	66	67	68	69	70
C	C	C	B	C	B	D	C	D	C

71	72	73	74	75
C	D	A	B	C

R. Gupta's®
GENERAL KNOWLEDGE BOOKS

Book Name	Code	Price (₹)
General Knowledge 2020	R-1716	45
General Knowledge For All 2020	R-1641	25
R. Gupta's® GK & Current Affairs including Latest Who's Who	R-1	35
General Knowledge Hand Book (Junior)	R-3	50
General Knowledge & Current Affairs	R-5	65
General Knowledge At a Glance	R-7	75
Popular General Knowledge	R-9	170
General Knowledge Encyclopaedia	R-11	270
Delhi General Knowledge	R-464	70
Kerala General Knowledge	R-1588	95
Comprehensive J&K GK, Current Affairs & Who's Who	R-564	95
J & K General Knowledge (small)	R-12	45
J & K General Knowledge – At a Glance	R-1066	55
Haryana General Knowledge	R-505	95
Himachal Pradesh General Knowledge	R-415	110
Uttarakhand General Knowledge	R-469	65
Odisha General Knowledge	R-518	140
West Bengal General Knowledge	R-1070	65
Arunachal Pradesh General Knowledge	R-1067	70
India At a Glance *(with Description of All States/Union Territories)*	R-489	75
Manipur General Knowledge	R-822	95
Manipur GK Handbook (with Multiple Choice Questions)	R-954	50
Maharashtra General Knowledge	R-1043	75

Ramesh Publishing House,
4457, Nai Sarak, Delhi-6

For Online Shopping: www.rameshpublishinghouse.com

R. Gupta's®

ENGLISH IMPROVEMENT BOOKS

Book Name	Code	Price (₹)
General English for Competitive Exams Objectivce MCQs	(R-1762)	110
The English Enhancement Book	(R-1720)	180
Common Errors in English (English-Hindi)	(R-1709)	230
Spoken English	(R-1654)	230
All About English	(R-1391)	260
Treasury of Synonyms & Antonyms (Words with Hindi Meanings)	(R-1348)	190
All Time English	(R-1100)	120
The Right & Wrong English (Volume-I) (A to G)	(R-1076)	140
The Right & Wrong English (Volume-II) (H to R)	(R-1077)	140
The Right & Wrong English (Volume-III) (S to Z)	(R-1078)	140
Dealing with English Made Easy	(R-1042)	120
Popular English Grammar for Competitions	(R-938)	110
Popular English Grammar (with Hindi Explanations)	(R-204)	180
English Grammar	(R-611)	210
English Grammar & Composition	(R-783)	130
English Grammar & Comprehension	(R-705)	140
Pocket English Grammar	(R-676)	45
A Concise English Grammar	(R-269)	65
General Grammar & Interactive English	(R-452)	140
English Literature & Grammar	(R-378)	110
English Reading Comprehension	(R-303)	190
Gloria English Speaking Course (Hindi-English)	(R-218)	370
पॉपुलर मिनी इंगलिश स्पीकिंग कोर्स	(R-657)	80
English Improvement Course	(R-358)	280
Dictionary of Synonyms & Antonyms	(R-205)	160
Dictionary of Prepositions	(R-270)	110
Handbook of Idioms & Phrases	(R-473)	80
Idioms, Phrases & Proverbs (with Hindi Meanings & Usage)(English-Hindi)	(R-353)	75
Handbook of Proverbs	(R-514)	110
Common Errors in English	(R-305)	190
Spoken & Communicative English	(R-1801)	295
Words Commonly Confused	(R-576)	120
Writing Correct English	(R-541)	110
Write English Right	(R-578)	140
How to Write Correct English (Hindi-English)	(R-451)	140
Multiple Uses of Words	(R-721)	95
Handbook of Quotations	(R-190)	130
Art of Communication in English	(R-419)	120
Modern English Usage	(R-388)	120
Objective General English	(R-229)	140
Advance General English	(R-230)	130
General English (With Multiple-Choice Questions)	(R-311)	160
Test of English Language	(R-310)	120

Ramesh Publishing House

12-H, New Daryaganj Road, Opp. Officer's Mess, Delhi-110002

For Online Shopping: www.rameshpublishinghouse.com

Jawaharlal Nehru University (JNU)
BA (Hons.) Entrance Examination, 2018

CLUSTER-1: French, German, Russian and Spanish

SECTION-A

Unit-I

*Answer **all** questions. Each question carries 1 mark.*

1. Here are some words translated from an artificial language.

   kamceno means sky blue

   cenorax means blue cheese

   aplmitl means star bright

   Which word could mean 'bright sky'?
   A. cenokam
   B. mitlkam
   C. raxmitl
   D. aplceno

2. Here are some words translated from an artificial language.

   granamelke means big tree

   pinimelke means little tree

   melkehoon means tree house

   Which word could mean 'big house'?
   A. granahoon
   B. pinishur
   C. pinihoon
   D. melkegrana

3. Here are some words translated from an artificial language.

   slar means jump

   slary means jumping

   slarnend means jumped

   Which word could mean 'playing'?
   A. clargslarend
   B. clargy
   C. ellaclarg
   D. slarmont

4. Here are some words translated from an artificial language.

   plekapaki means fruitcake

   pakishillen means cakewalk

   treftalan means buttercup

   Which word could mean 'cupcake'?
   A. shillenalan
   B. treftpleka
   C. pakitreft
   D. alanpaki

5. If in a certain code language, 'CHARCOAL' is coded as '45164913' and 'MORALE' is coded as '296137', then how would the word 'ALLOCHRE' be coded in that language?
   A. 13396875
   B. 16693985
   C. 13394567
   D. 19943785

6. If in a certain code language, 'MONKEY' is coded as 'XDJMNL', then how would 'TIGER' be written in that same code language?
   A. QDFHSB
   B. SDFHSC
   C. SHFDQD
   D. None of the above

7. Find the odd one out:
   A. Rigveda
   B. Atharveda
   C. Ayurveda
   D. Samaveda

8. Find the odd one out:
   A. Swim
   B. Listen
   C. Climb
   D. Run

9. Find the odd one out:
   A. RAM
   B. Flash Memory (Pen Drive)
   C. Hard Disc
   D. Floppy

10. Find the odd one out:
  A. Lion
  B. Zebra
  C. Tiger
  D. Crocodile

11. Find the odd one out:
  A. England
  B. America
  C. Asia
  D. Africa

12. If in each number, all the three digits are arranged in ascending order, which of the following will be the lowest number?
  A. 489
  B. 541
  C. 654
  D. 953

13. Find the missing number:
  6, 11, 21, 36, 56, ?
  A. 42
  B. 51
  C. 81
  D. 91

14. If with third, fourth and eleventh letters of the word 'CONTROVERSIAL', a meaningful word can be formed, then its first letter is the answer. If more than one words are possible, then M and if no meaningful words can be formed, then X is the answer.
  A. N
  B. T
  C. X
  D. M

15. Which numbered space in the figure represents teachers who are players as well as artists?

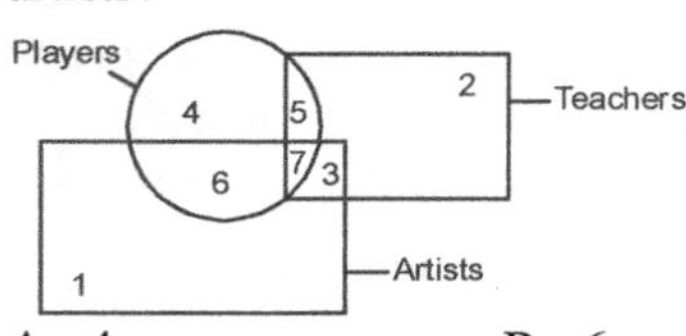

  A. 4
  B. 6
  C. 7
  D. None of the above

16. In the following diagram, the square represents women, triangle represents team leaders and circle represents graduate. Which numbered part represents women-graduate-team leaders?

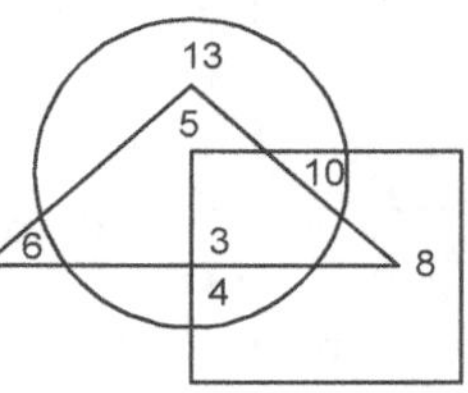

  A. 3
  B. 5
  C. 8
  D. 13

17. If 15 apples and 20 oranges cost as much as 20 apples and 15 oranges, how do you compare the cost of two?
  A. Apples are so costly as oranges
  B. Oranges are costly than oranges
  C. Apples are costly than oranges
  D. Nothing can be found from the given data

18. An analogue clock always has:
  A. numbers
  B. battery
  C. alarm
  D. needles

19. A book always has:
  A. chapters
  B. contents
  C. pages
  D. pictures

20. Children should avoid smoking because:
  A. it is a bad habit
  B. elders advise them not to do so
  C. it is an unnecessary expenditure
  D. it is injurious to health

21. Which one is the same as emancipate, free and release?
  A. Ignore
  B. Pardon
  C. Liberate
  D. Quit

22. Find out the word that expresses most effectively the general characteristics of these three words—wheat, barley, rice.
  A. Food
  B. Gram
  C. Cereal
  D. Agriculture

23. How was France known as?
  A. Elysium
  B. Francia
  C. Britannia
  D. Gaul

24. Which city is famous for its Film Festival?
  A. Cannes
  B. Grenoble
  C. Avignon
  D. Paris

25. Which of the following is a river of France?
  A. Thames
  B. Danube
  C. Seine
  D. Tigris

26. When is Bastille Day?
  A. July 14
  B. January 1
  C. July 4
  D. October 3

27. Which State of USA was once a French colony?
  A. Alaska
  B. California
  C. Louisiana
  D. Florida

28. Who won Wimbledon Women's Singles Title in 1991?
A. Steffi Graf   B. Monica Seles
C. Gabriela Sabatini D. Martina Navratilova

29. When did East Germany and West Germany unite?
A. 1990   B. 1986
C. 1998   D. 2000

30. Who followed the policy of Blood and Iron?
A. Helmut Kohl   B. Konrad Adenauer
C. Führer   D. Otto von Bismark

31. Which was the capital of West Germany?
A. Berlin   B. Bonn
C. Vienna   D. Prague

32. Who began reformation in the 16th century?
A. Martin Luther   B. Nestorius
C. John Wesley   D. John Calvin

33. Who became the King of Spain in 1975?
A. Philip II   B. Jorge III
C. Juan Carlos   D. Alfonso X

34. Which of the following is not a co-official language in Spain?
A. Catalan   B. Basque
C. Galician   D. Frisian

35. Which British colony is claimed by Spain?
A. Gibralter   B. Bermuda
C. Ivory Coast   D. Bahamas

36. Mainland Spain is the part of which peninsula?
A. Balkan   B. Alaskan
C. Iberian   D. Scandinavian

37. Where was Olympics 1992 (Summer) held?
A. Barcelona   B. Paris
C. Athens   D. Madrid

38. Which city is considered as Third Rome?
A. St. Petersburg   B. Tula
C. Kiev   D. Moscow

39. Which is the national animal of Russia?
A. Cow   B. Lion
C. Bear   D. Tiger

40. What are the colours of Russian Flag?
A. Green, red and white
B. White, blue and red
C. Blue and red
D. Red and white

41. Who was awarded the Nobel Prize in literature in 1970?
A. Anna Karenina
B. Alexander Solzhenitsyn
C. Andrei Sakharov
D. Vasily Shukshin

42. Which is the highest mountain in Russia?
A. Elbrus   B. Krestovski
C. Ushkovski   D. Ostri Tolbachik

Unit-II

*Answer **all** questions. Each question carries 2 marks.*

43. Find the minimum number of straight lines required to make the given figure:

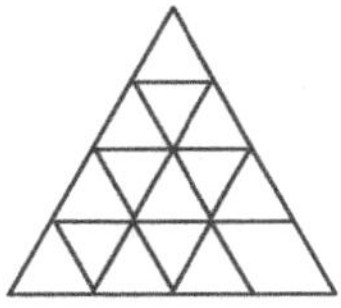

A. 9   B. 11
C. 15   D. 16

44. Choose the suitable figure from the four alternatives given below that would complete the figure matrix:

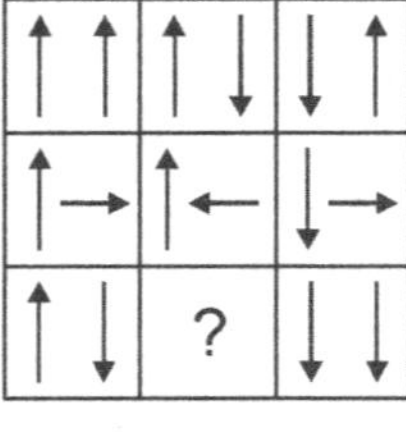

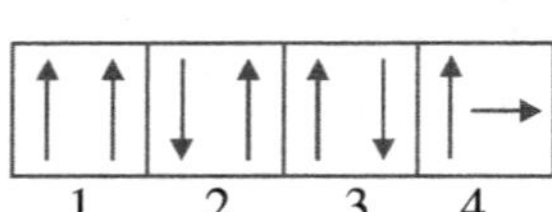

A. 1   B. 2
C. 3   D. 4

45. Choose the suitable figure from the four alternatives given below that would complete the figure matrix:

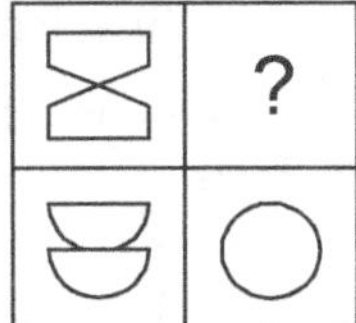

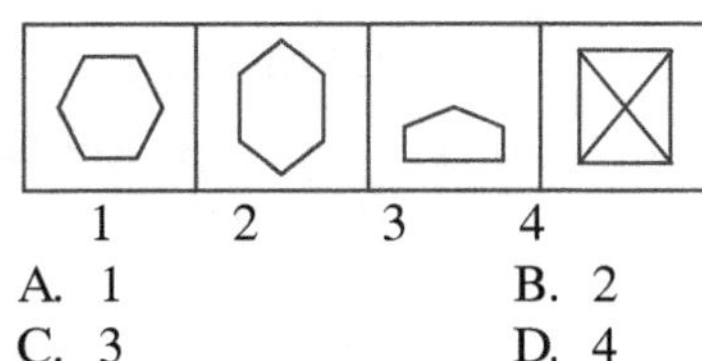

| 1 | 2 | 3 | 4 |

A. 1   B. 2
C. 3   D. 4

46. Choose the suitable figure from the four alternatives given below that would complete the figure matrix:

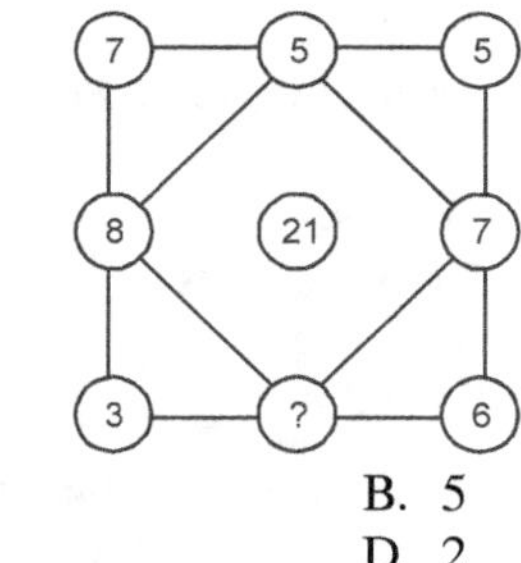

A. 3   B. 5
C. 1   D. 2

47. In the following questions, a statement is given, followed by two conclusions. On the basis of the statement, find out which one is the correct conclusion given below:

Statement: All the organised persons find time for rest, Reena in spite of her busy schedule, finds time for rest.

Conclusions:
I. Reena is an organised person.
II. Reena is a hardworking person.
A. Only conclusion I follows
B. Only conclusion II follows
C. Either I or II follows
D. Both I and II follow

48. There are three statements. Based on the first two statements, the third statement may be true, false, or uncertain.

Teena is older than Ramesh.
Nitin is older than Teena.
Ramesh is older than Nitin.
If the first two statements are true, the third statement is:
A. true
B. false
C. uncertain
D. None of the above

49. There are three statements. Based on the first two statements, the third statement may be true, false, or uncertain.

The temperature on Monday was lower than on Tuesday.
The temperature on Wednesday was lower than on Tuesday.
The temperature on Monday was higher than on Wednesday.
If the first two statements are true, the third statement is:
A. true
B. false
C. uncertain
D. None of the above

50. Six friends are sitting in a circle and are facing the centre of the circle. Aakansha is between Rahul and Vinod. Mansi is between Kumar and Mohit. Rahul and Kumar are opposite to each other.
Who is sitting right to Rahul?
A. Kumar
B. Aakansha
C. Vinod
D. Mohit

51. Among five students, Mohan is older than Raju but not as old as Lalit. Lalit is older than Neelesh and Kabir. Neelesh is younger than Raju but not the youngest. Who is the fourth in the descending order of age?
A. Mohan
B. Raju
C. Kabir
D. None of them

SECTION-B

*Answer **all** questions. (Marks : 40)*

A. *Read the text and answer to the questions given below:*

Antarctica is the coldest, driest, highest, windiest, most inaccessible and inhospitable area of the earth's surface. Although it covers one-tenth of the world's land surface, as large as China, Argentina and France. Nigeria and New Zealand combined, the only people on this harsh continent are scientists and the occasional explorers.

Seals and penguins, the only wildlife, inhabit the pack-ice and beaches. Mites, springtails, lice and midges are the main fauna. The only plants are fungi, algae, lichens and mosses. Shoals of krill, perhaps enough to double the world's fish catch, whales (mostly blue, humpback and fin species) and fish abound in the Antarctic seas.

And by geological analogy scientists believe that there is a very substantial amount of mineral resources, including gas and oil. Estimates made by the United States Geological Survey several years ago suggest an offshore recoverable resource of 15 billion barrels. Coal and iron ore are also present for exploitation beneath the large repository of ice.

The total volume of ice in Antarctica is 30 million cubic kilometres, about 70 per cent of the world's store of fresh water and 90 per cent of the world's ice. If it all melted, the world's oceans would rise between 45 and 90 metres.

Such is the intriguing promise of unexplored wealth on this continental land mass, which, when developed, may relieve the world's food shortage and energy crisis.

Tick the correct answer:

1. The opening sentence illustrates that Antarctica is:
  A. an uninhabitable place
  B. not worth developing
  C. a land of harsh extremes
  D. a virgin land

2. Which of the following statements about Antarctica is false?
  A. It is the home of seals and penguins
  B. It is rich in plant life
  C. The only people of Antarctica are scientists and explorers
  D. It covers 10 per cent of the earth's land surface

3. A significant potential food resource that Antarctica has is:
  A. its plant life
  B. its possibility of farming
  C. its fauna
  D. krill

4. Scientists believe that Antarctica:
  A. is very rich in mineral resources
  B. is moderately rich in mineral resources
  C. is more rich in gas and oil than anywhere else in the world
  D. has coal and iron, but not enough to be mined

5. Many nations are interested in Antarctica because:
  A. it offers a challenge to human initiative
  B. it is as yet unexplored
  C. it is a no-main's land
  D. it is rich in minerals

B. Write a short essay (in about 250-300 words) on the topic "Representation of women in Bollywood movies".

C. Describe the picture given below in about 150-200 words:

ANSWERS

SECTION-A

1	2	3	4	5	6	7	8	9	10
B	A	B	D	C	D	C	B	A	D

11	12	13	14	15	16	17	18	19	20
C	B	C	B	C	A	A	D	B	D

21	22	23	24	25	26	27	28	29	30
D	C	D	A	C	A	C	A	A	D

31	32	33	34	35	36	37	38	39	40
B	A	C	D	A	C	A	D	C	B

41	42	43	44	45	46	47	48	49	50
B	A	A	A	B	C	A	B	C	B

51
D

SECTION-B

1	2	3	4	5
C	B	D	A	B

EXPLANATORY ANSWERS

SECTION-A

1. kamceno → sky blue ...(i)

cenorax → blue cheese ...(ii)

aplmitl → star bright ...(iii)

From equation (i) and (ii),

ceno → blue

From equation (i),

kam → sky

From equation (iii), mitl → bright

∴ mitlkam → bright sky

Hence, option (B) is correct

2. granamelke → big tree ...(i)

pinimelke → little tree ...(ii)

melkehoon → tree house ...(iii)

From equation (i), (ii) and (iii),

melke → tree

From equation (i), grana → big

From equation (iii), hoon → house

∴ 'granahoon' means 'big house'.

3. slar → jump ...(i)

slary → jumping ...(ii)

slarnend → jumped ...(iii)

From equation (i), (ii) and (iii),

slar → jump

From equation (ii), y → ing

∴ clargy means playing.

4. plekapaki → fruitcake ...(i)

pakishillen → cakewalk ...(ii)

treftalan → buttercup ...(iii)

From equation (i) and (ii),

paki → cake

From equation (iii), alan → cup

∴ alanpaki → cupcake.

5. As,
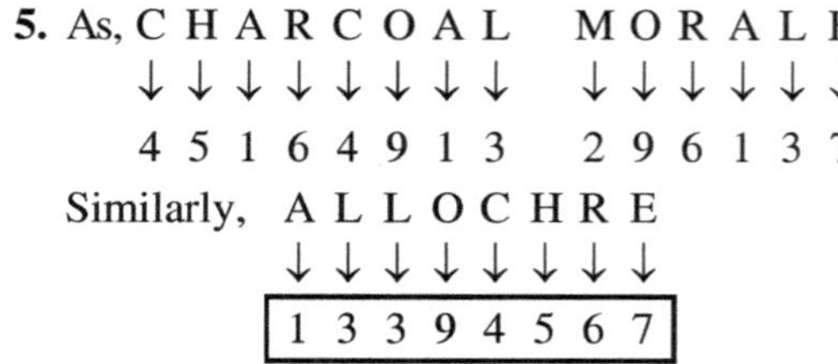

Similarly, A L L O C H R E
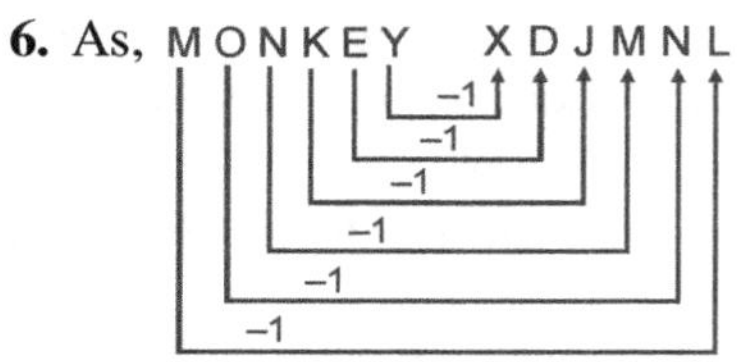

$$\boxed{1\ 3\ 3\ 9\ 4\ 5\ 6\ 7}$$

6. As, M O N K E Y   X D J M N L
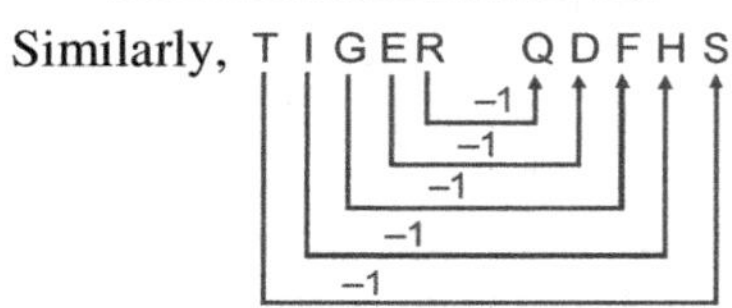

Similarly, T I G E R   Q D F H S

7. Except (C) Ayurveda, all others are the name of Vedas.

9. Except (A) RAM, all others are the Secondary Memory of the Computer.

10. Except (D) Crocodile, all others are mammals.

11. Except (C), all others are the name of a country.

12. Digit Arrange in Ascending order,
(A) 489 $\Rightarrow$ 489
(B) 541 $\Rightarrow$ 145 (Lowest)
(C) 654 $\Rightarrow$ 456
(D) 953 $\Rightarrow$ 359
Hence, (B) 541 is the lowest number.

13.
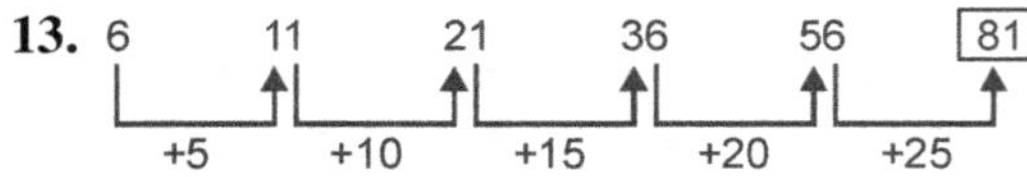

14. Third letter $\rightarrow$ N
Fourth letter $\rightarrow$ T
Eleventh letter $\rightarrow$ I
Meaningful word, TIN
$\therefore$ Answer will be first letter of the meaningful **word** *i.e.,* T will be the answer.

15. A number which is present in all the three figures, represent teachers who are players as well as artists *i.e.,* 7.

16. A number which is present in all the three figures, represent women-graduate-team leaders *i.e.,* 3.

17.
$$15A + 20O = 20A + 15O$$
$$5O = 5A$$
$$O = A$$
$\therefore$ Apples are so costly as oranges.

43. Total Vertical lines = 0
Total Horizontal lines = 4
Total inclined lines = 5
$\therefore$ Minimum straight lines = 0 + 4 + 5 = 9.

46. As, the sum of the corner number of the matrix
$(7 + 5 + 6 + 3) = 21$
Similarly, the sum of the middle number of the matrix
$$5 + 7 + ? + 8 = 21$$
$$? = 21 - 20 = 1.$$

48. I.   Teena > Ramesh
II.   Nitin > Teena
From I and II
Nitin > Teena > Ramesh
$\therefore$ Ramesh is older than Nitin is false.

49. I. $T_{Monday} < T_{Tuesday}$
II. $T_{Wednesday} < T_{Tuesday}$
We can not conclude these two inequality
$\therefore$ We are uncertain about third statement.

50.
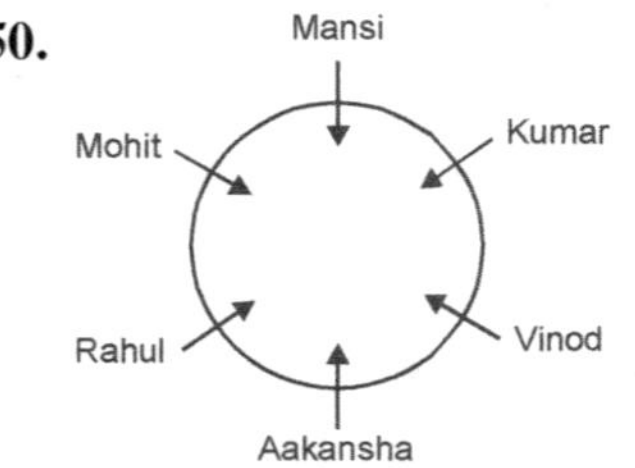

Aakansha is sitting right to Rahul.

51.
   1   2   3   4   5
Lalit > Mohan > Raju > Neelesh > Kabir
Oldest   Youngest
$\therefore$ Neelesh is fourth in the descending order of age.

SECTION-B

B. Representation of women in Bollywood movies

Hindi cinema has always been a major point of reference for Indian culture and society. The society and the world that we live in is changing and these changes are echoed in the cinema. Let's take the example of the humble and illiterate mother or 'ma' depicted in the Hindi movies of 60's, through the 70's right till the 80'. The 'ma' was a female figure, an epitome of sacrifice and hard work, caring and bothered about nothing but her children. She burned the midnight oil to stitch clothes to afford two meals a day and to pay for the hero's BA degree, has slowly got replaced with the modern, educated and sometimes even independent 'mom'.

The heroine who was normally a simple homely girl has now been replaced by a woman who is not only educated and bold but is also confident about her sexuality. The hero no longer falls in love with a innocent uneducated 'gaon-ki-gori'. Movies now portray live-in relationships, girlfriends and boyfriends, pre-marital sex, corruption, people following live and let live policy in life and family, liberal parents, colleges are depicted like dating parties and professors like friends.

The representation of women is often used as a selling point of the films. Audience likes to watch women on screen in various song and dance routines, in stereotypical images, in various costumes and the reflection of women on screen change from time to time with changing trends in the continuously evolving society. It is true that the changing ideologies of a society have the power over what is depicted on screen and how it is depicted but another truth is the fact that the patriarchal undercurrents in our society are still the same. Women are still depicted in a way that caters to the male gaze.

Women are still depicted or portrayed in the old moulds of feminity. Heroines are westernised, as is everything around them, but this has resulted in turning a woman into a commodity that needs to be made a spectacle of so that the film can sell well. The western influence and modernisation has led to more skin show in order to make the film commercially viable as it is now sold to Indian as well as western audiences.

C. The picture depicts world tourism in the modern era.

Tourism has turned out to be a very important industry in the modern age. In almost all the countries of the world there are separate ministries of tourism.

Tourist spots are being developed all over the world to attract the tourists. Tourism is, indeed, a good source of earning foreign exchange for every country that can manage it efficiently. All over the world there is a great interaction between people of different countries, races, communities, regions and religions. Business magnates visit other countries to promote their business.

Several newspaper agencies, journalists, scribes, radio and T.V. reports and others connected with mass media have to roam from place to place to trace out essential and interesting matter for reporting purposes.

Most of the tourists, however, are in search of entertainment, exploration and adventure, alongwith which they also want to enhance their knowledge in various fields.

Such men and women have to stay in hotels and they often stay in good hotels—five star or others. They are ready to pay adequately for the good food, lodging, comfort given and entertainment provided. Many tourists visit tourist spots such as beaches, hill stations, historical and picturesque places, religious and cultural programmes and congregations. Tourists are also fond of participating in adventure games and swimming bouts and visiting Sanctuaries of animals and birds and zoos, museums, exhibitions, etc.

Jawaharlal Nehru University (JNU)
BA (Hons.) Entrance Examination, 2018

CLUSTER-2: Japanese, Korean and Chinese

SECTION-A

*Answer **all** questions. Each question carries 1 mark.*

Choose the correct anawer:

1. In an artificial language,
   aptabuke means bookshelf
   aptagani means book reading
   valipuli means huge worm
   Which word could mean 'bookworm'?
   A. ganipuli   B. aptapuli
   C. puliapta   D. bukepuli

2. In an artificial language,
   malgalola means shoe-shop
   malgaport means shoe-lace
   mogagrop means book-stand
   Which word could mean 'book-shop'?
   A. malgalola   B. mogalola
   C. malgagrop   D. moggaport

3. In an artificial language,
   zanamiti means happy birthday
   mitihofze means birthday party
   menahatt means madness
   Which word could mean 'happiness'?
   A. hofzehatt   B. zanahofze
   C. hofzemiti   D. zanahatt

4. In an artificial language,
   celaprigg means jasmine tea
   celakram means jasmine flavour
   camenbril means guava jam
   Which word could mean 'tea flavour'?
   A. camenkram   B. priggbril
   C. kramcela   D. priggkram

5. If DANCER is coded as FDRHKY, how can ABSORB be written in that code?
   A. CEWTXI
   B. BCUQVF
   C. EDTSUD
   D. EJFBDG

6. If BEAD is coded as 2514, HIDE is coded as 8945, how can CHIEF be coded in that language?
   A. 39125   B. 36278
   C. 38956   D. 35876

7. If BIG BAG is coded as 297 and 217, DEAD FIG is coded as 4514 and 697, how can HIGH IDEA be coded in that language?
   A. 8672 and 7963
   B. 8978 and 9451
   C. 9865 and 7436
   D. 9263 and 4915

8. What comes next in the series?
   TTF   VVE   XXD
   A. ZZC   B. UUB
   C. ZZG   D. YYC

9. Which number comes next?
   284   465   646
   A. 947   B. 827
   C. 857   D. 927

10. If I _____ you, I would say sorry.
   A. am   B. was
   C. were   D. be

11. You _____ touch the exhibits in an antique shop.
    A. won't   B. mustn't
    C. can't   D. hadn't

12. When I was younger I ___ remember anything.
    A. would   B. have
    C. could   D. shall

13. The sun rises ____ the East.
    A. on   B. from
    C. in   D. above

14. Shanghai is ____ the southeast of Beijing.
    A. on   B. to
    C. in   D. by

15. Feed your baby _____ the same regular intervals each day.
    A. on   B. in
    C. at   D. with

16. The mechanic announced that the engine was _____ repair.
    A. over   B. upon
    C. about   D. beyond

17. There _____ not to be much noise in a hospital.
    A. should   B. ought
    C. must   D. shall

18. He studies hard so that he _____ serve the people well.
    A. can   B. may
    C. might   D. must

19. The news is unexpected, ____, it is true.
    A. however   B. moreover
    C. nevertheless   D. otherwise

20. The post office is just _____ the street.
    A. opposite   B. across
    C. above   D. beyond

21. Which islands did Netaji Subhash Chandra Bose rename as *Shaheed* and *Swaraj* in 1943?
    A. Lakshadweep and Minicoy
    B. Daman and Diu
    C. Andaman and Nicobar
    D. Basavaraj Durga Islands

22. Which is the deepest place on the Earth?
    A. Grand Canyon   B. Mariana Trench
    C. Lake Baikal   D. Milwaukee Deep

23. Which oriental nation does not use chopsticks?
    A. Japan   B. South Korea
    C. Thailand   D. China

24. The year 2018 in Chinese zodiac is the year of _____ .
    A. Dragon   B. Dog
    C. Horse   D. Rabbit

25. In the Second World War, Japan attacked Pearl Harbour on:
    A. 15 February 1942 B. 7 December 1941
    C. 1 January 1943   D. 18 March 1944

26. Which parallel divides North Korea and South Korea?
    A. 27th   B. 23rd
    C. 38th   D. 42nd

27. Doklam is situated in the tri-junction of ____.
    A. Bhutan, Nepal and China
    B. India, China and Nepal
    C. India, China and Bhutan
    D. India, Pakistan and China

28. Which country is known for having invented paper, printing and magnetic compass?
    A. Korea   B. China
    C. Japan   D. England

29. What is the name of the Korean script?
    A. Hanja   B. Hangeul
    C. Amharic   D. Kanji

30. Who was the first Japanese author to receive the Nobel Prize for literature?
    A. Oe Kenzaburo
    B. Kazuo Ishiguro
    C. Kawabata Yasunari
    D. Murakami Haruki

31. Who composed the national song *Vande Mataram*?
    A. Rabindranath Tagore
    B. Bankim Chandra Chattopadhyay
    C. Kazi Nazrul Islam
    D. Dwijendralal Ray

32. Tenali Rama was a famous jester poet in the kingdom of _____ .
   A. Vijayanagara   B. Krishnanagar
   C. Travancore   D. Mysore

33. Which of the following names is *not* associated with the name Ooty?
   A. Ottakalmandu   B. Udumalaippettai
   C. Udagamandalam   D. Ootacamund

34. Who was *not* a painter of India?
   A. Ramkinkar Baij   B. Nandalal Bose
   C. Jamini Roy   D. Manohar Aich

35. Who calculated the height of Mount Everest?
   A. Ramgopal Ghosh
   B. Rashbehari Bose
   C. Radhanath Sikdar
   D. Tenzing Norgay

36. The expressions *Jhala* and *Antara* belong to the discipline of:
   A. painting   B. music
   C. architecture   D. astronomy

37. Who invented the *Crescograph,* a pioneering discovery in plant physiology?
   A. Satyendranath Bose
   B. Jagadish Chandra Bose
   C. Prafulla Chandra Ray
   D. Shibnath Shastri

38. The throne of the Emperor of Japan is known as
   A. Chrysanthemum throne
   B. Cherry blossom throne
   C. Orchid throne
   D. The throne of the Rising Sun

39. Colloquially known as Bullet Train, what does the word *Shinkansen* mean?
   A. High-Speed Super Rail
   B. Super-Speed Maglev Rail
   C. New Super-Express Line
   D. New Trunk Line

40. The National Flag of which country literally means the 'Supreme Ultimate Flag' and is marked with the Yin-Yang symbols?
   A. Bhutan   B. North Korea
   C. South Korea   D. Cambodia

Directions (Qs. 41-50): *Read the following three passages and choose the correct answers:*

Passage-1

The major socio-economic problem being faced by India is 'Poverty'. Even after seven decades of independence, the country is still fighting against this social evil of property. It is estimated that nearly one-third of Indian population of 1.21 billion, *i.e.,* nearly 4.26 millions of people are living below poverty line. Many go without a meal a day. Though governments are struggling hard to eradicate poverty, the increasing population and mismanagement of government schemes, have fuelled the growth of poverty. The population is growing at an alarming rate. In last ten years the population has grown by 0.20 billion. The positive effects of development are nullified by increase in population. Hence, there is an urgent need to curtail population growth, by adopting strict family planning programmes by government.

41. According to the passage, what is the biggest obstacle in the path of development?
   A. Strict family planning programmes
   B. Seven decades of independence
   C. The alarming growth of population
   D. Doling out of mid-day meals

42. According to this passage, the most pressing need is to curtail:
   A. family planning programmes
   B. population growth
   C. government schemes
   D. mid-day meals

Passage-2

Marie Curie was one of the most accomplished scientists in history. Together with her husband, Pierre, she discovered radium, an element widely used for treating cancer, and studied uranium and other radioactive substances. Pierre and Marie's amicable collaboration later helped to unlock the secrets of the atom.

Marie was born in 1867 in Warsaw, Poland, where her father was a professor of physics. At an early age, she displayed a brilliant mind and a blithe personality. Her great exuberance for learning prompted her to continue with her studies after high school. She became disgruntled, however, when she learned that the university in Warsaw was closed to women. Determined to receive a higher education, she defiantly left Poland and in 1891 entered the Sorbonne, a French university, where she earned her master's degree and doctorate in physics. Marie was fortunate to have studied at the Sorbonne with some of the greatest scientists of her day, one of whom was Pierre Curie. Marie and Pierre were married in 1895 and spent many productive years working together in the physics laboratory. A short time after they discovered radium, Pierre was killed by a horse-drawn wagon in 1906. Marie was stunned by this horrible misfortune and endured heartbreaking anguish. Despondently she recalled their close relationship and the joy that they had shared in scientific research. The fact that she had two young daughters to raise by herself greatly increased her distress. Curie's feeling of desolation finally began to fade when she was asked to succeed her husband as a physics professor at the Sorbonne. She was the first woman to be given a professorship at the world famous university. In 1911, she received the Nobel Prize in chemistry for isolating radium. Although Marie Curie eventually suffered a fatal illness from her long exposure to radium, she never became disillusioned about her work. Regardless of the consequences, she had dedicated herself to science and to revealing the mysteries of the physical world.

43. According to the passage, what did Marie Curie discover?

A. Polonium
B. Neptunium
C. Helium
D. Radium

44. What was Marie curie by birth?

A. French
B. Swiss
C. Polish
D. German

45. How old was Marie Curie when she got married?

A. 24
B. 30
C. 27
D. 28

46. How old was Marie Curie when she won the Nobel Prize?

A. 40
B. 44
C. 34
D. 47

47. After serving as a Professor at Sorbonne, in which category did Marie Curie win the Nobel Prize?

A. Mathematics
B. Chemistry
C. Physics
D. Physiotherapy

Passage-3

One of the most intriguing stories of the Russian Revolution concerns the identity of Anastasia, the youngest daughter of Czar Nicholas II. During his reign over Russia, the Czar had planned to revoke many of the harsh laws established by previous Czars. Some workers and peasants, however, clamored for more rapid social reform. In 1918, a group of these people known as Bolsheviks overthrew the government. On July 17 or 18, they murdered the Czar and what was thought to be his entire family. Although witnesses vouched that all the members of the Czar's family had been executed, there were rumors suggesting that Anastasia had survived. Over the years, a number of women claimed to be Grand Duchess Anastasia. Perhaps the most famous claimant was Anastasia Tschaikovsky, who was also known as Anna Anderson. In 1920, 18 months after the Czar's execution, this terrified young woman was rescued from drowning in a Berlin river. She spent two years in a hospital, where she attempted to reclaim her health and shattered mind. The doctors and nurses thought that she resembled Anastasia and questioned her about her background. She disclaimed any connection with the Czar's family. Eight years later, however, she claimed that she was Anastasia. She said that she had been rescued by two Russian soldiers after the Czar and the rest of her family had been killed. Two brothers named Tschaikovsky had carried her into Romania. She had married one of the brothers, who had taken her to Berlin and left her there, penniless and without a vocation. Unable to invoke the aid of her mother's family in Germany, she had tried to drown herself. During the next few years, scores of the Czar's relatives, ex-servants, and acquaintances interviewed her. Many of these people said that her looks and mannerisms were evocative of the Anastasia that they had known. Her grandmother and other relatives denied that she was the real

Anastasia, however. Tired of being accused of fraud, Anastasia immigrated to the United States in 1928 and took the name Anna Anderson. She still wished to prove that she was Anastasia, though, and returned to Germany in 1933 to bring suit against her mother's family. There she declaimed to the court, asserting that she was indeed Anastasia and deserved her inheritance. In 1957, the court decided that it could neither confirm nor deny Anastasia's identity. Although it will probably never be known whether this woman was the grand Duchess Anastasia, her search to establish her identity has been the subject of numerous books, plays, and movies.

48. Where was Anastasia abandoned penniless?
   A. United States
   B. Russia
   C. Romania
   D. Germany

49. Who killed the Czar Nicholas II?
   A. Bolsheviks
   B. Mensheviks
   C. Tchaikovsky brothers
   D. Andersons

50. When was Anastasia discharged from the hospital?
   A. 1933   B. 1928
   C. 1922   D. 1920

Directions (Qs. 51-60): *Choose the appropriate prepositions to fill in the blanks:*

51. _______ every three people who agree, you'll find five who don't.
   A. With   B. For
   C. Within   D. Across

52. He has gained a lot of weight _______ not doing any exercise.
   A. over   B. for
   C. from   D. because

53. Would you like me to help you _______ the street?
   A. beyond   B. around
   C. over   D. across

54. Trash and food were strewn _______ the room.
   A. about   B. out
   C. over   D. within

55. I did it _______ of a sense of duty.
   A. because   B. out
   C. under   D. due

56. Almost half their sales are now made _______ the Internet.
   A. around   B. over
   C. across   D. within

57. How would they get ___ the new tax laws?
   A. around   B. under
   C. within   D. across

58. Simon has come _______ attack for his recent remarks.
   A. beneath   B. against
   C. under   D. over

59. The machine is not being operated _______ safety guidelines.
   A. without   B. within
   C. under   D. around

60. In just six years, the town had changed _______ all recognition.
   A. in   B. beyond
   C. from   D. without

SECTION-B

*Answer **all** questions. (Marks : 40)*

61. Follow the coded language below and convert the following signs into sentences according to the context and their given meanings:
The key to certain sign-words are as follows:
→ = I; ↔ = to; ≡ = everyday; / = to go; ∩ = school; √ = to wake up; ∟ = at, in ;

◊ = sweet; ↓ = he; | = five; ‖ = ten; + = twelve; ← = you; ⌂ = market; ⟡ = hour/ o'clock; ≃ = to study; ∞ = be able to; ⊨ = shop; ♀/♀ = and/with; ↑ = she; ⌐ = today.

(a) ↑ / ↔ ⌂ ≡ ∟ ∥ ♀ ↔ ∩ ≃ ∟ ∥∥ ☼

....

....

(b) ← ∞ √ → ⌐ ∟ | ♀ ≡ ∟ | ∥ ☼ ?

....

....

(c) ↓ / ∩ ♀ ≈ ⊥ ☼ ≡ ♀ →

....

....

(d) ← ∞ / ↔ ◊ ⊧ ∟ ⌂ ⌐ ∟ ⊥ ∥ ☼ ?

....

....

(e) ⌐ ↓ ∞ √ ← ♀ ∞ / ↔ ∩ ♀ ←

....

....

62. Write the full forms of the following:
(a) APEC

....

(b) OBOR

....

(c) ASEAN

....

(d) BCIM

....

(e) SCO

....

(f) www

....

(g) GST

....

(h) ICBM

....

(i) DRDO

....

(j) ADIZ

....

63. What is the objective behind your choosing to study a foreign language at the under-graduate level? How did you get interested in the language of your choice? What do you think about the future benefits of learning the language you have chosen? How do you think you can contribute for your society after studying a foreign language? (Write in 150 words)

64. Look at the picture below and write your thoughts on it—in the form of a short essay (in 100 words):

ANSWERS

SECTION-A

1	2	3	4	5	6	7	8	9	10
B	B	D	D	A	C	B	A	B	C
11	**12**	**13**	**14**	**15**	**16**	**17**	**18**	**19**	**20**
B	C	C	B	A	D	B	C	C	B
21	**22**	**23**	**24**	**25**	**26**	**27**	**28**	**29**	**30**
C	B	D	B	B	C	C	B	B	C
31	**32**	**33**	**34**	**35**	**36**	**37**	**38**	**39**	**40**
B	A	B	D	C	B	B	A	D	C
41	**42**	**43**	**44**	**45**	**46**	**47**	**48**	**49**	**50**
C	B	D	C	D	B	B	D	A	D
51	**52**	**53**	**54**	**55**	**56**	**57**	**58**	**59**	**60**
B	C	B	D	B	B	A	C	B	B

EXPLANATORY ANSWERS

SECTION-A

1. aptabuke → bookshelf ...(i)
aptagani → book reading ...(ii)
valipuli → huge worm ...(iii)
From equation (i) and (ii)
apta → book
From equation (iii), puli → worm
∴ aptapuli → bookworm.

2. malgalola → shoe-shop ...(i)
malgaport → shoe-lace ...(ii)
mogagrop → book-stand ...(iii)
From equation (i) and (ii)
malga → shoe
From equation (i), lola → shop
From equation (ii), moga → book
∴ mogalola → 'book-shop'.

3. zanamiti → happy birthday ...(i)
mitihofze → birthday party ...(ii)
menahatt → madness ...(iii)
From equation (i) and (ii)
miti → birthday
From equation (i), zana → happy
From equation (iii), hatt → ness
∴ zanahatt → 'happiness'.

4. celaprigg → jasmine tea ...(i)
celakram → jasmine flavour ...(ii)
camenbrill → guava jam ...(iii)
From equation (i) and (ii)
cela → jasmine
From equation (i), prigg → tea
From equation (ii), kram → flavour
∴ priggkram → 'tea flavour'.

5. As, 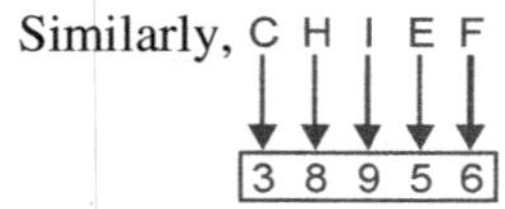
Similarly, 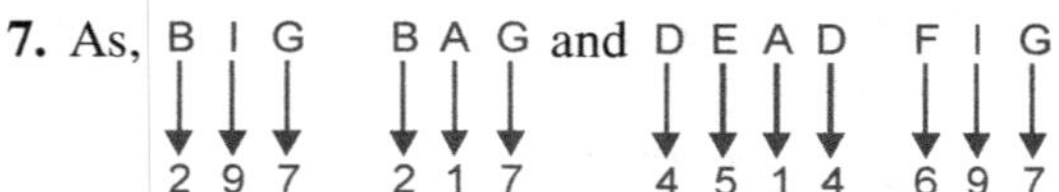

6. As, B E A D and H I D E
2 5 1 4   8 9 4 5
Serial number on english alphabet series
Similarly, 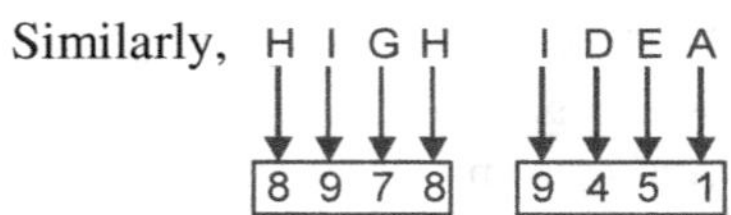

7. As, B I G   B A G and D E A D   F I G
2 9 7   2 1 7   4 5 1 4   6 9 7
Serial number on english alphabet series
Similarly, 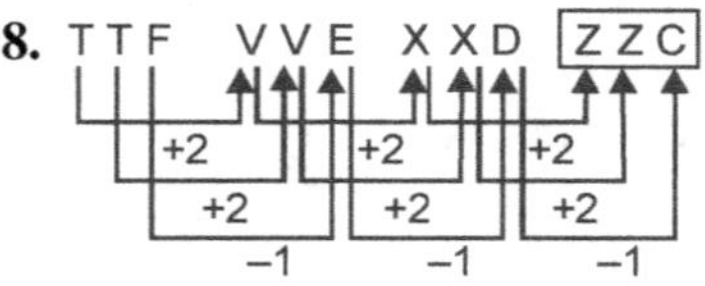

8. 

9. 284   465   646   827
        +181   +181   +181

SECTION-B

61. (a) She goes to market everyday at ten and to school to study at ten o'clock.
(b) Will you be able to wake me up at five today and everyday at five o'clock?
(c) He goes to school to study with me everyday at twelve o'clock.
(d) Will you be able to go to sweet shop at market at twelve o'clock today?

(*e*) He will be able to wake you up and be able to go to school with you.

62. (*a*) **APEC :** Asia-Pacific Economic Cooperation

(*b*) **OBOR :** One Belt One Road

(*c*) **ASEAN :** The Association of Southeast Asian Nations

(*d*) **BCIM :** The Bangladesh-China-India-Myanmar form for Regional Cooperation

(*e*) **SCO :** Shanghai Cooperation Organisation

(*f*) **WWW :** World Wide Web

(*g*) **GST :** Goods and Service Tax

(*h*) **ICBM :** An Intercontinental Ballistic Missile

(*i*) **DRDO :** Defence Research and Development Organization

(*j*) **ADIZ :** Air Defense Identification Zone

63. The main objective behind choosing to study a foreign language at the undergraduate level is that it provides a competitive edge in career choices.

I got interested in learning French when I came in contact with my new neighbour who works with the French Embassy. She told me about the great scope of learning it.

Learning French will help me in getting admission in some French university for further education. This will make me more employable in a multinational company also.

One can contribute to society in many ways after studying a foreign language in the following ways:

1. Foreign Language study creates more positive attitudes and less prejudice toward people who are different.

2. Analytical skills improve when students study a foreign language.

3. Dealing with another culture enables people to gain a more profound understanding of their own culture.

4. Creativity is increased with the study of foreign languages.

5. Skills like problem solving, dealing with abstract concepts, are increased when you study a foreign language.

6. One participates more effectively and responsibly in a multi-cultural world if one knows another language.

7. The study of foreign languages teaches and encourages respect for other peoples: it fosters an understanding of the interrelation of language and human nature.

8. Foreign languages expand one's view of the world, liberalize one's experiences, and make one more flexible and tolerant.

9. Foreign languages expand one's world view and limit the barriers between people: barriers cause distrust and fear.

10. Foreign languages open the door to art, music, dance, fashion, cuisine, film, philosophy, science.

64. The Picture depicts gender-equality

Gender equality in India or in any other part of the world would be achieved when men and women, boys and girls would be treated equally, like two individuals, not two genders. This equality needs to be practiced at homes, in the schools, offices, in marital relations, etc.

Gender equality in India would also mean that the females should feel safe and not driven by the fear of violence. The uneven sex ratio all over the country is a proof that preference for boys over girls is a ground level norm in our Indian society. And this blemish is not confined to just one religion or caste. To a large level, it infects the whole society.

The road to an absolute gender equality in India is tough but not impossible. We must be honest in our efforts and work on changing the social outlook toward females. For a full-fledged gender equality in India, both men and women must work together and bring a positive change in society.

Jawaharlal Nehru University (JNU)
BA (Hons.) Entrance Examination, 2018

CLUSTER-3: Persian, Arabic and Pashto

SECTION-A

Each question carries 1 mark

1. The pre-Islamic era is known as:
A. age of enlightenment
B. age of ignorance
C. age of Renaissance
D. age of knowledge

2. *Avesta* the holy book of the Zoroastrians was originally written in:
A. Avesta language   B. Pahlavi language
C. Old Persian   D. Middle Persian

3. The capital of Umayyad dynasty was:
A. Baghdad   B. Cairo
C. Khurasan   D. Damascus

4. The Ottoman dynasty fell in:
A. 1857   B. 1926
C. 1940   D. 1924

5. Ibn Khaldun was a/an:
A. architect   B. historian
C. Muhaddith   D. Sufi

6. Cordova is a city of:
A. Libya   B. Al-Andalus
C. Lebanon   D. None of the above

7. Umar Khayyam is known for his work:
A. Shahnamah   B. Siyasat-namah
C. Rubaiyat   D. None of the above

8. Which of the following is *not* correct in describing cultural influences on Islam?
A. Persian literature deeply influenced Islamic literary works
B. Indian numerals had a profound influence on the development of mathematical thinking among Muslims
C. The Caliphs adopted Persian ideas of kingship
D. Greek rational reasoning had a long-lasting influence on the theological development of Islam

9. Exposure to sunlight helps a person to improve his health because:
A. the infrared light kills bacteria in the body
B. resistance power increases
C. the pigment cells in the skin get stimulated and produce a healthy tan
D. the ultraviolet rays convert skin oil into vitamin D

10. Fire temple is the place of worship of which of the following religions?
A. Taoism
B. Judaism
C. Zoroastrianism (Parsi religion)
D. Shintoism

11. Who was the first Indian Chief of Army Staff of the Indian Army?
A. Gen. K.M. Cariappa
B. Vice-Admiral R.D. Katari
C. Gen. Maharaja Rajendra Singhji
D. None of them

12. G-15 is an economic grouping of:
  A. First World Nations
  B. Second World Nations
  C. Third World Nations
  D. None of the above

13. Which of the following is used in pencils?
  A. Graphite   B. Silicon
  C. Charcoal   D. Phosphorous

14. The members of the Rajya Sabha are:
  A. directly elected by the people on the basis of universal adult franchise
  B. elected by the members of the State Legislative Assemblies
  C. elected by the members of the State Legislative Councils
  D. elected by the members of the State Legislative Councils and State Legislative Assemblies

15. Which of the following pairs of artists and their areas of specialization is *not* correct?
  A. Pandit Ravi Shankar : Sitar
  B. M.S. Subbulakshmi : Dance
  C. Hari Prasad Chaurasia : Flute
  D. Ustad Zakir Hussain Khan : Tabla

16. The name of the union given in the Constitution is:
  A. Hindustan or Bharatavarsha
  B. India or Hindustan
  C. India or Bharat
  D. Bharatadesh or India

17. The book of Parsis is:
  A. *Torah*   B. *Bible*
  C. *Zend Avesta*   D. *Gita*

18. Pandit Jasraj has established his reputation in which of the following fields?
  A. Music   B. Literature
  C. Sanskrit   D. Dance

19. The preamble to our Constitution provided that India is:
  A. a sovereign, socialist and democratic republic
  B. a sovereign, socialist secular and democratic republic
  C. a sovereign republic with a socialist pattern of society
  D. a socialist, secular and democratic republic

20. Which of the following places is famous for its gigantic rock-cut statue of Buddha?
  A. Bamiyan   B. Borobudur
  C. Anuradhapuram   D. Angor Vat

21. The letters in the first set have certain relationship. On the basis of this relationship, what is the right choice for the second set?
AST : BRU :: NQV : ?
  A. ORW   B. MPU
  C. MRW   D. OPW

22. In a certain code, PAN is written as 31 and PAR as 35. In this code, PAT is written as:
  A. 30   B. 37
  C. 38   D. 39

23. Which of the following statements are mutually contradictory?
  1. All flowers are not fragrant.
  2. Most flowers are not fragrant.
  3. None of the flowers is fragrant.
  4. Most flowers are fragrant.
  A. 1 and 2   B. 1 and 3
  C. 2 and 3   D. 3 and 4

24. Which of the following was *not* founded by Dr. B.R. Ambedkar?
  A. Deccan Education Society
  B. Samaj Samata Sangh
  C. People's Education Society
  D. Depressed Classes Institute

25. The Indian Constitution was amended for the first time in:
  A. 1950   B. 1951
  C. 1952   D. 1953

26. Which of the following statement(s) is/are correct about Amir Khusro?
  1. He was a disciple of Nizamuddin Auliya.
  2. He was the founder of both Hindustani Classical Music and Qawwali.
  A. 1 only   B. 2 only
  C. Both 1 and 2   D. Neither 1 nor 2

27. Which one of the following pairs is *not* correctly matched?
A. Shiekh Shihabuddin Suharwardi : Sufi Saint
B. Chaitanya Mahaprabhu : Bhakti Saint
C. Minhaj-us Siraj : Founder of Sufi order
D. Lalleshwari : Bhakti Saint

28. Which one of the following scripts of ancient India was written from right to left?
A. Brahmi   B. Nandnagari
C. Sharada   D. Kharoshti

29. What is the value of 'X' in the following sequence?
20, 19, 17, X, 10, 5
A. 15   B. 14
C. 13   D. 12

30. Who receives the 'Dronacharya' Award?
A. Scientists   B. Movie actors
C. Sports coaches   D. Sportspersons

31. In which year India joined the United Nations?
A. 1945   B. 1955
C. 1956   D. 1957

32. Which *does not* belong to the Indo-Aryan languages?
A. Gujarati   B. Tamil
C. Oriya   D. Marathi

33. Who administers the oath of office to the President?
A. The Chief Justice of India
B. The Speaker of the Lok Sabha
C. The Prime Minister
D. The Vice President

34. India helped the Rohingya refugees in Bangladesh through:
A. operation Rohingya
B. operation Manavta
C. operation Insaniyat
D. operation Refugee

35. Which Indian city has been declared as India's first 'World Heritage City'?
A. Amritsar   B. Ahmedabad
C. Rishikesh   D. Haridwar

36. The digital initiative 'Swayam' and 'Swayam Prabha' launched by the President Pranab Mukherji is associated with:
A. e-education   B. skill development
C. automation   D. Make in India

37. 2017 FIFA Confederations Cup title was won by:
A. Barcelona   B. England
C. Chile   D. Germany

38. Which city is declared World Book Capital, 2019 by UNESCO?
A. Riyad   B. Cairo
C. Jerusalem   D. Sharjah

39. Which Mosque did the Prime Minister Narendra Modi visit during one of his foreign visits?
A. Al-Aqsa Mosque
B. Sheikh-Zayed Grand Mosque
C. Al-Azhar Mosque
D. Masjid An-Nabawi

40. A block in the Parliament of which country is named after Atal Bihari Vajpayee, former Prime Minister of India?
A. Nepal   B. Bhutan
C. Afghanistan   D. Israel

41. Saudi Arabia has issued a decree that allows women to:
A. drive cars
B. contest elections
C. open bank accounts
D. participate in international games

42. GST has been primarily categorized into how many tax slab rates?
A. Six   B. Three
C. Four   D. Two

43. A veteran actor and Padmashri Awardee who featured in 'Shatranj Ke Khilari', 'Junoon' and 'Kranti' is:
A. Tom Alter   B. Vinod Khanna
C. Dharmender   D. Tom Cruise

44. At which place Gautama Buddha delivered his first sermon?
A. Sarnath   B. Lumbini
C. Bodh Gaya   D. Vaishali

45. TAPI Gas Pipeline connects:
  A. Tajikistan, Azerbaijan, Palestine, Israel
  B. Tajikistan, Afghanistan, Pakistan, India
  C. Turkmenistan, Afghanistan, Pakistan, India
  D. Turkmenistan, Afghanistan, Pakistan, Iran

46. Nirmala Sitharaman is a:
  A. Women Empowerment Minister
  B. Defence Minister
  C. Higher Education Minister
  D. Foreign Minister

47. Film and Television Institute of India is located at:
  A. Pune   B. Rajkot
  C. Pimpri   D. New Delhi

48. Which word *does not* belong with the others?
  A. Tyre   B. Steering wheel
  C. Engine   D. Car

49. Which word *does not* belong with the others?
  A. Noun   B. Preposition
  C. Punctuation   D. Adverb

50. Sponge is to porous as rubber is to:
  A. massive   B. solid
  C. elastic   D. inflexible

Directions (Qs. No. 51-60): *Choose the word or phrase which best completes each sentence.*

51. The children won't go to sleep ____ we leave a light on outside their bedroom.
  A. except   B. otherwise
  C. unless   D. but

52. She came to live here ____ a month ago.
  A. quite   B. beyond
  C. already   D. almost

53. Fortunately, ____ for a bump on the head, she suffered no serious injuries from her fall.
  A. other   B. except
  C. besides   D. apart

54. The clock was the first complex machine to enter the home, ____ it was too expensive.
  A. despite   B. although
  C. otherwise   D. average

55. Don't you get tired ____ watching TV every night?
  A. with   B. by
  C. of   D. at

56. The singer ended the concert ____ her most popular song.
  A. by   B. with
  C. in   D. as

57. Anyone ____ after the start of the play is not allowed in until the interval.
  A. arrives   B. has arrived
  C. arriving   D. arrived

58. By the time you ____ to the party, we ____ for several hours.
  A. have come; had been drinking
  B. come; will be drinking
  C. come; have been drinking
  D. came; had been drinking

59. I'll give you my spare keys in case you ____ home before me.
  A. would get   B. got
  C. will get   D. get

60. We shall take an umbrella with us ____ we don't get wet.
  A. in case   B. in order to
  C. so that   D. despite

SECTION-B

(Marks : 40)

Directions (Qs. No. 61-65): *Read the passage carefully and based on your understanding of it, answer the following questions briefly in your own words.*

For lasting and clear eyesight, eyes need care in the form of preventive measures, a continuous life-long exercise. Eyes don't just see, they do the talking. Eyes need care in the form of prevention, and knowing some preventive methods in eye care can make your eyes look bright and healthy and leave you with excellent eyesight. For bright and healthy eye good habits and good health care is important. One should eat good helpings of vegetables, fruits, omega-3 fatty acids, beta carotenes with vitamins A, C and E, enjoy good sleep and avoid direct sunlight. Eyes are windows to the human body. Doctors look in the eye to find conditions such as glaucoma, abnormal blood pressure, diabetes, heart diseases and other health concerns much before you notice its adverse impact.

It is never too early to begin eye checkups. By the time a child is four, it is imperative to have a checkup regularly to look for squint, signs of opacity, to decide whether or not glasses are needed. Ultraviolet-protective sunglasses from childhood can help protect eyes from the harmful UV-rays. An emerging and alarming trend is the Computer Eye Syndrome, which appears to be catching on in early adult life. We cannot escape the use of computers. Continuous staring at the monitors reduces blinking, causes strain to the eyes and can lead to dry eyes as well.

Glaucoma or raised pressure in eyes and diabetic retinopathy are silent killers of eyesight. If afflicited with diabetes, diet, exercise and drugs are to be remembered in that order to keep the doctor away. Some also require reading glasses in a condition known as presbyopia. Lasers are fast replacing glasses. One can develop cataract-defined as the loss of transparency in the natural lens of the eye. It's treated by replacing the opaque lens with an artificial lens called the intraocular lens. That said, eye care is, inevitably a continuous exercise through life.

61. How do we keep our eyes bright and healthy?

62. Explain 'Eyes don't just see, they do the talking'.

63. How is excessive computer usage harmful for the eyes?

64. Find word(s) from the passage which is/are equivalent(s) of the following:
 (*a*) Grievously affected especially by disease
 (*b*) By necessity
 (*c*) Necessarily
 (*d*) Non-transparent

65. Give a proper title to the passage.

Directions (Qs. No. 66-69): *Rearrange the following jumbled sentences in proper order.*

66. The Chief administers Justice of India Office the oath of President to the

67. chose India was a cozy home here for generations lived for Jews who

68. The process of mixed reaction demonetization well as critics received as it had both supporters as

69. monitors continuous at the reduces staring blinking

70. Write an essay on any one of the following topics within 200 words:
 (*a*) My idea of 'New India'
 (*b*) 'Corruption and Politics'
 (*c*) Women empowerment
 (*d*) Clean India Mission

71. Write a short note on any one of the following (within 150 words)
 (*a*) One suffers from it inequality due to improper education
 (*b*) Women must be treated on par with men
 (*c*) Role of students in the nation-building
 (*d*) Monuments are cultural heritage of a country
 (*e*) Effects of media on the young generation

72. Write your opinion about any one of the following (100 words):
 (*a*) Mobile should be banned in educational institution.
 (*b*) Study of a foreign language should be made compulsory.

ANSWERS

SECTION-A

1	2	3	4	5	6	7	8	9	10
B	A	D	D	B	D	C	C	D	C

11	12	13	14	15	16	17	18	19	20
A	C	A	B	B	C	C	A	B	A

21	22	23	24	25	26	27	28	29	30
D	B	B	A	B	C	C	D	B	C

31	32	33	34	35	36	37	38	39	40
A	C	A	C	B	A	D	D	A	C

41	42	43	44	45	46	47	48	49	50
A	C	A	A	C	B	A	D	C	C

51	52	53	54	55	56	57	58	59	60
C	D	B	B	C	B	C	D	D	C

EXPLANATORY ANSWERS

SECTION-A

21. 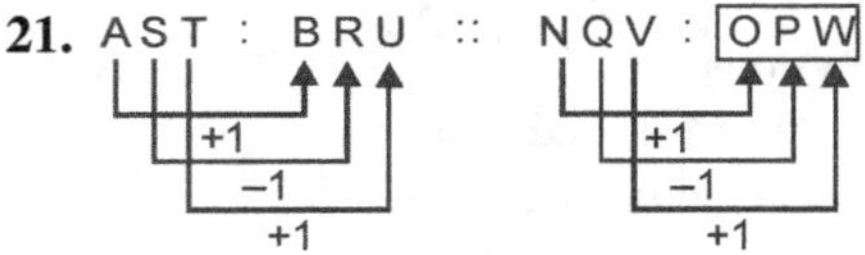

22. As,
$$PAN = 16 + 1 + 14 = 31$$
$$PAR = 16 + 1 + 18 = 35$$
Similarly, $PAT = 16 + 1 + 20 = 37$.

29. 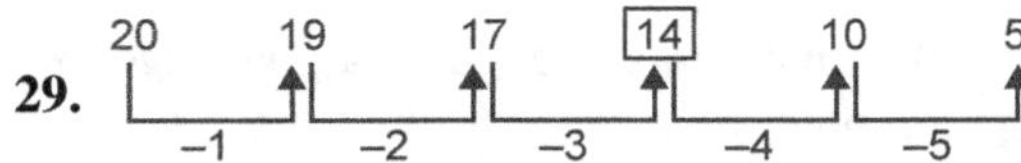

Hence, the value of 'X' is 14.

SECTION-B

61. We may keep our eyes bright and healthy through good habits and good health care. We should eat fruits and vegetables, healthy oils and diet with vitamins A, C & E. We should enjoy good sleep and avoid direct sunlight. We should go for regular eye-checkups. We should avoid sitting before the computers for longer durations. A good diet, exercise and drugs are a must in case of diabetes for better eye care.

62. In fact our eyes are made by nature to connect with others. Our eyes reveal our thoughts and feelings. Our eye contact should our attention. The eye contact creates an intimate bond with the other person. Eyes tell whether a person is shy, confident, happy, sad or hiding some emotions. If a person tells a lie it really difficult for him to make an eye contact with the other person.

63. These days, many of us have jobs that require us to stare at computer screens for hours at a time. That can put a real strain on your eyes.

Eye problems caused by computer use fall under the heading computer vision syndrome (CVS). It isn't one specific problem. Instead, it includes a whole range of eye strain and pain. Research shows that between 50% and 90% of people who work at a computer screen have at least some symptoms.

Working adults aren't the only ones affected. Kids who stare at tablets or use computers during the day at school can have issues, too, especially if the lighting and their posture are less than ideal.

CVS is similar to carpal tunnel syndrome and other repetitive motion injuries we might get at work. It happens because our eyes follow the same path over and over. And it can get worse the longer we continue the movement.

When we work at a computer, our eyes have to focus and refocus all the time. They move back and forth as we read. We may have to look down at papers and then back up to type. Our eyes react to changing images on the screen to create so our brain can process what we're seeing. All these jobs require a lot of effort from our eye muscles. And to make things worse, unlike a book or piece of paper, the screen adds contrast, flicker, and glare.

We're more likely to have problems if we already have eye trouble, if we need glasses but don't have them, or if we wear the wrong prescription for computer use.

Computer work gets harder as we age and the lenses in our eyes becomes less flexible. Somewhere around age 40, our ability to focus on near and far objects will start to go away. Our eye doctor call this condition presbyopia.

There's no proof that computer use causes any long-term damage to the eyes. But regular use can lead to eye strain and discomfort.

We may notice:

- Blurred vision
- Double vision
- Dry, red eyes
- Eye irritation
- Headaches
- Neck or back pain
- If we don't do anything about them, it could affect more than our eyes. We could also have issues with our work performance.

64. (*a*) Grievously affected especially by disease : **Retinopathy/Cataract**

(*b*) By necessity : **Imperative**

(*c*) Necessarily : **Inevitably**

(*d*) Non-transparent : **Opaque**

65. EYE CARE.

66. The Chief Justice of India administers the oath of office to the President.

67. India was chose a cozy home for Jews who lived here for generations.

Jews who lived here for generations chose India was for a cozy home.

68. The process of demonetization received mixed reaction as it had both supporters as well as critics.

69. Continuous staring at the monitors reduces blinking.

70. (*a*) It is believed that India is likely to become a fully developed nation by 2020. In any case, I can have a dream about India. The India of my dreams will be a fully developed nation.

In the India of my dreams, there will be no poverty, no illiteracy, no disease, no unemployment, no scams, no shortages of food and no serious problems.

In such an India population will have stabilized. All the people will be literate, highly learned and skilled.

It will be an egalitarian society in India that I dream of. There will be no wide disparity in incomes and possesion of property and hence no heart-burning.

In the India of my dreams, there will be no communalism. All communities, even while observing their own different rituals and having different faiths and creeds, will live in peace and respect each othe's sentiments.

Such an India will be a strong world power both in economic and military terms. No other country would ever dare attack

India. The people will be highly patriotic and will defend every inch of the Indian land with all their might.

There will be no terrorism and no evils of dowry system, drinking, smoking, gambling and drug-taking in this India. Great attention will be given to women, children, the youth and the old people.

The houses, cities and villages will be clean and beautiful and free from garbage and pollution. All will lead a long, happy healthy, and carefree life.

71. (*c*) The future of India depends on our students. A country's name and fame rest on the youth. If the power of young men or students is directed to constructive purposes, the whole nation will move to all round development. This responsibility has increased immensely with the dawn of independence. An eminent educationist has rightly said, "Give me the children and I will change the nation." A nation can make progress only when it gets the co-operation form all its citizens. So it is essential that students must know about their duties.

India is a developing country. The young men may do a lot in the development work. They may go to the villages for adult education, for doing social service to the poor villagers, for teaching new technology in farming and other such vocations. The trained and learned young men may bring about green revolution in the country. They may preach ideas of secularism in the country.

By leading an ideal simple life they may lead literate. In emergencies, they may do a lot in controlling floods etc. We can mobilize student power to preach communal harmony. In brief, the student power may be used at every moment whenever the nation needs their services.

72. (*a*) Mobile Phones are causing distress and disruption as students are using phones in schools/colleges, in streets, almost everywhere.

Mobile phones unvaryingly introduce students to the world of social media. In a country like India, where online ethics are invisible in the school curriculum, this also increases antisocial activities like bullying. The introduction of mobile phones, thus, cannot go without these problems.

Apart from a small lot, majority students will easily be distracted by the numerous attractive applications present in their phones. Thus, resulting in a waste of time.

We are becoming slaves to mobile phones in today's time. Even for small calculations, students use mobiles and calculators which is making their basics weak and also degrading their thinking ability.

Jawaharlal Nehru University (JNU)
BA (Hons.) Entrance Examination, 2017

CLUSTER-1: French, German, Russian and Spanish

UNIT–1

1. Here below is a series. Fill in the blank with one of the options given below:

B_2CD, _____ , BCD_4, B_5CD, BC_6D.

A. B_2C_2D B. BC_3D
C. B_2C_3D D. BCD_7

2. On the basis of the paragraph below, find out which one is the correct statement among the four statements that follow:

Tato is twelve years old. For three years, he has been asking his parents for a dog. His parents have told him that they believe a dog would not be happy in an apartment, but they have given him permission to have a bird. Tato has not yet decided what kind of bird he would like to have.

A. Tato's parents like birds better than they like dogs.
B. Tato does not like birds.
C. Tato and his parents live in an apartment.
D. Tato and his parents would like to move.

3. Choose the picture that would go in the empty box so that the two bottom pictures are related in the same way as the top two are related:

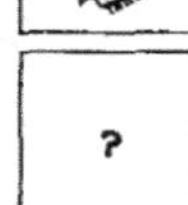

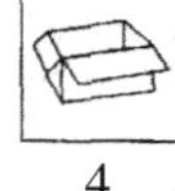

A. 1   B. 2
C. 3   D. 4

4. Choose the picture that would go in the empty box so that the two bottom pictures are related in the same way as the top two are related:

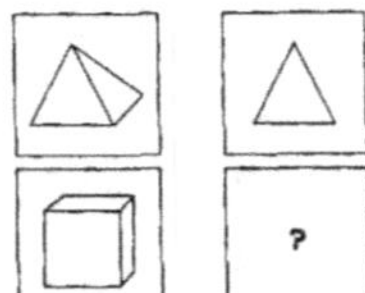

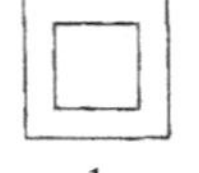
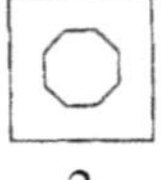

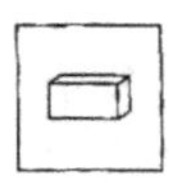

A. 1   B. 2
C. 3   D. 4

5. Each problem consists of three statements. Based on the first two statements, the third statement may be true, false, or uncertain.

    Smrithi is older than Jean.
    Olivier is older than Smrithi.
    Jean is older than Olivier.

If the first two statements are true, the third statement is:

A. true   B. false
C. uncertain   D. None of the above

6. Shera weighs less than Bruno.

Shera weighs more than Boomer.

Of the three dogs, Boomer weighs the least.

If the first two statements are true, the third statement is

A. true   B. false

C. uncertain D. None of the above

7. Find the odd one out:

A. Pendulum   B. Pencil

C. Penicillin   D. Pesticide

8. Find the odd one out:

A. Poet   B. Novelist

C. Critic   D. Dramatist

9. Find the odd one out:

A. Roar   B. Bark

C. Howl   D. Quack

10. Find the odd one out:

A. Wheat   B. Ragi

C. Millet   D. Corn flakes

11. There are five suitcases. The weight of each one is given below.

 Suitcase A weighs 33 kg

 Suitcase B weighs 35 kg

 Suitcase C weighs 60 kg

 Suitcase D weighs 42 kg

 Suitcase E weighs 15 kg

Which is the odd one out?

A. Suitcase A   B. Suitcase B

C. Suitcase C   D. Suitcase D

12. In the left-hand side, fill up the position of @ the correct mathematical operations like addition, subtraction, multiplication, division etc., so as to arrive at the correct right-hand side number

35@16@5 = 112

Options:

A. Addition and subtraction

B. Multiplication and subtraction

C. Multiplication and division

D. Division and addition

13. Who ruled Russia in 1914?

A. Tsar Nicolas II B. Novgorod Rurik

C. Peter the Great D. Ivan IV

14. Jadidists were:

A. the merchants selling the stone called Jade

B. Jews living outside Germany

C. Muslim reformers within the Russian empire

D. Supporters of the king of France during the French Revolution

15. The Nuremberg Tribunal judged:

A. the Tsars of Russia after Revolution

B. the Nazis after the Second World War

C. the supporters of Lenin after his death

D. the deputies of Weimar Republic

16. After the First World War, who demilitarized Germany to weaken its power?

A. United Nations

B. The axis powers

C. The newly formed USSR

D. The allied powers

17. The National Anthem of France called *Marseillaise* was written by:

A. Rouget de Lisle B. Charles Baudelaire

C. La Martine   D. Rousseau

18. Nanine Vallain was a

A. French traveller who came to India in 19th century

B. French female painter in the Court of the last Tsar of Russia

C. German female painter whose works represented hope in post Second World War Germany

D. French female painter who painted on themes related to the French Revolution

19. The French speaking province of Canada is:

A. Nova Scotia   B. Quebec

C. Manitoba   D. Saskatchewan

20. The Spanish working class responded with a Revolution in 1936 to the troops of

A. Franco   B. Salazar

C. Mussolini   D. Hitler

21. Felipe VI is a king of:
A. England
B. Monaco
C. Spain
D. Belgium

22. Santiago is the capital city of:
A. Chile
B. Brazil
C. Peru
D. Cuba

23. Machu Picchu is in:
A. Bali province of Indonesia
B. South America
C. Africa
D. North America

24. The painting *Mona Lisa* is in which museum?
A. Musée d'Orsay
B. Musée du Louvre
C. Museo del Prado
D. Galleria Nazionale d'Arte Moderna

25. *Oktoberfest* is celebrated in:
A. Marseille
B. Monaco
C. Madrid
D. Munich

26. *Dia de muertos* is celebrated in:
A. Argentina
B. Mexico
C. Spain
D. Chile

27. *Hermitage* Museum is in which city?
A. Saint Petersburg
B. Moscow
C. Berlin
D. Barcelona

28. Neymar Jr., the famous footballer plays for which football club?
A. FC Barcelona
B. Real Madrid
C. Paris Saint-Germain FC
D. FC Bayern Munich

Directions (Qs. No. 29-33): *Based on the given statements, answer the questions that follow:*

Anita and Amit play hockey and cricket.

Amit and Madhu like to play chess and hockey.

Alok and Anita play football and cricket.

Alok and Srishti play golf and football.

Srishti is good at golf, football and chess.

29. Who among the following plays chess, hockey and cricket?
A. Anita
B. Alok
C. Srishti
D. None of them

30. Who among the following plays golf, football and cricket?
A. Srishti
B. Anita
C. Alok
D. None of them

31. Who among the following plays hockey and chess but not cricket?
A. Srishti
B. Alok
C. Madhu
D. Amit

32. Who among the following plays golf, football and chess?
A. Srishti
B. Alok
C. Madhu
D. Amit

33. Who among the following plays cricket, hockey and football?
A. Amit
B. Anita
C. Srishti
D. Madhu

Directions (Qs. No. 34-35): *Based on the given statements, answer the questions that follow:*

Vaibhav is son of Mahesh's father's sister. Prateek is son of Rekha, who is mother of Vineet and grandmother of Mahesh. Mukesh is father of Neeti and grandfather of Vaibhav. Rekha is wife of Mukesh.

34. How is Vaibhav related to Rekha?
A. Grandson
B. Son
C. Nephew
D. Data inadequate

35. How is Vineet's wife related to Neeti?
A. Sister
B. Niece
C. Sister-in-law
D. Data inadequate

UNIT–2

(Reading Comprehension)

Directions (Qs. No. 36-40): *Reading Comprehension Questions.*

A quarter of all global deaths of children under five are due to unhealthy or polluted environments, including dirty water and air, second-hand smoke and a lack of adequate hygiene, the World Health Organization (WHO) said on Monday.

Such unsanitary and polluted environments can lead to fatal cases of diarrhoea, malaria and pneumonia, the WHO said in a report, and kill 1.7 million children a year.

"A polluted environment is a deadly one—particularly for young children," WHO Director-General Margaret Chan said in a statement. "Their developing organs and immune systems, and smaller bodies and airways, make them especially vulnerable to dirty air and water."

In the report—"Inheriting a sustainable world : Atlas on children's health and the environment"—the WHO said harmful exposure can start in the womb, and then continue if infants and toddlers are exposed to indoor and outdoor air pollution and second-hand smoke.

This increases their childhood risk of pneumonia as well as their lifelong risk of chronic respiratory diseases such as asthma. Air pollution also increases the lifelong risk of heart disease, stroke and cancer, the report said.

The report also noted that in households without access to safe water and sanitation, or that are polluted with smoke from unclean fuels such as coal or dung for cooking and heating, children are at higher risk of diarrhoea and pneumonia.

Children are also exposed to harmful chemicals through food, water, air and products around them, it said.

Maria Neira, a WHO expert on public health, said this was a heavy toll, both in terms of deaths and long-term illness and disease rates. She urged governments to do more to make all places safe for children.

"Investing in the removal of environmental risks to health, such as improving water quality or using cleaner fuels, will result in massive health benefits," she said.

[Source : *The Hindu,* March 6, 2017)

36. The newspaper article primarily discusses:
    A. the environmental risk to health
    B. environmental hazards leading to global deaths of children
    C. hazards of air pollution
    D. pollution leading to long-term illness

37. Fatal cases of diarrhoea, malaria and pneumonia in children are caused due to
    A. low immune system in children
    B. bad water quality
    C. unsanitary and polluted environments
    D. harmful chemicals through food

38. In order to improve the situation and lower the death rates in children, Maria Neira, a WHO expert on public health, suggests which of the following?
    A. Improving water quality or using cleaner fuels
    B. Government should do more to improve the environment
    C. Avoid harmful exposure to chemicals
    D. Work with WHO

39. An antonym used for 'resilient' in the article is:
    A. unsafe   B. endangered
    C. unprotected   D. vulnerable

40. Harmful exposure to children can start in the womb due to:
    A. indoor and outdoor air pollution and second-hand smoke
    B. using unclean fuels
    C. dirty air and water
    D. unhygienic sanitation

UNIT–3

(Artificial Language)

Directions (Qs. No. 41-45): *Given below is a list of three words in an artificial language and their English meanings. The question that follows requires you to translate an English word into the artificial language. Choose one from the choices given:*

41. Here are some words translated from an artificial language.

   Bezbota means without employment
   Dostobota means enough employment
   Okhranvedomost means defense ministry
   Which word could mean 'employment ministry'?
   A. Botavedomost   B. Bezokhran
   C. Dostookhran   D. Botaokhran

42. Here are some words translated from an artificial language.

   Narodproxy means mass protest
   Jenaproxy means women protest
   Phoebeteti means February revolution
   Which word could mean 'February women revolution'?
   A. Phoebenarodteti   B. Jenaphoebeproxy
   C. Phoebejenateti   D. Phoebejenaproxy

43. Here are some words translated from an artificial language.

   Contrarose means human respect
   Acontrarose means mutual respect
   Altropenja means self being
   Which word could mean 'being human'?
   A. Altrocontra   B. Panjaacontra
   C. Penjarose   D. Penjacontra

44. Here are some words translated from an artificial language.

   Conteskult means people's culture
   Contesnulkht means people's narrative
   Kultpassant means cultural tradition
   Which word could mean 'people's narrative tradition'?
   A. Contesnultpassant
   B. Nulktcontespassant
   C. Passantnulktcontes
   D. Contesnulkhtpassant

45. Here are some words translated from an artificial language.

   Husslebussle means artistic music
   Musslebussle means rock music
   Tusslenussle means commercial cinema
   Which word could mean 'artistic cinema'?
   A. Hussletussle   B. Musslenussle
   C. Nusslehussle   D. Husslenussle

UNIT–4

1. Please rearrange the order of the given sentence in correct form:
   French King Louis XVI/the French Revolution/was tried/on January 21, 1793/and executed/after/the

2. Please rearrange the order of the given sentence in correct form:
   the Hollywood Theatre/is a not-for-profit organization/whose mission is to entertain,/inspire,/educate/and connect/the community/through the art of film

3. Please rearrange the order of the given sentence in correct form:
   touch/told/woman/anything/museum/to/me/the/not/the/in

4. Write the full forms of the following:
   NASA :
   GST   :
   ISRO :
   ATM   :
   HTTP :
   GDP   :

5. Write a short essay on the advantages and disadvantages of Social Media like Facebook, Twitter and WhatsApp, etc. Is social media a medium to empower people or is it used to enslave people and cripple communication skills? Support your answer with concrete examples.

6. Look at the image, read the passage and write about what you think of the festival. Argue your position clearly, in a coherent and logical manner by taking into account the various arguments that are involved in sports that involve animal participants and the tradition of a particular society.

Jallikattu (or Sallikkattu), also known as *Eru thazhuvuthal* and *Manju virattu,* is a traditional sport in which a bull is released into a crowd of people, and multiple human participants attempt to grab the large hump on the bull's back with both arms and hang on to it while the bull attempts to escape.

ANSWERS

UNIT-1

1	2	3	4	5	6	7	8	9	10
B	C	A	A	B	A	D	C	D	D

11	12	13	14	15	16	17	18	19	20
B	C	A	C	B	D	A	D	B	A

21	22	23	24	25	26	27	28	29	30
C	A	B	B	D	B	A	C	D	C

31	32	33	34	35
C	A	B	A	C

UNIT-2

36	37	38	39	40
B	C	A	D	A

UNIT-3

41	42	43	44	45
A	C	D	D	D

EXPLANATORY ANSWERS

UNIT-1

1. Here,

$$B_2CD \rightarrow B\ C\ D \rightarrow B\ C\ D$$
$$(2+1)\qquad (2+1+1)$$
$$\rightarrow \quad B \qquad C D \rightarrow B \quad C \quad D$$
$$(2+1+1+1)\qquad (2+1+1+1+1)$$

11. Sum of the digits of the weight is:

$A \Rightarrow 3 + 3 = 6$

$B \Rightarrow 3 + 5 = 8$

$C \Rightarrow 6 + 0 = 6$

$D \Rightarrow 4 + 2 = 6$

$E \Rightarrow 1 + 5 = 6.$

12. $\Rightarrow 35 \times 16 \div 5$

$\Rightarrow 33 \times \dfrac{16}{5}$

$= 7 \times 16 = 112.$

17. The French National Anthem is called *La Marseillaise.* It was written in Strasbourg in 1792 (not in Marseille as the name implies) with the encouragement and support of the Mayor of Strasbourg, who felt the revolution needed a stirring song for its troops to march by. Claude Rouget de Lisle, a young engineer in the army, composed and named it *Chant de Guerre de l'Armée du Rhinwhich,* translates as 'War Song of the Rhine Army'. Of course, he didn't know that it would eventually become the National Anthem of France. It began to be sung at banquets and throughout the city after copies were distributed. The revolutionaries from Marseilles marched into Paris singing it and thereafter it became known as 'La Marseillaise'.

19. French is the mother tongue of about 7.3 million Canadians (22% of the Canadian population, second to English at 58.4%) according to Census Canada 2011. Most native speakers of the French language in Canada live in Quebec, where French is the majority official language. About 80% of Quebec's population are native francophones, and 95% of the population speak French as their first or second language. Additionally, about one million native francophones live in other provinces, forming a sizable minority in New Brunswick, which is officially a bilingual province, where about one-third of the population are francophone.

21. **Felipe VI** is the King of Spain. He ascended to the throne on 19 June 2014 following the abdication of his father, King Juan Carlos I. He is the only son of Juan Carlos and his wife Sofía of Greece and Denmark. When Juan Carlos was chosen in 1969 to be Francisco Franco's successor, Felipe became second in line to the Spanish throne.

22. Santiago de Chile, or simply Santiago, is the capital and largest city of Chile as well as one of the largest cities in the Americas. It is the centre of Chile's largest and the most densely populated conurbation. The city is entirely located in the country's central valley, at an elevation of 520 m (1,706 ft) above the mean sea level.

24. The *Mona Lisa,* is a half-length portrait painting by the Italian Renaissance artist Leonardo da Vinci that has been described as "the best known, the most visited, the most written about, the most sung about, the most parodied work of art in the world". The *Mona Lisa* is also one of the most valuable paintings in the world. The painting is thought to be a portrait of Lisa Gherardini, the wife of Francesco del Giocondo, and is in oil on a white Lombardy poplarpanel. It had been believed to have been painted between 1503 and 1506; however, Leonardo may have continued working on it as late as 1517.

Recent academic work suggests that it would not have been started before 1513. It was acquired by King Francis I of France and is now the property of the French Republic, on permanent display at the Louvre Museum in Paris since 1797.

27. The **Hermitage Museum** in St. Petersburg, Russia is one of the largest and oldest art galleries and museums of human history and culture in the world. The vast Hermitage collections are displayed in six buildings, founded by Catherine II of Russia in 1764 and opened in public since 1852. The main building is the Winter Palace. This was the official residence of the Russian Tsars.

For Qs. 29-33: From the given statements,
Anita plays = Hockey, Cricket & Football
Amit plays = Hockey, Cricket & Chess
Madhu plays = Chess & Hockey
Alok plays = Football, Cricket & Golf
Srishti plays = Golf, Football & Chess

UNIT-3

43. Here,
$\Rightarrow$ Contra + rose = human + respect
$\Rightarrow$ Acontra + rose = mutual + respect
$\Rightarrow$ Altro + penja = self + being
$\therefore$ Penja + contra = being + human

44. Here,
$\Rightarrow$ contes + kult = people's + culture
$\Rightarrow$ contes + nulkht = people's + narrative
and $\Rightarrow$ kult + passant = cultural + tradition
$\therefore$ contes + nulkht + passant
= people's + narrative + tradition.

45. Here,
$\Rightarrow$ Huss + lebussle = artistic + music
$\Rightarrow$ Muss + lebussle = rock + music
$\Rightarrow$ Tuss + lenussle = commercial + cinema
$\therefore$ Huss + lenussle = artistic + cinema.

UNIT-4

1. The French King Louis XVI was tried after the French Revolution and executed on January 21, 1793.

2. The Hollywood Theatre is a not-for-profit organization whose mission is to entertain, educate, inspire and connect the community through the art of film.

3. The woman told me not to touch anything in the museum.

4. NASA : National Aeronautics and State Administration.
GST : Goods and Services Tax
ISRO : Indian Space Research Organisation.
ATM : Automated Teller Machine
HTTP : Hypertext Transfer Protocol
GDP : Gross Domestic Product

5. Man invented technology to make his life better and it became a revolution. Now-a-days technology can be seen everywhere. Use of technology has affected the human life to that extent that we are literally dependent on the technology in our daily lives. The technology has also changed the way we communicate with other people. With the use of social media, people are connected with each other in an electronic way. Any Website, Portal, App which brings the social aspect of the human life online can be called as social media site. YouTube, Twitter, WhatsApp, Instagram and Facebook affect the social aspect of the community. It's been always debated whether social media is a boon or a bane. There are both advantages and disadvantages of it. So we will discuss the pros and cons of social media. Social media is a great way to connect with people in your life. It enables you to share important events, information and the moments in your life with people that matter. Social networking sites brought the opportunity of expression to each and everyone in their palm. Now we can support policy changes, petitions, social causes, show sympathy to disasters and calamity survivors. On YouTube we can share our knowledge by making videos, on Quora we can help others by answering their questions. Social media also gave medium to raise voices against serious issues like eve teasing, women safety, feminism, etc. Social networking sites gave us a channel to help others too.

Now-a-days social media is the main distribution channel for news, updates, weather forecast, etc.; gone are those days when one had to wait till news time. The real time updates, news and the current affairs definitely help us to stay up to date with the time and the situation around us. These sites also expose us to information around the world.

As every coin has two sides even the social media has its own dangers and disadvantages. There is no doubt that social media brought new opportunities in communication but at the same time it suppressed the old ones. After all, we are human beings and there is no better way of interaction than face to face communication. Social media created a new type of crime called Cyber crime. It has also created a threat to our privacy as all the social media sites access your personal information when you use them.

Like any other technology, solution, invention social media also has both brighter and darker sides. On one side social media brings lots of opportunities but at the same time they get used for cyber bullying terrorist propagandas too. Better parental control features need to be implemented on these social media sites so that younger children are protected from such online harms. For adults, it's up to them, what to choose, what not to say and what to say as they are free to make choices. In short,

social media sites are not bad, it's up to us users to make it boon or bane. Social media is definitely a medium to empower people if it is used intelligently and with restraint. It is not at all used to enslave people and cripple communication skills. It is for the people who use it not to become its slaves and cripple their communication skills by overusing it in place of direct communications.

6. Jallikattu is typically practised in the state of Tamil Nadu as a part of Pongal celebrations on Mattu Pongal day, which occurs annually in January. On Mattu Pongal day a harvest festival is celebrated in Tamil Nadu state. Ancient Tamil Sangams described the practice as Eru Thazhuvuthal, literally "bull embracing". The modern term *Jallikattu* or *Sallikattu* is derived from *Salli* (coins) and *Kattu* (Package), which refers to a prize of coins that are tied to the bull's horns and that participants attempt to retrieve. *manju virattu* literally means "bull chasing".

Jallikattu has been known to be practised since the Tamil classical period (400 – 100 BC). It was common among the ancient people Aayars who lived in the 'Mullai' geographical division of the ancient Tamil country. Later, it became a platform for display of bravery and prize money was introduced for participation encouragement.

An investigation by the Animal Welfare Board of India concluded that "Jallikattu is inherently cruel to animals". Animal welfare organisations, the Federation of Indian Animal Protection Organisations and PETA India have protested against the practice. The legal situation surrounding Jallikattu is as yet not clearly resolved.

While the people who have been celebrating the event for so many years insist they cannot let go the event due to religious reasons.

Jawaharlal Nehru University (JNU)
BA (Hons.) Entrance Examination, 2017

CLUSTER-2: Japanese, Korean and Chinese

SECTION-A

Directions: *Question Nos. 1-45 are of 1 mark each and Question Nos. 46-50 are of 2 marks each. All questions are compulsory.*
Encircle the correct answer:

1. In an artificial language,
    gorblflur means fan belt
    pixngorbl means ceiling fan
    arthtusl means tile roof
    Which word could mean 'ceiling tile'?
    A. gorbltusl   B. flurgorbl
    C. arthflur   D. pixnarth

2. In an artificial language,
    granamelke means big tree
    pinimelke means little tree
    melkehoon means tree house
    Which word could mean 'big house'?
    A. granahoon   B. pinishur
    C. pinihoon   D. melkegrana

3. In an artificial language,
    lelibroon means yellow hat
    plekafroti means flower garden
    frotimix means garden salad
    Which word could mean 'yellow flower'?
    A. lelifroti   B. lelipleka
    C. plekabroon   D. frotibroon

4. In an artificial language,
    malgauper means peach cobbler
    malgaport means peach juice
    moggagrop means apple jelley

Which word could mean 'apple juice'?
    A. moggaport   B. malgaaupar
    C. gropport   D. moggagrop

5. If FRIEND is coded as HUMJTK, how can CANDLE be written in that code?
    A. DEQJQM   B. DCQHQK
    C. EDRIRL   D. ESJFME

6. If PALE is coded as 2134, EARTH is coded as 41590, how can PEARL be coded in that language?
    A. 25430   B. 29530
    C. 25413   D. 24153

7. If 'eraser' is called 'box', 'box' is called 'pencil', 'pencil' is called 'sharpener', and 'sharpener' is called 'bag', what will a child write with?
    A. Eraser   B. Bag
    C. Pencil   D. Sharpener

8. How often do you play tennis?
    A. On Tuesday
    B. For two hours
    C. Almost everyday
    D. With Anil

9. Do not go out __ you've finished your work.
    A. as   B. while
    C. until   D. after

10. Ram wasn't tired, __ he took a nap.
    A. otherwise   B. hence
    C. nevertheless   D. furthermore

11. Meena can bring some food,
    A. won't she?   B. will she?
    C. can't she?   D. can she?

12. "Where is the library?"
"It is ___ your right."
    A. in   B. at
    C. on   D. by

13. Amita started her current job _________ September 24.
    A. in   B. at
    C. on   D. to

14. What did you do yesterday?
    A. I am swimming   B. I swim
    C. I will swim   D. I swam

15. He didn't earn enough money. ____, his wife decided to get a job.
    A. Moreover   B. Therefore
    C. Although   D. Otherwise

16. My friend is very good __ singing.
    A. at   B. in
    C. with   D. of

17. Don't brood ___ your mistakes and failures.
    A. with   B. at
    C. by   D. over

Directions (Qs. 18-20): *What comes next in the series? Encircle the correct answer to fill in the blanks in the series:*

18. SCD,TEF, UGH, __ , WKL
    A. CMN   B. UJI
    C. VIJ   D. IJT

19. B2CD, __ , BCD4, B5CD, BC6D
    A. B2C2D   B. BC3D
    C. B2C3D   D. BCD7

20. 3, 4, 6, 9, 13, __
    A. 16   B. 17
    C. 18   D. 19

Directions (Qs. 21-23): *Each of the following problems consists of three statements. Based on the first two statements, the third statement may be true, false, uncertain or none of the above. Encircle the correct answer:*

21. The hotel is two blocks East of the drugstore. The market is one block West of the hotel. The drugstore is West of the market.
If the first two statements are true, the third statement is
    A. true   B. false
    C. uncertain   D. None of the above

22. Town A is North of Town B.
Town B is East of Town C.
Town C is North-West of Town A.
If the first two statements are true, the third statement is
    A. true   B. false
    C. uncertain   D. None of the above

23. Houses in Kanpur cost less than houses in Lucknow.
Houses in Varanasi cost more than houses in Lucknow.
Of the three cities, the houses in Varanasi cost the most.
If the first two statements are true, the third statement is
    A. true   B. false
    C. uncertain   D. None of the above

Directions (Qs. 24-25): *Find the statement that must be true according to the given information. Encircle A, B, C or D:*

24. When they heard news of the cyclone, Maya and Ria decided to change their vacation plans. Instead of travelling to the beach resort, they booked a room at a new spa in the mountains. Their plans were a bit more expensive, but they had heard wonderful things about the spa and they were happy to find availability on such short notice.
    A. Maya and Ria take beach vacations every year
    B. The spa is overpriced
    C. It is usually necessary to book at least six months in advance at the spa
    D. Maya and Ria decided to change their vacation plans because of the cyclone

25. Rashmi has four children. Two of the children have blue eyes and two of the children have brown eyes. Half of the children are girls. If the above three statements are facts, which of the following must also be a fact?
(*i*) At least one girl has blue eyes
(*ii*) Two of the children are boys
(*iii*) The boys have brown eyes
A. (*i*) only
B. (*ii*) only
C. (*ii*) and (*iii*) only
D. None of the statements is a known fact

Directions (Qs. 26-27): *Encircle the correct answer.*

26. What is Ikebana?
A. Flower viewing   B. Flower painting
C. Paper folding   D. Flower arrangement

27. Ban Ki-moon, the Ex-Secretary General of the UN was a national of which country?
A. ROC   B. DPRK
C. PRC   D. ROK

28. When was Macao handed over to China?
A. 2001   B. 1999
C. 2004   D. 1997

29. Which of the following is the first level of administrative division for jurisdiction in Japan?
A. District   B. State
C. Country   D. Prefecture

30. Which of the following is a Japanese martial art?
A. Taekwondo   B. Karate
C. Shaolin   D. Kung Fu

31. The year 2017 in Chinese Zodiac is the year of
A. Horse   B. Sheep
C. Rooster   D. Dragon

32. What was Taiwan formerly known as?
A. Formosa   B. Canton
C. Taipei   D. Macau

33. Who is the present emperor of Japan?
A. Akihito   B. Hirohito
C. Naruhito   D. Yoshihito

34. The 'Gangnan' in popular Korean pop music 'Gangnam style' refers to:
A. stylish women   B. psy the singer
C. a district in Seoul D. a dance style

35. Kimchi is a dish made of:
A. fermented fish and spices
B. fermented soyabean and spices
C. fermented vegetables and spices
D. fermented meat and spices

36. Hallyu or Korean Wave is the word for the South Korean Wave of:
A. popular products B. popular culture
C. popular food   D. popular dress

37. The words 'Satyameva Jayate' inscribed below the baseplate of the emblem of India are taken from the:
A. Rigveda
B. Satapatha Brahmana
C. Mundak Upanishad
D. Ramayana

38. Who composed the famous song 'Sare Jahan Se Accha'?
A. Jaidev
B. Muhammed Iqbal
C. Bankim Chandra Chatterjee
D. Rabindranath Tagore

39. R. K. Narayan and his stories are centred on which fictional place?
A. Malgudi   B. Malguri
C. Talgudi   D. Hemkhanakhan

40. How much time approximately does it take for sunlight to reach the earth?
A. 8 seconds   B. 8 minutes
C. 8 hours   D. 8 days

Directions (Qs. 41-42): *Read the following passages and encircle the correct answer.*

PASSAGE-1

BPA is a chemical that is put into plastics that are used as food containers. Unfortunately, some of the BPA passes from the containers into the foods that they are meant to protect. When people and animals eat those foods, BPA goes into their bodies.

There are studies that have found that BPA can increase our chances of getting a number of serious diseases. Many food companies are concerned about that risk and are starting to use containers that contain no BPA.

That's good right? Not necessarily. Some scientists caution that the substitute chemicals being used might turn out to be dangerous as well. They could possibly be even worse!

41. According to this passage, BPA
   A. is used to make food taste better
   B. leaks into food
   C. means better plastic articles
   D. makes us strong

42. Food companies are starting to
   A. tell people not to worry about BPA
   B. pretend that they don't use BPA in their containers
   C. charge more for BPA
   D. use containers that do not contain BPA

PASSAGE-2

Dolphins are regarded as the friendliest creatures in the sea and stories of them helping drowning sailors have been common since Roman times. The more we learn about dolphins, the more we realize that their society is more complex than people previously imagined. They look after other dolphins when they are ill, care for pregnant mothers and protect the weakest in the community, as we do. Some scientists have suggested that dolphins have a language but it is much more probable that they communicate with each other without needing words. Could any of these mammals be more intelligent than man? Certainly the most common argument in favour of man's superiority over them that we can kill them more easily than they can kill us is the least satisfactory. On the contrary, the more we discover about these remarkable creatures, the less we appear superior when we destroy them.

43. It is clear from the passage that dolphins
   A. are proven to be less intelligent than once thought
   B. have a reputation for being friendly to humans
   C. are the most powerful creatures that live in the oceans
   D. are capable of learning a language and communicating with humans

44. The fact that the writer of the passage thinks that we can kill dolphins more easily than they can kill us
   A. means that they are better adapted to their environment than we are
   B. shows that dolphins have a very sophisticated form of communication
   C. proves that dolphins are not the most intelligent species at sea
   D. does not mean that we are superior to them

45. One can infer from the reading that:
   A. communication is the most fascinating aspect of the dolphins
   B. dolphins have skills that no other living creatures have, such as the ability to think
   C. it is not usual for dolphins to communicate with each other
   D. dolphins have some social traits that are similar to those of humans

PASSAGE-3

Esperanto is what is called a planned, or artificial, language. It was created more than a century ago by Polish eye doctor Ludwik Lazar Zamenhof.

Zamenhof believed that a common language would help to alleviate some of the misunderstandings among cultures. In Zamenhof's first attempt at a universal language, he tried to create a language that was as uncomplicated as possible.

This first language included words such as ab, ac, ba, eb, be, and ce. This did not result in a workable language, in that, these monosyllabic words, though short, were not easy to understand or to retain.

Next, Zamenhof tried a different way of constructing a simplified language. He made the words in his language sound like words that people already knew, but he simplified the grammar tremendously. One example of how he simplified the language can be seen in the suffixes : all nouns in this language end in o, as in the noun amiko, which means "friend", and all adjectives end in -a, as in the adjective beta, which means "pretty". Another example of the simplified language can be seen in the prefix mal-, which makes a word opposite in meaning; the word *malamiko* therefore means "enemy", and the word *malbela* therefore means "ugly" in Zamenhof's language.

In 1887, Zamenhof wrote a description of this language and published it. He used a penname, Dr. Esperanto, when signing the book. He selected the name Esperanto because this word means "a person who hopes" in his language. Esperanto clubs began **popping up** throughout Europe, and by 1905 Esperanto had spread from Europe to America and Asia.

In 1905, the First World Congress of Esperanto took place in France with approximately 700 attendees from 20 different countries. Congresses were held annually for nine years and 4000 attendees were registered for the Tenth World Esperanto Congress scheduled for 1914, when World War I erupted and forced its cancellation.

Esperanto has had its ups and downs in the period since World War I. Today, years after it was introduced, it is estimated that perhaps a quarter of a million people are fluent in it.

Current advocates would like to see its use grow considerably and are taking steps to try to make this happen.

46. The passage is about:
   A. one man's efforts to create a universal language
   B. a language developed in the last few years
   C. how language can be improved
   D. language as a means of communication

47. What can the words 'popping up' in the passage be replaced with?
   A. Opening B. Jumping
   C. Hiding D. Leaping

48. It can be inferred from the passage that malespera in Esperanto language means
   A. hopeful B. hopeless
   C. hope D. hopelessness

49. The Third World Congress of Esperanto took place in
   A. 1907 B. 1905
   C. 1909 D. 1913

50. What was Zamenhof's belief in making Esperanto?
   A. That it would alleviate misunderstandings
   B. That it would be as uncomplicated as possible
   C. That it would be monosyllabic
   D. That he would create an artificial language in the first attempt

SECTION-B

All questions are compulsory

Directions (Qs. 1-5): *Rewrite the sentences correctly:*

1. A greater amount of people are eating better than before.

2. He was the only person that wanted to come to the party.

3. She is married with a dentist.

4. Every students like the teacher.

5. You speak English good.

Directions (Qs. 6-15): *Fill in the blanks using appropriate words. Use a single word in each sentence:*

6. Could you .... me some money please? I will return it by tomorrow.

7. The earth .... around the sun.

8. The vegetables in this market are .... than those in the Sunday Bazar.

9. I need .... egg for this recipe, but we do not have any.

10. Take .... umbrella with you.

11. Are .... in the cinema? I can't find them here.

12. Sunaina made this dress ....

13. We haven't heard .... about Tarun. Is he ill?

14. Can I have .... to eat? I am really hungry.

15. That is an .... story. Where did you read it?

Directions (Qs. Nos. 16-20): *Rearrange the following words and phrases to make meaningful sentences:*

16. a deep connection / for close to 20 years / their hometown / many children / and feel / with their childhood school / live in

17. is challenging enough / or a father figure / I shouldn't play / I don't see why / if the role / an older man

18. I tried / but over 90 percent / was sensational / to the final menu / of the food / not every dish / will make it

19. they absorb a great deal of salt / and they carry this salt out to sea / as streams and rivers flow across the land / from rocks and the earth

20. getting into a time machine / and pressing some buttons / for an encounter with the famous people of the past / all of us dream about / to zip across centuries

Short Essay-type:

21. Write about demonetization in India.

22. Look at the picture below and write your thoughts on it, in the form of a short essay:

23. Why do you want to study a foreign language at the B.A. level? What made you interested in the language that you have chosen?

Long Essay-type

24. Write the summary of any book, novel or story you have read, and your interpretation/views on it.

ANSWERS

SECTION-A

1	2	3	4	5	6	7	8	9	10
D	A	B	A	C	D	D	C	C	C

11	12	13	14	15	16	17	18	19	20
C	C	C	D	B	A	D	C	B	C

21	22	23	24	25	26	27	28	29	30
C	A	A	D	B	D	D	B	D	B

31	32	33	34	35	36	37	38	39	40
C	A	A	B	C	B	C	B	A	B

41	42	43	44	45	46	47	48	49	50
B	D	B	D	D	A	A	B	A	B

EXPLANATORY ANSWERS

SECTION-A

1. Here,

gorbl + flur = fan + belt

pixn + gorbl = ceiling + fan

arth + tusl = tile + roof

∴　pixn + arth = ceiling + tile

2. Here,

grana + melke = big + tree

pini + melke = little + tree

melke + hoon = tree + house

∴　grana + hoon = big + house

3. Here,

leli + broon = yellow + hat

pleka + froti = flower + garden

froti + mix = garden + salad

∴　leli + pleka = yellow + flower

5.

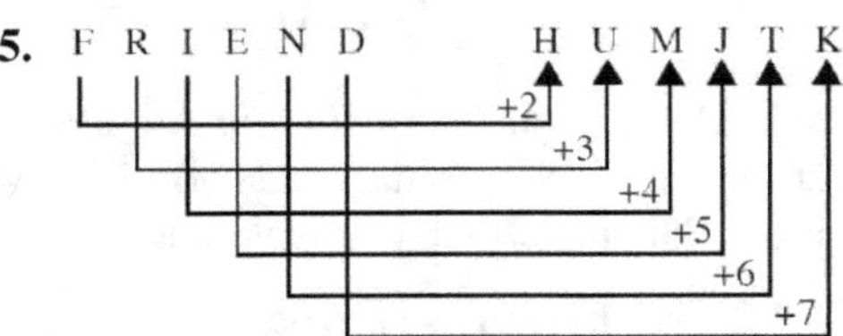

6. Here,

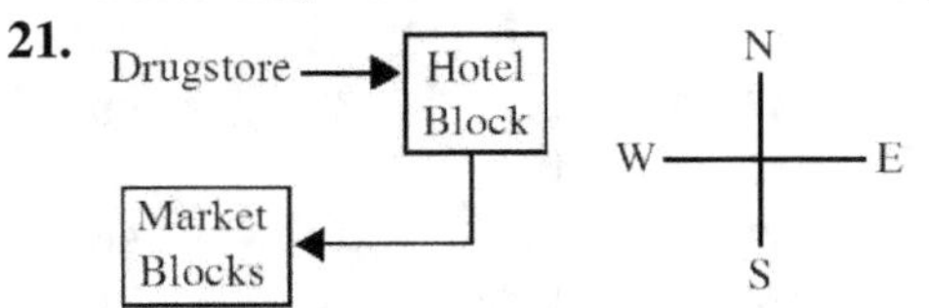

7. Here pencil is called 'sharpener'

Therefore, the child will write with Sharpener.

21.

Drugstore ⟶ Hotel Block

Market Blocks ⟵

N

W —|— E

S

SECTION-B

22.

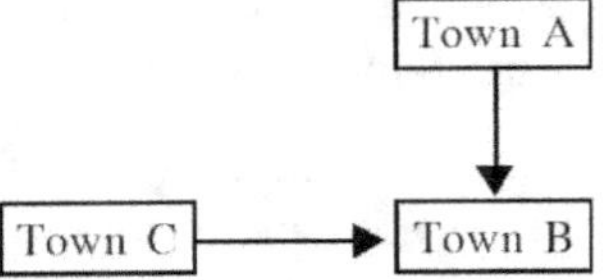

1. A larger number of people are eating better than before.

2. He was the only person who wanted to come to the party.

3. She is married to a dentist.

4. Every student likes the teacher.

5. You speak a fair English.

6. lend

7. moves

8. cheaper

9. an

10. an

11. they

12. herself

13. anything

14. something

15. obsolete

16. Many children live in their hometown and feel a deep connection with their childhood school for close to 20 years.

17. I don't see why I shouldn't play an older man or a father figure if the role is challenging enough.

18. Not every dish I tried will make it to the final menu but over 90 per cent of the food was sensational.

19. As streams and rivers flow across the land they absorb a great deal of salt from rocks and the earth and they carry this salt out to sea.

20. All of us dream about getting into a time machine and pressing some buttons to zip across centuries for an encounter with the famous people of the past.

21. Demonetization refers to discontinuity of the existing currency from circulation and replacing it with a new currency. On 8 November 2016, the government of India, under the primeministership of Narendra Modi, announced the demonetization of all 500 and 1000 bank notes of the Mahatma Gandhi series. The sudden and the abrupt nature of this announcement and the shortage of cash in the following weeks created disruption throughout the economy and threatened economic output. However, most of the Indians appreciated this strong decision of Modi, though the poor were shocked by this move. It is hoped that, this bold step of the government will definitely help India to become corruption-free.

There are both advantages and disadvantages of demonetization. These are stated below:

Advantages

The advantages of demonetization include blackmoney tracking, reduction in illegal acting, tax payment and Jan Dhan Yojana. This effort will help the government to track unaccounted black money or cash on which income tax has not been paid. Secondly, it is hoped that the illegal activities will be stopped by banning high value currency as the cash provided for such activities has no value now. The black money is also used to fund illegal activity, terrorism and money laundering. Therefore, because of demonetization, the circulation of fake currency will come to a halt. Thirdly, tax payers who have been hiding some income can come forward to declare income and pay tax on the same and finally,

individuals will deposit enough cash in their Jan Dhan Yojana which they were reluctant to do earlier.

Disadvantages

Demonetization can cause an initial inconvenience for a few days for exchanging notes or depositing or withdrawing amounts. Delay in the circulation of new currency can create chaos in the country. Secondly, there will be a loss in economy because, after the announcement of demonetization many individuals have burnt their old notes. Thirdly, the government has to bear the cost of printing new currency.

In conclusion, we may say that in the long run we will see the advantages of demonetization. Corruption, money laundering and black money will be reduced to a very large extent.

22. It is a symbol of national integration and brotherhood. In a multi-religious and multilingual country like India, where there are differences in people *e.g.,* difference in culture, food items, mentality, etc., it is necessary to maintain integrity among us. Only maintaining integrity, we can bring peace, prosperity and development in our country.

23. A language can bring people closer. We know that English is a lingua franca, and yet knowing any other language is very much helpful to a person, because he can make the world nearer to him than he could do it with mere English. More importantly, ours is an age of globalization. As a result, the world has come closer to us. Therefore, from the commercial point of view, knowing a foreign language is very essential. Many multinational companies have set up offices in India. Therefore, despite having other qualifications, it is better if one more language, especially a European language is learnt, other than English. In that case, it will be easy to grab a prestigious position in a multinational company. In short, learning a foreign language is necessary for one's work, because in an increasingly competitive job market a candidate should give himself every possible edge to grab a job. Again, with the ever-increasing level of international trade and business, tourism, immigration and random cross-cultural experiences, one may have chances to speak in a foreign language with such a foreigner whose English is worst than the speaker's.

Secondly, learning a foreign language will help a person if he wants to travel overseas. If the country travelled is a non-English-speaking one, learning the language of that country will make the thing easier to the person. Even knowing some basic words can help break ice when one is in a foreign country. It also helps a person to learn others' cultures.

Next, according to a new research published on the New York Times, learning one more language actually makes one smarter. Lastly, according to St. John's university, "In a world that is increasingly interdependent, we can no longer afford to remain monolingual, learning foreign languages is no longer a pastime, it is a necessity." Because of these reasons I want to study a foreign language at BA level.

24. Recently I have read a short story, viz., "The Ugly Duckling" written by Hans Christian Anderson. Its summary is as follows:

There was a duck who was very plain-looking, or rather ugly. He was born in a barnyard and was teased and mocked at by his brothers and sisters and other birds and animals because of his ugliness. So he used to avoid his flock and stay with a flock of wild ducks and geese till then flock was shot down by the hunters. He became alone and took shelter to a old woman's house, but was teased by her cat and hen.

He wandered and met a flock of migrating swans, but could not join them, as he was too young to fly well enough. Winter came and the duckling was rescued by a farmer, but again he fled, because of farmers children and other animals who teased and frightened him. He hide himself in a lonely cave throughout the winter. In the spring when he came out of the cave, he met a flock of swan. When he approached them, he was happy to know that they accepted him and treated him like one of them. He was taken aback and looked in the lake. To his astonishment, he found that he was changed into a beautiful swan. When the swans flew, he joined them, being happy to find a family accepting him.

Interpretation

In this short story, one's identity is being searched. The cat and the hen discourage the duck to be taken seriously, because they advise him to behave in certain ways. But the little duck is not discouraged but is in quest of his heritage by swimming, which he loves most. When he is put down for such "silly" desires, he leaves the firm, so that he can find someone more like himself. The determination to discover his identity bears the message to 'never give up'.

Jawaharlal Nehru University (JNU)
BA (Hons.) Entrance Examination, 2017

CLUSTER-3: Persian, Arabic and Pashto

SECTION-A

Each questions carries 1 mark

Directions (Qs. No. 1-45): *Encircle the correct answer.*

1. The recent 'Heart of Asia' Conference was held in:
   A. Amritsar
   B. Patiala
   C. Kabul
   D. Lahore

2. Which are the two official languages of Afghanistan?
   A. Persian and Dari
   B. Urdu and Pashto
   C. Dari and Pashto
   D. Persian and Tajik

3. 'Tajik', the official language of Tajikistan, is a dialect of:
   A. Russian
   B. Arabic
   C. Uzbek
   D. Persian

4. *Ain-i-Akbari* is a part of the __ book.
   A. *Alamgirnamah*
   B. *Akbarnamah*
   C. *Shahnamah*
   D. *Humayun-namah*

5. Which city of Iran is called 'Half of World'?
   A. Tehran
   B. Shiraz
   C. Esfahan
   D. Mashad

6. Which of the following languages does not belong to the Indo-European family of languages?
   A. Persian
   B. Sanskrit
   C. Pashto
   D. Arabic

7. The Chief Guest at the Republic Day Parade this year (2017) belonged to:
   A. Saudi Arabia
   B. United Arab Emirates
   C. Egypt
   D. Afghanistan

8. 'The Heart of Asia' process is also known as the:
   A. Geneva process
   B. Kabul process
   C. Istanbul process
   D. Delhi process

9. The terrorist group 'ISIS' stands for:
   A. Islamic State of Iran and Syria
   B. Islamic System of Intelligence Support
   C. Islamic Support for International State
   D. Islamic State of Iraq and Syria

10. A Russian Ambassador was recently killed in Turkey by a:
   A. diplomat
   B. politician
   C. terrorist
   D. policeman

11. The festival of Nourooz is celebrated to mark:
   A. the beginning of New Year in the solar Persian calendar
   B. the beginning of New Year in the lunar Persian calendar
   C. the beginning of New Year in the Islamic-Hijri calendar
   D. the victory of Iranians over Turanians

12. The translation of *Panchatantra* into Arabic and Persian is known as
   A. Gulistan
   B. Kalila wa Dimna
   C. Baharistan
   D. Kitab-e-Janwaran

13. Which of the following pair of countries is land-locked?
A. Iraq and Afghanistan
B. Iran and Afghanistan
C. Saudi Arabia and Afghanistan
D. Tajikistan and Afghanistan

14. In the context of the Central Asian Countries, the term CIS stands for
A. Consortium of Independent States
B. Commonwealth of Independent States
C. Council of Independent States
D. Common Integrated States

15. Persepolis is a historical city located in
A. Iran   B. Afghanistan
C. Iraq   D. Egypt

16. Match the following:
(*a*) Hamid Karzai   1. Poet/Writer
(*b*) Khalil Gibran   2. Scientist
(*c*) Avicenna   3. Politician
(*d*) Ali Khamenei   4. Supreme Spiritual Leader

	(*a*)	(*b*)	(*c*)	(*d*)
A.	1	2	3	4
B.	3	1	2	4
C.	4	3	2	1
D.	2	1	4	3

17. Match the following books with their authors:
(*a*) Rubaiyat   1. Ferdowsi
(*b*) Shahnameh   2. Saadi Shirazi
(*c*) Gulistan   3. Omar Khayyam
(*d*) The Prophet   4. Khalil Gibran

	(*a*)	(*b*)	(*c*)	(*d*)
A.	1	2	3	4
B.	4	3	2	1
C.	3	1	2	4
D.	3	2	1	4

18. OPEC, the Organization of Petroleum Exporting Countries is headquartered in
A. Tehran   B. Dubai
C. Vienna   D. Riyadh

19. The Nile River does not cover __ in its course.
A. Egypt   B. Sudan
C. Iraq   D. Kenya

20. Rabat is the Capital city of
A. Morocco   B. Tunisia
C. Algeria   D. Oman

21. The Greeks established the __ Empire in Persia after its invasion by Alexander.
A. Sasanian   B. Achaemenian
C. Seleucid   D. Median

22. Which of the following is the only country in the Arab world with both Red Sea and Persian Gulf coast?
A. Saudi Arabia   B. Yemen
C. Oman   D. UAE

23. The famous Al-Azhar University is located in
A. Damascus   B. Cairo
C. Baghdad   D. Dubai

24. The most populous country in the Arab world is
A. Saudi Arabia   B. Iraq
C. Egypt   D. Sudan

25. Which one of the following countries is not a part of the Arabian Peninsula?
A. Yemen   B. Qatar
C. Kuwait   D. Egypt

26. Tigris and Euphrates, two rivers provide significant amounts of fertile land to which country?
A. Iran   B. Afghanistan
C. Iraq   D. Egypt

27. Mesopotamia, often referred to as the cradle of civilization, was located in modern day:
A. Afghanistan   B. Syria
C. Egypt   D. Iraq

28. Consider the following statements about Egypt:
I. It has among the longest histories of any modern country.
II. It emerged as one of the world's first nation-States in the 10th Millennium BC.
III. It is the most populous country in Africa.
A. All of the above are correct
B. Only I and II are correct
C. Only I and III are correct
D. Only III is correct

29. Which one of the following is **not** a city of Afghanistan?
A. Ghazni
B. Zahedan
C. Balkh
D. Bamyan

30. The National Sport of Saudi Arabia is
A. camel racing
B. basketball
C. soccer
D. scuba diving

31. Consider the following series :
81, 64, __ , 36, 25, ...
What number should fill in the blank?
A. 60
B. 42
C. 49
D. 56

32. Which one of the following does not belong with others?
A. Highway
B. Interstate
C. Expressway
D. Thoroughfare

33. Reptile is to snake as flower is to:
A. stem
B. bud
C. daisy
D. petal

34. Speculation is something when one considers a situation and assumes that to be true based or uncertain evidence. Which is a good example of speculation below?
A. After consulting many physicians, I was confident of my good health.
B. The Police appealed in a higher court against him even after his acquittal by a lower court.
C. She regretted her performance in exams after only missing a question in the paper.
D. When he opened the door in tears; I guessed someone had died in his family.

35. Statement : Government has spoiled many educational institutions by appointing bureaucrats as Vice-Chancellors of these institutions.
Conclusions:
I. Government should appoint only those persons as head of educational institutions who have expertise in the field of education.
II. The VCs of an educational institute should have expertise equal to the academic work carried out by the institute.
A. Only conclusion I follows
B. Only conclusion II follows
C. Neither I nor II follows
D. Both I and II follow

36. Consider the following words/sentences translated from an artificial language:
Dishab means yesterday night
Shabrooz means day night
Zoodsubh means early morning
What could mean zooddirooz?
A. Early last night
B. Early yesterday morning
C. Early yesterday night
D. Early yesterday

37. *roobahzirakast* means fox is clever
zirakpeasar means clever boy
seyahroobah means black fox
What could mean 'boy is clever'?
A. seyahzirakast
B. roobahastaan
C. pesarastroobah
D. pesarzirakast

38. *aan yek mard ast* means 'that is a man'
wa aan mard yek ketab darad means 'and that man has a book'
wa aan ketab do aks darad means 'and that book has two pictures'

Then *aan yek ketab ast wa yek mard do aks darad* would mean:
A. this is a book and has two pictures of a man
B. that book has two pictures of a man
C. that is a book and a man has two pictures
D. it is a book and has a picture of two men

39. *ambeshirin* means sweet mango
shirinharf means sweet word
durustast means it is right
What could more appropriately mean, 'mango is sweet'?
A. ambesatshirin
B. astambedurust
C. asteshirinambe
D. ambeshirinast

40. *amoozgardabistan* means 'school teacher'
amoozgaranjabood means 'teacher was there'
anjadabistanast means 'school is there'
What would *amoozgar anja dar dardabistan bood* mean more appropriately?
A. Teacher is in school there.
B. Teacher was there in the school.
C. There is school and teacher.
D. School teacher was therein.

41. Consider the following statements:
I. The demonetization process of the Modi Government at the Centre was received with mixed reactions by the common public.
II. BJP leaders have claimed that its landslide victory in UP Assembly Elections was helped by its demonetization process.
A. II is the definite effect of the I.
B. I is the cause of the II effect.
C. I and II are independent processes and have no relation of cause and effect.
D. I and II have possible relation of cause and effect.

42. Statement : All educated are literates.
All illiterates are not uneducated.
Conclusions :
I. All literates are not uneducated.
II. All illiterates are not educated.
III. Some illiterates are uneducated.
IV. Some educated are illiterates.
A. Only conclusions I and II follow
B. Only conclusions I and IV follow
C. Only conclusions II and IV follow
D. Only conclusions I and III follow

43. Choose the odd one:
A. Poet : Panegyric
B. Writer : Playwright
C. Lyricist : Song
D. Guitarist : Note

44. Fill in the blank:
Cardiovascular diseases : Cardiologist
Bone fractures : Orthopaedician
Skin problems : Dermatologist
Diabetes : _____
A. Dietician   B. Oncologist
C. Endocrinologist   D. Diabetician

45. Which is not associated with Pedagogy?
A. Education   B. Eradication
C. Erudition   D. Edification

Directions (Qs. No. 46-55): *Select and encircle the most appropriate/correct answers.*

46. This couplet is _____ to Khayyam.
A. returned   B. ascribed
C. implied   D. prescribed

47. This passage is _____ from the book.
A. deferred   B. dedicated
C. derived   D. deducted

48. The book consists _____ four chapters.
A. from   B. for
C. to   D. of

49. The magistrate _____ him free.
A. set   B. cleared
C. claimed   D. denounced

50. Both parties agreed _____ a deal.
A. unless   B. up to
C. upon   D. until

51. The bomb was _____ by a squad.
A. diffused   B. difused
C. defuzed   D. defused

52. The Police have _____ the call by a terrorist.
A. inferred   B. intervened
C. intercepted   D. entered

53. The gang _____ a plan for robbery.
A. heaved   B. hired
C. hacked   D. hatched

54. Birds of the same feather _____ together.
A. block   B. clock
C. flock   D. stock

55. Cleanliness is next to _____ .
A. gentleness   B. godliness
C. usefulness   D. friendliness

SECTION-B

Directions (Qs. 56-60): *Read the passage carefully and based on your understanding of it, answer the following questions briefly in your own language.*

Some of the most recent languages evolved due to the Atlantic slave trade. At that time, slaves from a number of different ethnicities were forced to work together under colonizer's rule. Since they had no opportunity to learn each other's languages, they developed a make-shift language called a pidgin. Pidgins are strings of words copied from the language of the landowner. They have little in the way of grammar, and in many cases it is difficult for a listener to deduce when an event happened, and who did what to whom. Speakers need to use circumlocution in order to make their meaning understood. Interestingly, however, all it takes for a pidgin to become a complex language is for a group of children to be exposed to it at the time when they learn their mother tongue. Slave children did not simply copy the strings of words uttered by their elders, they adapted that words to create a new, expressive language. Complex grammar systems which emerge from pidgins are termed creoles, and they are invented by children.

Some linguists believed that many of the world's most established languages were creoles at first. The English past tense -ed ending may have evolved from the verb 'do'. 'It ended' may once have been 'It end-did'. Therefore it would appear that even the most widespread languages were partly created by children. Children appear to have innate grammatical machinery in their brains, which springs to life when they are first trying to make sense of the world around them. Their minds can serve to create logical, complex structures, even when there is no grammar present for them to copy.

56. What do you think the writer is talking about? Give the passage a suitable title.

57. According to the passage, what can be attributed as a consequence of the Atlantic slave trade?

58. What is pidgin?

59. What are creoles?

60. How are children involved in evolution and development of a language?

Directions (Qs. No. 61-65): *Rearrange the following jumbled sentences in proper order.*

61. a case filed the Police in a higher court by secured he has a respite.

62. a shortfall expected by economists minor after in demonetization the GDP is rate growth.

63. developed in the modern had Arabic prose he distinct writing of a style.

64. to secure the desirable failed obtain he and in his class grade first position.

65. to raise in progress of UP he will continue play and people's problems a constructive role.

66. Write an essay on any one of the following topics within 200 words:
(*a*) Demonetization in India
(*b*) Most memorable event in my life
(*c*) Knowledgeable are powerful
(*d*) The relevance of Higher Education in India

67. Write a short note on any one of the following:
(*a*) Dr. B.R. Ambedkar
(*b*) Maulana Abul Kalam Azad
(*c*) Munshi Prem Chand
(*d*) Amir Khusrau

68. In your opinion, how can the study of a foreign language be useful in your life?

ANSWERS

SECTION-A

1	2	3	4	5	6	7	8	9	10
A	C	D	B	C	C	B	C	D	D

11	12	13	14	15	16	17	18	19	20
A	B	D	B	A	B	C	C	C	A

21	22	23	24	25	26	27	28	29	30
B	A	B	C	D	C	D	C	B	C

31	32	33	34	35	36	37	38	39	40
C	B	C	D	A	C	D	C	D	B

41	42	43	44	45	46	47	48	49	50
D	D	A	C	B	B	C	D	A	C

51	52	53	54	55
D	C	D	C	B

EXPLANATORY ANSWERS

SECTION-A

1. Recently concluded Sixth Ministerial Conference of the Heart of Asia—Istanbul Process on Afghanistan in Amritsar. The Sixth Ministerial Conference of the Heart of Asia-Istanbul Process on Afghanistan was held in Amritsar on 3-4 December. The conference adopted the Amritsar Declaration which puts focus on the Heart of Asia countries and supporting countries and organizations working together to comprehensively address the menace of terrorism. Issues of terrorism took centre stage at the event.

2. Afghanistan is a multilingual country in which two languages—Pashto and Dari—are both official and most widely spoken. Both Pashto and Persian are Indo-European languages from the Iranian languages sub-family. Other regional languages, such as Uzbek, Turkmen, Balochi, Pashayi and Nuristani are spoken by minority groups across the country.

4. The *Ain-i-Akbari,* is a 16th-century, detailed document recording the administration of emperor Akbar's empire, written by his vizier, *Abu'l-Fazl ibn Mubarak.* It makes the Volume III and the final part of the much larger document, the Akbarnama, the Book of Akbar, also by Abul Fazl, and it itself is in three volumes.

5. Isfahan, historically also rendered in English as Ispahan, Sepahan, Esfahan or Hispahan, is the capital of Isfahan Province in Iran, located about 340 kilometres (211 miles) south of Tehran. The Greater Isfahan Region had a population of 3,793,104 in the 2011 Census, the second most populous metropolitan area in Iran after Tehran. The counties of Isfahan, Borkhar, Najafabad, Khomeynishahr, Shahinshahr, Mobarakeh, Falavarjan, Tiran o Karvan, Lenjan and Jay all constitute the metropolitan city of Isfahan.

31.

81	64	49	36	25
$\downarrow$	$\downarrow$	$\downarrow$	$\downarrow$	$\downarrow$
$(9)^2$	$(8)^2$	$(7)^2$	$(6)^2$	$(5)^2$

36. Here, di + shab = yesterday + night

shab + rooz = day + night

zood + subh = early + morning

Therefore,

zood + di + rooz = early + yesterday + night

37. Here,

roobah + zirak + ast = fox + is + clever

zirak + peasar = clever + boy

seyah + roobah = black + fox

Therefore,

pesar + ast + roobah = boy + is + clever

39. Here,   ambe + shirin = sweet + mango

shirin + hart = sweet + word

duru + st + ast = it + is + right

Therefore,

ambe + shirin + ast = mango + is + sweet

SECTION-B

56. **Title: Evolution of a New Language**

According to me, the writer depicts the scenario of a creation of a new language, which was the need of that time.

He also explains the consequences of that language on the offspring's of the slaves engaged under colonizer's rule.

57. Slaves from a number of different ethnicities were forced to work together under colonizer's rule. This incident is the consequence of the Atlantic Slave Trade, according to the passage.

58. Pidgins are strings of words copied from the language of the landowner. They have little in the way of grammar, and in many cases it is difficult for a listener to deduce when an event happened and who did what to whom. In fact, it is a make-shift language.

59. Complex grammar systems which emerge from Pidgins are termed as creoles and they are invented by offspring's of the slaves engaged under colonizer's rule.

60. Pidgin is a complex language for a group of children to be exposed to it at the time when

they learn their mother tongue. Slave children did not simply copy the strings of words uttered by their elders So, they adapted that words to create a new expressive language.

61. The Police has filed a case in a higher court by the secured a respite.

62. After demonetization a minor shortfall is expected by economists in the GDP growth.

63. He had developed a distinct style of writing in the modern Arabic prose.

64. He failed to obtain the desirable grade and secure first position in his class.

65. He will continue to raise people's problems and play a constructive role in progress of UP.

66. **The Relevance of Higher Education in India**

High quality and relevant higher education is able to equip students with the knowledge, skills and core transferable competences they need to succeed after graduation, within a high quality learning environment which recognises and supports good teaching. There is a strong need for flexible, innovative learning approaches and delivery methods to improve quality and relevance while expanding student numbers. One key way of achieving this on Rethinking Education, is to exploit the transformational benefits to enrich teaching, improve learning experiences and support personalised learning.

India's higher education system is the third largest in the world, next to the United States and China. The main governing body at the tertiary level is the University Grants Commission, which enforces its standards, advises the government, and helps coordinate between the centre and the state. Accreditation for higher learning is overseen by 15 autonomous institutions established by the University Grants Commission (UGC). Some institutions of India, such as the Indian

Institutes of Technology(IITs), National Institute of Technology (NITs), Indian Institutes of Information Technology (IIITs), Indian Institutes of Management (IIMs), International Institute of Information Technology (IIIT), University of Mumbai and Jawaharlal Nehru University have been globally acclaimed for their standard of education.

Driven by market opportunities and entrepreneurial zeal, many institutions are taking advantage of the lax regulatory environment to offer 'degrees' not approved by Indian authorities, and many institutions are functioning as pseudo non-profit organisations, developing sophisticated financial methods to siphon off the 'profits'. Thus, for making India prosperous Higher Education is highly needed for performing in each and every sector.

67. Munshi Prem Chand

He was born at Lamahi near Banaras (now Varanasi) on 31st July, 1880. His father Munshi Ajaib Lal was a clerk in the postal department. Premchand's early education was in a *madarsa* under a *maulvi, where* he learnt Urdu. Premchand was only eight years old when his mother died. His grandmother took the responsibility of raising him but she too died soon. He was married when he was 15 and in the 9th class. His father also died and after passing the intermediate he had to stop his study. He got a job as a teacher in the primary school. In 1919, he passed his B.A., with English, Persian and History. After a series of promotions he became Deputy Inspectors of Schools. In response to Mahatma Gandhi's call of non-cooperation with the British, he quit his job. He was a pioneer of modern Hindi and Urdu social fiction, Munshi Premchand's real name was Dhanpat Rai. He wrote nearly 300 stories and novels. Among his best known novels are: *Sevasadan, Rangmanch, Gaban, Nirmala* and *Godan.* Much of Premchand's best work is to be found among his 250 short stories, collected in Hindi under the title *Manasarovar.* Three of his novels have been made into films. Premchand's literary career started as a freelancer in Urdu.

His first story appeared in the magazine *Zamana* published from Kanpur. In his early short stories, he depicted the patriotic upsurge that was sweeping the land in the first decade of the past century. *Soz-e-Watan,* a collection of patriotic stories published by Premchand in 1907, attracted the attention of the British Government In 1914, when Premchand switched over to Hindi, he had already established his reputation as a fiction writer in Urdu. While writing Urdu novels and short stories, he emphasised in presenting the realities of life and he made the Indian villages his theme of writing. His novels describe the problems of the urban middle-class and the country's villages and their problems. He also emphasised on the Hindu-Muslim unity. His famous works include *Godan, Maidan-e-Amal, Bay-wah, Chaugaan etc.* It would not be wrong to say that Premchand was the Father of Urdu short- stories. Short stories or *afsanas* were started by Premchand. As with his novels, his *afsanas* also mirror the society that he lived in. With a simple and flowing writing some of his works depict excellent use of satire and humour. His later works used very simple words and he started including Hindi words too to honestly potray his characters. His famous afsanas are *Qaatil Ki Maan, Zewar Ka Dibba, Gilli Danda, Eidgaah, Namak Ka Daroga* and *Kafan.* His collected stories have been published as *Prem Pachisi, Prem Battisi, Wardaat* and *Zaad-e-Raah.*

Premchand was the first Hindi author to introduce realism in his writings. He pioneered the new form-fiction with a social purpose. He supplemented Gandhiji's work in the political and social fields by adopting his revolutionary ideas as themes for his literary writings.

Besides being a great novelist, Premchand was also a social reformer and thinker. His greatness lies in the fact that his writings embody social purpose and social criticism rather than mere entertainment. Literature according to him is a powerful means of educating public opinion. He believed in social evolution and his ideal was equal opportunities for all. Premchand died in 1936 and has since been studied both in India and abroad as one of the greatest writers of the century.

Premchand translated several non-Hindi works into Hindi. These included the writings of Ratan Nath Dhar Sarshar, Leo Tolstoy, Charles Dickens (*The Story of Richard Doubledick*), Oscar Wilde (*Canterville*), John Galsworthy (*Strife*), Sadi, Guy de Maupassant, Maurice Maeterlinck (*Sightless*) and Hendrik van Loon (*The Story of Mankind*).

Satyajit Ray filmed two of Premchand's works—*Sadgati* and Shatranj Ke Khiladi. *Sadgati* (Salvation) is a short story revolving around poor Dukhi, who dies of exhaustion while hewing wood for a paltry favour. *Shatranj ke Khiladi* (The Chess Players) revolved around the decadence of nawabi Lucknow, where the obsession with a game consumes the players, making them oblivious of their responsibilities in the midst of a crisis.

Sevasadanam (first published in 1918) was made into a film with M.S. Subbulakshmi in the lead role. The novel is set in Varanasi, the holy city of Hindus. *Sevasadan* ("House of Service") is an institute built for the daughters of courtesans.

In 1934, Premchand came to Mumbai and got his first assignment as a scriptwriter for the film Mazdoor. However, he did not like the non literary commercial outlook of the Bombay Film Industry and therefore decided to leave the city before his annual contract came to an end. Himanshu Roy, the founder of the Bombay Talkies persuaded him to stay but to no avail.

Prem Chand moved to Benaras where he remained ill for a long time. Even in his last days, he **chaired the first All-India conference of Indian Progressive Writer's Association** in year 1936. Despite his health and financial problems, he embarked on the task to complete his last novel Mangalsutra which he did not manage to complete as he finally breathed his last on October 8, 1936 after several days of sickness. Premchand's last published short story was Cricket Match which appeared in the magazine Zamana in 1937.

68. Language is our primary source of communication. It's the method through which we share our ideas and thoughts with others. Some people even say that language is what separates us from animals and makes us human.

There are thousands of languages in this world. Countries have their own national languages in addition to a variety of local languages spoken and understood by their people in different regions. Some languages are spoken by millions of people, others by only a few thousand.

Language impacts the daily lives of members of any race, creed, and region of the world. Language helps express our feelings, desires, and queries to the world around us. Words, gestures and tone are utilized in union to portray a broad spectrum of emotion. The unique and diverse methods human beings can use to communicate through written and spoken language is a large part of what allows to harness our innate ability to form lasting bonds with one another; separating mankind from the rest of the animal kingdom.

In today's era, multilingualism has become more than just 'important'. Knowing a foreign language other than native language has evolved to be extremely beneficial. Whether viewed from the financial or social aspect, being able to communicate in a foreign language helps to make 'real' connection with people and provides a better understanding of your language. Learning a foreign language open up employment opportunities. For businesses, it is essential to develop and sustain a strong footing in the global economy. Apart from the financial gains learning a foreign dialect can offer a unique experience to travellers. People, who love to explore different parts of the world, know about diverse cultures, places, and lifestyle, knowing the local language can offer a life changing experience. Through language we can connect with other people and make sense of our experiences. Imagine what it must be like for your child to develop these skills that we take for granted. As a parent, teacher, or other type of caregiver, you shape a child's language development to reflect the identity, values, and experiences of your family and community.

Learning a second language opens up a ton of career opportunities. The world is changing fast. More companies than ever are doing business in several – often dozens of – countries around the world, but they can't do it without hiring globally-minded people who can speak at least one foreign language. Ever wanted to be like those people you see in the airport travelling to foreign countries "on business" all the time? Even in small, local companies, chances are that the ability to speak a second language will set us apart from other applicants.

Speaking a second language each day really can keep the doctor away! Study has demonstrated the cognitive benefits of learning another language, age is not a matter. Memory improvement, longer attention span, and a reduced risk of age-related cognitive decline, are just a few of the known positive effects of speaking two or more languages. Some important things which are to be considered:

(*i*) Establish Deep Connections and Cross-Cultural Friendships.

(*ii*) Get an Outsider's Perspective about my Own Culture.

(*iii*) Become More Interesting and Meet More Interesting People.

(*iv*) Conquer Your Fear of "Looking Stupid".

(*v*) Enjoy Works of Art in their Original Language.

(*vi*) Become a Better Learner.

So in the light of above mentioned facts, we can say that learning foreign language is very essential in our day-to-day life. We definitely upgrade our lifestyle through learning alien language. In every walks of life, it has very essential. So, we must know at least one language other than our native language.

———————

Previous Paper (Solved)

Jawaharlal Nehru University (JNU)
BA (Hons.) Entrance Examination, 2016

CLUSTER-1: French, German, Russian and Spanish

UNIT–1

A. REASONING

LOGICAL PROBLEMS

Direction (Qs. 1 and 2): *Each problem consists of three statements. Based on the first two statements, the third statement may be true, false, or uncertain.*

1. I. Blueberries cost more than strawberries.
   II. Blueberries cost less than raspberries.
   III. Raspberries cost more than strawberries and blueberries.

   If the first two statements are true, the third statement is:
   A. true   B. false
   C. uncertain

2. I. All the trees in the park are flowering trees.
   II. Some of the trees in the park are bougainvillea.
   III. All bougainvillea in the park are flowering trees.

   If the first two statements are true, the third statement is:
   A. true   B. false
   C. uncertain

ESSENTIAL PART

Direction (Qs. 3 and 4): *Each question has an underlined word followed by four answer choices. You will choose the word that is a necessary part of the underlined word.*

3. <u>Language</u>
   A. Tongue   B. Slang
   C. Writing   D. Words

4. <u>Election</u>
   A. President   B. Voter
   C. November   D. Nation

LETTER AND SYMBOL

Direction (Qs. 5 and 6): *Here below is a series. Fill in the blank with one of the options given below.*

5. QPO, NML, KJI, _____, EDC
   A. HGF   B. CAB
   C. JKL   D. GHI

6. JAK, KBL, LCM, MDN, _____
   A. OEP   B. NEO
   C. MEN   D. PFQ

LETTER AND SYMBOL SERIES

Direction (Qs. 7-8): *Look carefully at the squence of symbols to find the pattern. Select the correct pattern.*

7. I ⌐ ⌐ | ☐ ☐ ☐ | ☐ ?
   A. ☐☐   B. ☐ ☐
   C. I⌐   D. ⌐ I

1

8. 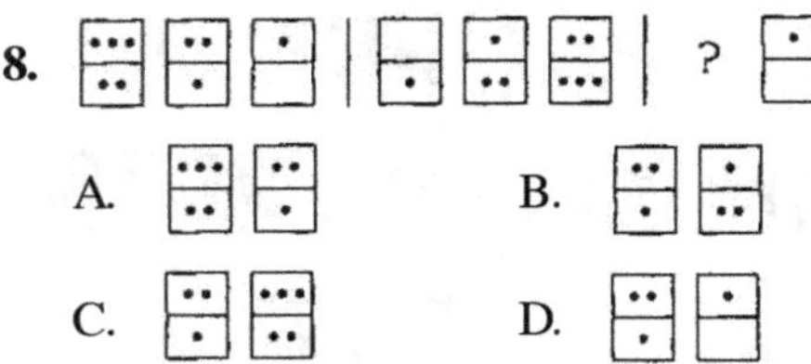

ANALOGIES

Direction (Qs. 9-11): *While trying to find out the relationship between two words, it's best to try and make a sentence with the two. Then use the same sentence to find out which of the answer choices completes the same relationship with the third word.*

9. Play is to actor as concert is to:
   A. symphony   B. musician
   C. piano   D. percussion

10. Sponge is to porous as rubber is to:
   A. massive   B. solid
   C. elastic   D. inflexible

11. Appetizer is to desert as introduction is to:
   A. acquaintance   B. friendship
   C. conclusion   D. None of the above

VERBAL CLASSIFICATION

Direction (Qs. 12 and 13): *Three of the words will be in the same classification, the remaining one will not be. Your answer will be the one word that **does not** belong in the same classification as the others.*

12. Which word **does not** belong with the others?
   A. Tyre   B. Steering wheel
   C. Engine   D. Car

13. Which word **does not** belong with the others?
   A. Noun   B. Preposition
   C. Punctuation   D. Adverb

COURSE OF ACTION

Direction (Qs. 14): *In the question below is a statement followed by two courses of action I and II. Assume everything in the statement is true and on the basis of the information given in the statement, decide which of the suggested courses of action logically follow(s). Choose one of the options given below.*

14. **Statement** : Vegetable prices are soaring in the market.
   Conclusion : I. Vegetables are becoming a rare commodity.
                 II. People cannot eat vegetables.
   A. Only I follows
   B. Only II follows
   C. Either I or II follows
   D. Neither I nor II follows
   E. Both I and II follow

THE ENVIRONMENT

Direction (Qs. 15 and 16): *Find the word that **does not** belong in each row.*

15. A. Croak   B. Scream
   C. Bray

16. A. Botany   B. Zoology
   C. Seismology

LOGICAL DEDUCTION

Direction (Qs. 17 and 18): *Two statements are followed by two conclusions. You have to take the given two statements to be true even if they seem otherwise. Read the conclusion and then decide which of the given conclusion(s) logically follow(s) from the given statements.*

17. **Statement** : Some frogs are bricks.
               All bricks are cakes.
   Conclusion : I. Some cakes are not frogs.
                 II. All frogs are cakes.
   A. Only I follows
   B. Only II follows
   C. Either I or II follows
   D. Neither I nor II follows
   E. Both I and II follow

18. **Statement** : All papers are bags.
               No bag is green.
   Conclusion : I. No paper is green.
                 II. Some bags are papers.
   A. Only I follows
   B. Only II follows

C. Either I or II follows
D. Neither I nor II follows
E. Both I and II follow

VERBAL REASONING

Direction (Qs. 19 and 20): *Find the statement that must be true according to the given information.*

19. Manju is twelve years old. For three years, she has been asking her parents for a dog. Her parents have told her that they believe a dog would not be happy in an apartment, but they have given her permission to have a bird. Manju has not yet decided what kind of bird she would like to have.
    A. Manju's parents like birds better than they like dogs.
    B. Manju does not like birds.
    C. Manju and her parents live in an apartment.
    D. Manju and her parents would like to move.

20. On weekends, Mr. Sharma spends many hours working in his vegetable and flower gardens. Mrs. Sharma spends her free time reading and listening to classical music. Both Mr. Sharma and Mrs. Sharma like to cook.
    A. Mr. Sharma enjoys planting and growing vegetables.
    B. Mr. Sharma does not like classical music.
    C. Mrs. Sharma cooks the vegetables that Mr. Sharma grows.
    D. Mrs. Sharma enjoys reading nineteenth century novels.

B. READING COMPREHENSION

Direction (Qs. 21-25): *Read the following passage and answer the questions that follow:*

The dodo, an extinct bird, whose name has entered popular culture as a symbol of stupidity, may have been actually quite intelligent. A study has found that the size of its brain in relation to body size was on par with pigeons–birds whose ability to be trained implies they are no dummies. The dodo *(Raphus cucullatus)* was a large, flightless bird that lived on the island of Mauritius in the Indian Ocean, where they were last seen alive in 1662.

When sailors discovered the island in the late 1500s, the dodo did not fear these new arrivals. That led to the birds being herded onto passing boats as an easy meal for passing sailors.

"Because of that behaviour and invasive species that were introduced to the island, they disappeared in less than 100 years after humans arrived," said Eugenia Gold, a research associate at the American Museum of Natural History's Richard Gilder Graduate School.

"Today, they are almost exclusively known for becoming extinct, and I think that's why we've given them this reputation of being dumb," said Ms. Gold.

Though the bird has become iconic in popular culture, most aspects of the dodo's biology are still unknown, partly because specimens are extremely rare, researchers said.

To examine the brain of the dodo, Gold tracked down a well-preserved skull from the collections of London's Natural History Museum and imaged it there with high-resolution computed tomography (CT) scanning, which can produce images of the brain inferred from the shape of the skull.

Ms. Gold CT-scanned the skulls of seven species of pigeons for comparison, while colleagues at the Natural History Museum of Denmark and National Museum of Scotland sent her the endocasts for the dodo's closest relative, the now-extinct Rodrigues solitaire *(Pzeophaps solitaria)*. The results found that the dodo's brain was about average for its body size.

"So if you take brain size as a proxy for intelligence, dodos probably had a similar intelligence level to pigeons," said Ms. Gold, also an instructor at the Stony Brook University. "Of course, there's more to intelligence than just overall brain size, but this gives us a basic measure." Ms. Gold said. While the brains of dodos might not have been small, they did show some unexpected surprises, researchers said.

The study found that both the dodo and the Rodrigues solitaire had large and differentiated olfactory bulbs, an unusual trait in birds, which depend on sight and thus usually have more heavily developed optical lobes.

The researchers suggest that because dodos and solitaires were ground-dwellers, they relied on smell to find food, making an oddly large olfactory lobe an asset.

The study was published in the *Zoological Journal of the Linnean Society.*

[Source : The Hindu, February 25, 2016, p. 20]

Reading Comprehension questions :

21. The article primarily discusses
    A. extinction of the dodo
    B. mass of the brain of the dodo
    C. cleverness of the dodo
    D. ability to fly of the dodo

22. 'Invasive species' in paragraph 3 is closest in meaning to:
    A. non-native organisms that can crowd out or replace native species
    B. tending to intrude upon native species
    C. meddling with native species
    D. harmful to native species

23. Where in the article is a term used that refers to the site for processing information on odours?
    A. Paragraph 2   B. Paragraph 5
    C. Paragraph 6   D. Paragraph 9

24. A synonym used for 'extinct' in the article is:
    A. dumb   B. rare
    C. unusual   D. disappeared

25. The bird is called a dodo because:
    A. it was too stupid to survive
    B. it was docile
    C. it was large and flightless
    D. its brain size is that of a pigeon

C. ARTIFICIAL LANGUAGE

Direction (Qs. 26-30): *Given below is a list of three words in an artificial language and their English meanings. The question that follows require you to translate an English word into the artificial language. Choose one from the choices given.*

26. Here are some words translated from an artificial language.
    goddevil means black diamond
    talladevil means black belt
    ballgruch means magic hall
    Which word corresponds to 'black magic'?
    A. Gruchdevil   B. Tallball
    C. Godball   D. Gruchgod

27. Here are some words translated from an artificial language.
    bionota means mango tree
    bryonota means mango leaf
    biopeg means banana tree
    What would 'mango jam' mean?
    A. Brymuth   B. Hupponota
    C. Biocrin   D. Crinpeg

28. Here are some words translated from an artificial language.

telibroom means yellow hat
lenkafroti means flower garden
frotimix means garden salad
What would 'yellow flower' mean?
    A. Telifroti   B. Mixlenka
    C. Lenkabroom   D. Frotibroom

29. Here are some words translated from an artificial languae.
    monogabel means saddle horse
    conowir means trail ride
    gabelguru means horse blanket
    What would 'horse ride' mean?
    A. Gabelwir   B. Monoguru
    C. Monowir   D. Conomono

30. Here are some more words translated from an artificial language.
    tamceno means sky blue
    cenorax means Prussian blue
    aplimitl means gouda cheese
    What would 'blue cheese' mean?
    A. Cenotam   B. Mitltam
    C. Raxmitil   D. Aplceno

D. GRAMMAR

31. Chinese and Hindi are ________ language in the world.
A. the most spoken B. the more spoken
C. much spoken D. the least spoken
E. most spoken

32. David Smith has been told he will have to pay the fine ____ his high rank in the military.
A. furthermore B. on grounds that
C. despite D. even if
E. on purpose that

33. It was stated ________ the bottom of the form, that applicants must hand ______ their forms ______ person.

A. be/at/by B. below/in/for
C. at/in/in D. on/for/at
E. at/in/by

34. Maria and Ruth spoke to ________ yesterday.
A. themselves B. yorself
C. each other D. herself
E. myself

35. The economy in India is booming; ______ many foreign investors are planning to enter the Indian market.
A. nonetheless B. so as to
C. that's why D. even if
E. in addition to

UNIT–2

ESSAY-TYPE (300 WORDS)

1. Write a short essay about any film that you have seen and disliked because you considered it harmful to human relations. What did you dislike about its possible effect on human relations? Support your answer with clearly explained references to the film. [Avoid simply summarizing the story as your response; focus instead, on what made you criticize the film]

UNIVERSITY AND YOU (200 WORDS)

2. It is important to know a foreign language in today's world. Support this claim with arguments and examples.

OPINION (150 WORDS)

"Earth provides enough to satisfy every man's needs, but not every man's greed."

—*Mahatma Gandhi*

3. Look at the image, read the quotation and write about what you think of the need for development and its impact on the environment. Argue your position clearly, in a coherent and logical manner by taking into account both image and text.

LANGUAGE

4. Please point out three possible consequences if there were no computers in the world.

ANSWERS

UNIT-1

1	2	3	4	5	6	7	8	9	10
A	A	D	B	A	B	D	A	B	C

11	12	13	14	15	16	17	18	19	20
C	D	C	D	B	C	A	E	C	A

21	22	23	24	25	26	27	28	29	30
C	C	D	D	B	A	B	C	A	D

31	32	33	34	35
E	C	C	C	C

UNIT-1 (Explanatory Answers)

1. Because the first two statements are true, raspberries are the most expensive of the three.

2. All of the trees in the park are flowering trees, so all bougainvillea in the park are flowering trees.

3. Words are a necessary part of language. Slang is not necessary to language.

   Not all languages are written. Not all languages are spoken.

4. An election does not exist without voters. The election of a president is a byproduct. Not all elections are held in November, nor are they nationwide.

5. Given series consists of letters in a reverse alphabetical order, so missing series is HGF.

6. This is an alternating series in alphabetical order. The middle letters follow the order ABCDE. The first and third letters are alphabetical begining with 'J'. The third letter is repeated as first letter in each subsequent three letter segment.

9. An actor performs in a play. A musician performs at a concert. Option A, C & D are incorrect because none is people who performs.

10. A sponge is a porous. Rubber is an elastic material.

14. The availability of vegetables is no mentioned in the given statement. So conclusion-I does not follow. Also, conclusion-II is not directly related to the statement and so it also does not follow.

17. Clearly, it follows from the Venn diagram that some cakes are frogs i.e., conclusion-I follows.

   But conclusion-II cannot follow.

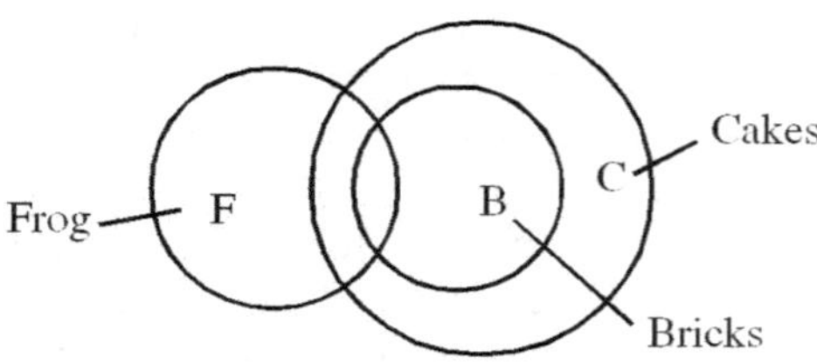

18. 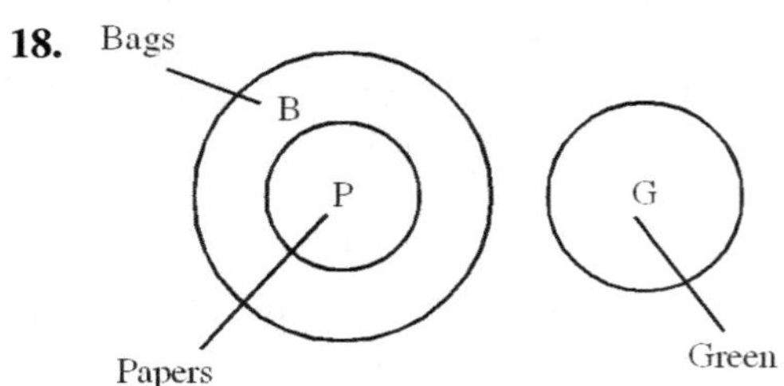

26. Here,   devil = Black

        God = Diamond

        Talla = Belt

        Gruch = Magic

∴   Black Magic = Gruch devil.

27. In this language, the adjective follows the noun. from 'bionota' and 'bryonota' you can determine that 'onota' means mango. From 'bionota' and 'biopeg', you can determine that 'bi' means 'tree'.

28. Here,   froti = Garden

        lenka = Flower

        mix = Salad

29. Here,

        Gabel = Horse

        Mono = Saddle

        Guru = Blanket

        Wir = Ride

∴   Gabelwir = Horse ride

30. Here,

        Tam = sky

        Ceno = blue

        Rax = Prussian

        Apl = Cheese.

UNIT-2

1. *Brokendown Palace* is an American dramatic film about two best friends who find themselves imprisoned in Thailand for drug smuggling.

Brokendown Palace tells the story of two young American high school graduates, Alice and Darlene, who go on a short vacation to Thailand. There they meet and make friends with an Australian man, Nick Parks, and decide to accept his invitation to join him on a business trip to Hong Kong for a few days. However, while at the airport, the girls are found to be carrying a large amount of heroin in their bag, and are sentenced to long-term imprisonment. It is in the Thai Correctional Institution where the girls are kept that most of the film takes place.

The main question that the viewers find themselves wondering about, for a great part of the film, is whether either of the girls knew anything about the drugs in their luggage, or if both were completely innocent and knew nothing of the criminal operation of which they became a part. When watching the movie, I found myself changing my mind about the matter a few times, suspecting one girl or the other, or deciding they were both unaware of the drugs in their bag. From this perspective, the director has succeeded in keeping the audience in suspense and creating some sort of a mystery, or rather, uncertainty, about the guilt of both of the main characters. However, there are a few serious oversights that, in my opinion, have accentuated the lapses in the film.

The plot itself was not new, especially considering the recent success of another film with a similar storyline –"Return to Paradise".

But, while in the latter movie the director paid plenty of attention to developing each character more fully, showing the tensions and inner conflicts between saving yourself or saving your friend, portraying the process of making this life-changing decision of the main character in all the details and nuances, I cannot say this was done in "Brokedown Palace." The relationship between the main characters, who were lifelong girlfriends, starts to sour as they begin suspecting each other of actually knowing about the drugs they were carrying. But there just is not enough emotional strain or enough feelings and acting panache to show the development of this key point in the film – "friendship and trust vs. hardships and caring for one's personal interests above all."

The film was not as successful as it could have been should the story have been developed a little deeper, with the main emphasis being put on the relationship between the two friends and the sacrifice that one makes for the other, rather than the imperfections and corruption of the Thai legal system. The film might be a decent way to kill time on a lazy weekend afternoon, even though one should not expect it to impress more cinematically-sophisticated viewers.

2. **Importance of Learning a Foreign Language:** One of the most phenomenal benefits of learning a foreign language? Doors are opened to you around the world. If you're learning in a group setting, you immediately have new friends to share your new language with. If not, then once you go somewhere and are actually able to employ what you've learned, you'll be surprised how open people are when you speak their mother tongue.

If your C.V. accolades include fluency in a second language, your chances of employment in today's economy are much greater for you than for those who speak only one language.

Multilingual people are able to communicate and interact within multiple communities. Potential employers consider this a valuable asset in an employee's skill set, as they're able to connect with a broader range of people. In this new age of start-ups, companies are increasingly breaking into new markets. You up your personal and professional value if you're able to negotiate with manufacturers in another country or communicate with customers who don't speak your native language.

Not to mention, your ability to speak a second language conveys that you're motivated and driven to learn new skills, and this also gives you a competitive edge over those who haven't yet become bilingual.

Many would argue that bilingualism is becoming a progressively necessary and essential skill for anyone who wants to keep up with today's rapidly increasing global economy.

As more and more people recognize the importance of learning an additional language, those who only speak one language will begin to get left behind in our shift towards a more integrated and connected global society.

Austrain philosopher Ludwig Wittgenstein is credited with saying that "the limits of your language are the limits of your world," and he was right.

Knowing more than one language opens up your vacation destination possibilities. Travelling through a foreign country becomes much easier if you can speak the language of that country. Fluency isn't required. Locals anywhere appreciate that you've taken the time to at least attempt to learn and communicate in their tongue. It shows a greater level of respect and is an easy way to meet new people. Also, getting to a comfortable speaking level in a foreign language in a new country.

As you begin to learn a second language, you'll find that the acquisition techniques you're using can be applied to learning additional languages as well.

The positive congnitive effects of learning to speak a second language can train the brain to analyze and process different linguistic structures. It's not specific to your first target language—it's a skill that can be applied to learning any language.

You're increasing your ability to replicate the process with multiple languages. This is called "metalinguistic awareness," where your brain learns to identify the techniques of learning a language and break them down into a series of steps. After learning one language, you retain the muscle memory. Your brain will intrinsically understand how to learn a language and how different languages are structured, through increased awareness of syntax, grammar and sentence structure.

Acquiring a second language improves your memory and increases your attention span. The process of becoming bilingual exercises your brain, challenges you to concentrate and boosts your problem solving skills.

Bilingual students tend to score higher on standardized tests than monolingual students, especially in the areas of vocabulary, reading and math. As you learn to toggle from one language to another, you improve your multitasking abilities. Bilingual individuals have also been shown to be more logical and rational, have better decision-making skills and be more perceptive and aware of their surroundings.

Learning a second language also improves your native language, as it teaches you the mechanics and structure behind *any* language—not just *new* languages.

Recent research has shown that bilingualism can stave off the effects of Alzheimer's and dementia by years. Regardless of their education level, gender or occupation, bilingual subjects in the linked study experienced the onset of Alzheimer's on average, 4½ years later than monolingual subjects did.

3. **Need of Development its Impact on the Environment:** Development has had far-reaching effects on our lifestyle. It has led to faster access to technology, improved communication and innovation. Apart from playing an important role in bringing people of different cultures together, it has ushered a new era in the economic prosperity and has opened up vast channels of development. However, development has also created some areas of concern, and prominent among these is the impact that it has had on the environment.

Development has led to an increase in the consumption of products, which has impacted the ecological cycle. Increased consumption leads to an increase in the production of goods, which in turn puts stress on the environment. It has also led to an increase in the transportation of raw materials and food from one place to another. Earlier, people used to consume locally-grown food, but with globalization, people consume products that have been developed in foreign countries. The amount of fuel that is consumed in transporting these products has led to an increase in the pollution levels in the environment. It has also led to several other environmental concerns such as noise pollution and landscape intrusion. Transportation has also put a strain on the non-renewable sources of energy, such as gasoline. The gases that are emitted from the aircraft have led to the depletion of the ozone layer apart from increasing the greenhouse effect. The industrial waste that is generated as a result of production has been laden on ships and dumped in oceans. This has killed many underwater organisms and has deposited many harmful chemicals in the ocean.

4. If there were No Computers

There would be the following three possible consequences if there were no computers in the world:

1. At present, the entire information technology and telecommunication system are based on computers. The computers have been installed and are being installed in banks, post offices, all government and commercial houses and offices, stock-exchanges, big business concerns etc. If the computers were no more there, the entire system of interaction would collapse and the world, instead of having a futuristic orientation, would relapse into a retrospective world of "narrow domestic walls".

2. India's most flourishing trade is at present in the software. She has a vast potential of exports in this sector. If there were no computers there, India's exports would get a terrible set back which would have an awfully adverse effect on her economy.

3. Millions of people in India and in the world are engaged in the computer and computer-related business and services. If there were no computers, the genie of unemployment would show its horrible, ugly teeth to such people, the youth in particular, who might feel greatly frustrated with life. many of entertainments in T.V. etc. are also based on computers and in their absence, the world would look dull and drab.

Jawaharlal Nehru University (JNU)
BA (Hons.) Entrance Examination, 2016

CLUSTER-2: Japanese, Korean and Chinese

SECTION-A

Direction: *Question Nos. 1-40 are of 1 marks each. Question Nos. 41-45 are of 2 marks each.*

1. _______ getting the highest marks in the class, Ashish still had problems with the teacher.
   A. Despite of
   B. In spite of
   C. Eventhough
   D. Nonetheless

2. _______ he was seen to be an aggressive politician, he was a quiet and loving family man at home.
   A. Although
   B. Despite
   C. In spite of
   D. Nevertheless

3. This method is widely used _______ algorithm is not only effective but also very simple.
   A. because its
   B. because
   C. it is because
   D. because of its

4. That is a story of hardship _______ our own situation into perspective.
   A. puts
   B. it puts
   C. that it puts
   D. that puts

5. The police were greatly outnumbered by rioters, _______ ran into hundreds.
   A. whose figures
   B. those figures
   C. that its figures
   D. its figures that

6. It is said that he was a man, _______ to have the vision of an eagle and courage of a lion.
   A. who appeared
   B. he appeared
   C. that appears
   D. and appears

7. After the discovery of the abandoned gateway vehicle, _______ believed to be hiding in the nearby riverside forest region.
   A. that the bank robber is
   B. the bank robber who
   C. the bank robber is
   D. the bank robber who is

8. You'd better take a taxi. _______ , you'll be late.
   A. Therefore
   B. Consequently
   C. Furthermore
   D. Otherwise

9. Mohan wasn't tired. _______ , he took a nap.
   A. Otherwise
   B. In spite of
   C. Hence
   D. Nevertheless

10. The weather was terrible. _______ , we decided to delay our trip.
    A. Furthermore
    B. Therefore
    C. Besides
    D. Otherwise

Direction: *Encircle the correct meaning of the underlined idioms.*

11. He is <u>out and out</u> a reactionary.
    A. no more
    B. thoroughly
    C. in favour of
    D. deadly against

12. Leaders should not only make speeches they should also be prepared <u>to bell the cat</u>.
    A. to take lead in danger
    B. to tie a bell to a cat's neck
    C. to be alert of the enemy
    D. to make noise

13. <u>Oily tongue</u>
   A. Flattery   B. Hungry person
   C. Strong critic   D. Rich food

Direction: *Encircle the correct answer.*

14. I like ______ red T-shirt over there. The one with the white dots.
   A. a   B. an
   C. the   D. None of the above

15. What do you usually have for ________ breakfast?
   A. a   B. an
   C. the   D. None of the above

16. My friend is good ______ volleyball.
   A. in   B. to
   C. with   D. at

17. Sunil apologized ______ being late.
   A. with   B. to
   C. for   D. in

18. Which of the following is a synonym for Apparent?
   A. Masked   B. Obscure
   C. Distinct   D. Indistinct

19. Architect : Building :: Sculptor : ?
   A. Museum   B. Stone
   C. Chisel   D. Statue

20. 'Boat is to water'. Therefore, 'Plane is to ______ '.
   A. fly   B. sky
   C. float   D. air

Direction: *Find the odd one out and encircle the correct answer:*

21. A. Crusade   B. Cruise
   C. Expedition   D. Campaign

22. A. Cornea   B. Retina
   C. Vision   D. Pupil

Direction: *Encircle the correct answer:*

23. The words in italics are translated from an artificial language.
agnoscrenia means poisonous spider
delanocrenia means poisonous snake
agnosdeery means brown spider

Which word could mean 'black widow spider'?
   A. deeryclostagnos
   B. agnosdelano
   C. agnosvitriblunin
   D. trymuttiagnos

24. The words in italics are translated from an artificial language.
jalkamofti means happy birthday
maftihoze means birthday party
mentogunn means goodness

Which word could mean 'happiness'?
   A. jalkagunn   B. mentohoze
   C. mofthihoze   D. hozement

25. The words in italics are translated from an artificial language.
myncabel means saddle horse
conowir means rail ride
cabelalma means horse blanket

Which word could mean 'horse ride'?
   A. cabelwir   B. conocabel
   C. almamyn   D. conoalma

Direction: *In the following letter series, some of the letters are missing, which are given in that order as one of the alternatives below. Choose and encircle the correct alternative.*

26. _a_b_abaa_bab_abb
   A. a a a b b   B. a b a b b
   C. b a b a b   D. b a b b a

27. gfe_ig_eii_fei_gf_ii
   A. e i f g i   B. f i g i e
   C. i f g i e   D. i f i g e

Direction: *Encircle the correct answer.*

28. Look at the series 80, 10, 70, 15, 60, ____.

What number should come next?
   A. 20   B. 25
   C. 30   D. 50

29. Look at the series 2, 6, 18, 54, ____.

What number should come next?
   A. 108   B. 148
   C. 162   D. 216

30. There are eight mango trees in a straight line. The distance between each mango tree is three metres. What is the distance between the first mango tree and the eighth mango tree?
A. 24 m
B. 27 m
C. 30 m
D. 21 m

Direction: *Each question given below consists of a statement, followed by two Arguments I and II. You have to decide which of the arguments is a strong argument and which is a weak argument.*

31. Statement: Should all the annual examinations up to Std V be abolished?

Argument I: Yes. The young students should not be burdened with such examinations which hampers their natural growth.

Argument II: No. The students will not study seriously as they will get automatic promotion to the next class and this will affect them in future.
A. Only argument I is strong
B. Only argument II is strong
C. Neither argument I nor argument II is strong
D. Both arguments I and II are strong

32. Statement: Should there be a cap on maximum number of contestants for parliamentary elections in any constituency?

Argument I: Yes. This will make the parliamentary elections more meaningful as the voters can make a considered judgment for casting their votes.

Argument II: No. In a democracy any person fulfilling the eligibility criteria can contest parliamentary elections and there should be no restrictions.
A. Only argument I is strong
B. Only argument II is strong
C. Neither argument I nor argument II is strong
D. Both arguments I and II are strong

Direction: *Encircle the correct answer.*

33. Who has the leader to announce the establishment of the People's Republic of China atop Tiananmen Square on October 1, 1949?
A. Lu Xun
B. Deng Xiaping
C. Sun-Yatsen
D. Mao Zedong

34. The Chinese currency 'Yuan' is also known as
A. Yen
B. RMB
C. Won
D. Dong

35. The largest island of Korea also considered as a vacation paradise by Koreans is
A. Koje-do
B. Ullung-do
C. Nami-do
D. Cheju-do

36. What percentage of Korea is mountainous?
A. 70%
B. 40%
C. 50%
D. 25%

37. Which Asian country will host the 2020 Olympics?
A. Korea
B. Japan
C. China
D. Singapore

38. What is the national flower of Japan?
A. Cherry blossom
B. Chrysanthemum
C. Wisteria
D. Rose

39. Plastic Bags : Think Twice

Almost every store puts its products into plastic bags. They are easy, convenient, strong and lightweight. They are also terrible for the environment. Plastic bags are typically used for only a few hours—may be even a few minutes. However, it can take hundreds of years for them to break down in a landfill. When plastic bags end up in the wild, they can be very dangerous to animals, who might eat the bags or get tangled up in them. The next time you go shopping, be sure to bring reusable bags with you.

Which of the following best describes the order of ideas as presented in the passage?
A. Benefits are put forth, drawbacks are articulated, a judgment is made
B. A question, is asked, an answer is given, an answer is rejected
C. A fact is described, a question is asked, an opinion is examined
D. A problem is explained, evidence is provided, a solution is offered

40. Land of Few

New Zealand is one of the most beautiful countries in the world. It was first discovered by Europeans in 1642. It was one of the last places of Earth to be settled by humans. Today, New Zealand is home to almost five million people. That may sound like a lot. But it's actually not compared to other countries with the same amount of land. New Zealand has few people. But it has many sheep—just over 30 million of them. That means there are about 7 sheeps for every 1 person. That may sound strange. But it makes sense. Wool is one of New Zealand's biggest exports.

The author wrote this passage mostly to
A. illustrate New Zealand's beauty
B. examine New Zealand's export
C. discuss New Zealand's population
D. identify New Zealand's problem

Direction: *Read the following passage and encircle the correct answer.*

Among the most important themes in the Disney movie *The Little Mermaid* are those of questioning conventional thinking, and pursuing a dream. Not only is Ariel, the little mermaid, demonstrating original thought (something that many seem to think she is lacking), but also she is rebelling against her speciesist father. When Ariel expresses her love for the human prince, King Trident is furious. When Ariel points out angrily that he does not understand her, or even know the man whom she loves, Trident retorts, "know him? I don't need to know him! He's a human!" In a very real way Disney is encouraging children to question pre-conceived ideas that we may have against a certain group.

Disney also teaches children to pursue what they love. We see that Ariel's love for Prince Eric is more important than all else. In turning to the Sea Witch, Ursula, for help, Ariel makes a mistake, but no true hero or heroine is flawless. Ariel puts herself, her family, and all men folk in danger, but we see that with the help of her prince, she is able to put everything right. At the end of the film, when Ursula has forced King Trident to sacrifice his kingdom for his daughter's soul, the Sea Witch rises out of the water, gigantic and terrifying, wearing the king's crown and holding his magic trident. She laughs evilly and declares that she is the ruler of all mermen and women. "So much for true love" she screams victoriously. Eric, however, succeeds in piloting the prow of his ship straight through her belly, vanquishing her. The moral here is that while we all make mistakes, what is truly important is, how we right the wrongs we may do to others.

41. The author's attitude towards *The Little Mermaid* is primarily one of
A. appreciation
B. frustration
C. stoicism
D. ambivalence

42. Ursula's quote "So much for true love" primarily suggests
A. the marriage was unacceptable to her
B. she was mocking true love
C. she is speciesist
D. Trident was her true love

43. Which of the following would best illustrate assertion made in the lines "Disney is encouraging children to question pre-conceived ideas that we may have against a certain group"?
A. A movie about the development of the iPod
B. A movie that details the horrors of war
C. A movie about a girl who overcomes her fear of snakes
D. A movie that documents the travels of a rock band

44. Why does the author use parentheses around the comment (Something that many seem to think she is lacking)?
A. To indicate a side comment to the reader
B. To indicate that it is unimportant
C. To indicate a humorous tone
D. To indicate a shift in meaning

45. The author's main point in the passage is
A. Ariel should not have been allowed to marry Prince Eric
B. Only Prince Eric truly understood Ariel
C. Ariel demonstrated original thought
D. *The Little Mermaid* teaches children to follow their heart

SECTION-B

All Questions are Compulsory

Direction: *Fill in the blanks with appropriate articles/prepositions:*

1. The potatoes are ten rupees __________ kilogram.
2. The car does 100 kilometres _______ hour.
3. I met him at _______ school playground.
4. She stays _________ bed until ten every morning.
5. I am prepared _______ any questions.

Direction: *Rearrange the following words and phrases to form meaningful sentences.*

6. of humankind/the habit/reading is/one of/resources/of/the greatest.
7. are/we enjoy/that/belong to us/than if/much more/they/borrowed/reading books.

Direction: *Rewrite the sentences correctly:*

8. The man to who I sold my house was a cheat.
9. The performance of our players was rather worst than I had expected.

10. A lot of travel delay is caused due to the inefficiency and lack of good management on behalf of the railways.

11. Observe the following two pictures on cleanliness, drive undertaken by schools:

Write a few lines on what is common and uncommon in them.

12. How do you think the language you have chosen to study is going to benefit you in the future?

13. Choose any social/cultural/political news you may have read or seen on television and summarize it in 300 words. What are your views on the piece of news?

ANSWERS
SECTION-A

1	2	3	4	5	6	7	8	9	10
B	A	A	D	A	A	C	D	D	B
11	12	13	14	15	16	17	18	19	20
B	A	A	C	C	D	C	C	D	D
21	22	23	24	25	26	27	28	29	30
B	C	C	A	A	D	C	A	C	D
31	32	33	34	35	36	37	38	39	40
D	D	D	B	D	A	B	B	A	C
41	42	43	44	45					
A	B	C	A	D					

SECTION-A

23. In this language, the noun appears first and the adjectives follow. Since 'agnos' means spices and should appear first, options 'A' and 'D' can be ruled out. Choice 'B' can be ruled out because 'delano' means snake.

24. Here,   Jalka = Happy

Mofti = Birthday

Hoze = Party

Mento = Good

Gunn = Ness

∴ Happiness = Jalkagunn

25. Here, Myn = Saddle

Cabel = Horse

Cono = Rail

Wir = Ride

Therefore, Cabelwir = Horseride

26. The series is : baa/bba/baa/bba/baa/bb.

27. The series is : gfeii/gfeii/gfeii/gfeii.

28. This is an alternating addition and subtraction series. In the first pattern, 10 is substracted from each number to arrive at the next. In the second 5 is added to each number to arrive at the next.

29. 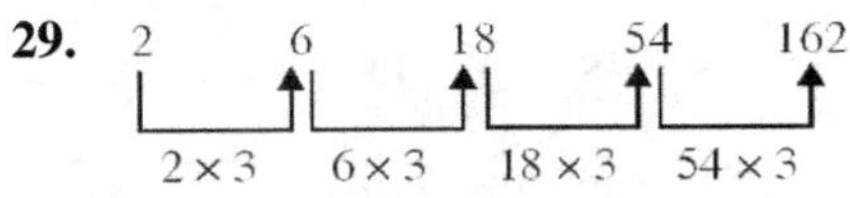

2   6   18   54   162

2×3 6×3 18×3 54×3

30. 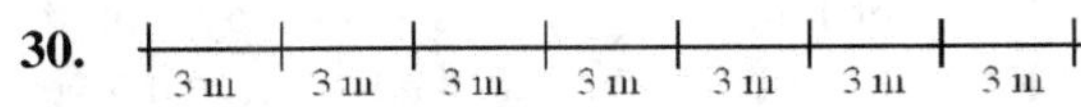

3 m   3 m   3 m   3 m   3 m   3 m   3 m

SECTION-B

1. a

2. per

3. the

4. in

5. for

6. The habit of reading is one of the greatest resources of human kind.

7. We enjoy reading books much more that are borrowed than if they belong to us.

8. The man to whom I sold my house was a cheat.

9. The performance of our players was rather worse than I had expected.

10. Much of travel delay is caused due to the inefficiency and poor management of the railways.

11. Both the pictures depict cleanliness drive undertaken by schools. Students participating in the drive is a common features between the two pictures.

While the picture on the right hand side shows students cleaning the premises of the school, the picture on the left side shows them cleaning a public place.

Cleanliness is a clean habit which is very necessary to all of us. Cleanliness is a habit of keeping ourselves physically and mentally clean including with our home, pet animals, surroundings, environment, pond, river, schools, etc. We should keep ourselves neat, clean and well dressed all time. It helps in making a good personality and impression in the society as it reflects a clean character. We should maintain the environment and natural resources (water, food, land, etc) cleanliness together with our body cleanliness in order to make the possibility of life existence forever on the earth.

Cleanliness makes us healthy in every aspect like mental, physical, social and intellectual. Generally, we all noticing in our homes that our grandmothers and moms are very strict about the cleanliness before worship, it is not another thing, they just try to make cleanliness our habit. But they follow wrong way as they never describe us the benefits and purpose of cleanliness that's why we get problem in following cleanliness. Every parent should logically describe and discuss their kids about the benefits, purpose, necessity, etc. of the cleanliness. They must tell us that cleanliness is the first and foremost thing in our lives like food and water.

We should always take care and observe our personal and surrounding cleanliness to make our future bright and healthy. We should take bath with soap, cut our nails, wear well washed and pressed clothes on daily basis. We should learn from our parents about how to keep home neat and clean. We should not make our surrounding areas dirty as it spread diseases. We should wash our hands with soap every time we go to eat something. We should drink safe, clean and well purified water all through the day. We never eat junk foods, stale foods or other ready-made liquids.

12. Analytical skills improve when students study a foreign language. Creativity is increased with the study of foreign languages. International travel is made easier and more pleasant through knowing a foreign language. Foreign language study enhances one's opportunities in government, business, medicine, law, technology, military, industry, marketing, etc. A second language improves your skills and grades in Math and English and on the SAT and GRE.

13. When PM Modi announced that Rs with the denomination of 500/- and 1000/- would cease to be the legal tender from 9th of Nov, the whole country was stunned. This decision caused sensation in the whole country. Social Media was flooded with messages and information. People started counting the trash they had accumulated for years legally or illegally.

Rumours became rife. Some tried to invest their dying currency in gold. Some contacted their near and dear ones in this miserable hour. People could get only ₹ 4000/ of old denomination exchanged with the new one. Big lines became the order of the day.

Instead of getting shorter, these queues were getting longer with every passing day. The last date for the whole process was 30th of December. The persons could deposit the old cash worth ₹ 2.5 lac till the said date.

The main objective of this move was to curb the black money, corruption and fake money menace. All the people but those who were indulged in malpractices welcomed the move. The whole opposition shook hand against this move under one pretence or the other.

They called this decision a draconian law and wanted the govt to roll back it. Tirades were made to target the decision. Govt also carried out counter attacks.

The new currency which replaced the old one is of denomination of 500/- and 2000/-. Though the people faced a lot of inconvenience owing to shortage of funds, they did not criticize the govt for the move. Even they lauded the Modi govt for this big move. Prime Minister also addressed the people many times telling the people that it was a *mahayajna* (महायज्ञ) and they must offer their own *ahuti* (आहुति) in it.

He further said he was aware the hardships they were suffering from but he sought only 50 days for setting the things right. He jibed at the chief political leaders who have stashed big amount of money and now joined hand to force govt to take the decision back.

The most interesting thing regarding the demonetisation is that people are devising various unique methods for transforming their black money in to white one. Some of these methods are as follows:

- Depositing money in the accounts of their poor relatives and friends.
- Enticing the people with some percentage of money for exchange.
- Asking their employees to stand in the long queues in front of Banks and ATMs for getting money exchanged.
- Hiring labours for some Rupees ranging from Rs 500/- to 700/- for becoming the part of long queues in front of banks/ATMs.
- Converting black money in to gold.
- Paying a few months salaries in advance.
- Paying back loans forcibly.
- Using their influence/links with bank employees and so on.

Jawaharlal Nehru University (JNU)
BA (Hons.) Entrance Examination, 2016

CLUSTER-3: Persian, Arabic and Pashto

SECTION-A

Each question carries 1 mark

Direction: *Encircle the correct answer.*

1. Match the following:
   - (*a*) Al-Farabi   1. Philosopher
   - (*b*) Ferdowsi   2. Poet
   - (*c*) Shirin Ibadi   3. Scientist
   - (*d*) Ahmad Zuwail   4. Nobel Peace Laureate

	(*a*)	(*b*)	(*c*)	(*d*)
A.	4	1	2	3
B.	1	2	4	3
C.	3	4	1	2
D.	1	2	3	4

2. Naguib Mahfouz is a celebrated writer of
   - A. Arabic
   - B. Persian
   - C. Pashto
   - D. Urdu

3. The *Rubaiyat* is popularly associated with the poet
   - A. Ferdowsi
   - B. Omar Khayyam
   - C. Mahmoud Darwesh
   - D. Khushal Khattak

4. The tales of *Arabian Nights* are believed to be drawn from their prototype tales, *Hazar Afsan* written in
   - A. Persian
   - B. Pashto
   - C. Urdu
   - D. None of the above

5. Who among the following founded the Arab Socialist Ba'th Party?
   - A. Michel Aflaq
   - B. Saddam Hussein
   - C. Salah Sabur
   - D. Hafez al-Assad

6. To which of the following language families does Pashto belong?
   - A. Semitic
   - B. Indo-European
   - C. Turkic
   - D. None of the above

7. In which year the Islamic Revolution of Iran took place?
   - A. 1970
   - B. 1975
   - C. 1979
   - D. 1985

8. Gamal Abdul Nasser, a popular Arab leader belonged to which country?
   - A. Egypt
   - B. Syria
   - C. Iraq
   - D. Saudi Arabia

9. The 'Arab Spring' originated from which country?
   - A. Libya
   - B. Egypt
   - C. Tunisia
   - D. Algeria

10. The largest ethnic group in Afghanistan is
    - A. Tajik
    - B. Hazara
    - C. Uzbek
    - D. Pashtoon

11. The Egyptian actor known for his prominent roles in the blockbuster Hollywood movies *The Lawrence of Arabia* and *Dr. Zhivago* passed away in 2015. Who is he among the following?
    - A. Yousef Shaheen
    - B. Omar Sharif
    - C. Adil Imam
    - D. Behrouz Vossoughi

12. Which of the following is correct about Navroz Festival?
- A. Literally translated, navroz means 'New Day'
- B. It is the first day of Persian Year
- C. The festival is celebrated on the dawn of the vernal equinox, when daytime and night are of approximately equal duration as the sun crosses the celestial equator
- D. All of the above

13. The national game of Afghanistan is
- A. Football
- B. Volleyball
- C. Buzkashi (goat grabbing)
- D. None of the above

14. Pashto is an official language of which of the following countries?
- A. Iran
- B. Kazakhastan
- C. Afghanistan
- D. None of the above

15. The largest contiguous sand desert in the world 'Empty Quarter' is a desert largely located in
- A. Saudi Arabia
- B. Sudan
- C. Algeria
- D. Egypt

16. Match the following classics with their authors:

(a) *Gulistan*		1. Saadi Shirazi
(b) *Chahar Maqala*		2. Nizami Aruzi Samarqandi
(c) *Kitab al-Hind*		3. Al-Beruni
(d) *Akbarnama*		4. Abul Fazal Faizi

	(a)	(b)	(c)	(d)
A.	4	3	1	2
B.	1	2	3	4
C.	2	1	4	3
D.	1	2	4	3

17. OPEC stands for
- A. Oil Producing and Exporting Countries
- B. Organization of the Petroleum Exporting Countries
- C. Oil and Petroleum Exploring Countries
- D. None of the above

18. The currency of Afghanistan is
- A. Afghan Afghani
- B. Rupiyah
- C. Riyal
- D. Dirham

19. Achaemenian kings ruled in
- A. Afghanistan
- B. Iran
- C. India
- D. None of the above

20. Casablanca is a famous city in
- A. Egypt
- B. Iran
- C. Morocco
- D. Algeria

21. 'Islam' is an Arabic word which means
- A. Peace
- B. Surrender
- C. Love
- D. Perfection

22. Other than Iran and Afghanistan, which of the following countries has Persian as an official language?
- A. Kazakhastan
- B. Azerbaijan
- C. Tajikistan
- D. Russia

23. Ibn-Batuta, the famous Arab traveler who served as a judge in India during the reign of Muhammad bin Tughlaq hailed from
- A. Algeria
- B. Tunisia
- C. Afghanistan
- D. Morocco

24. The Iranian Foreign Minister credited with clinching Iran's nuclear deal with P+1 nations in 2015 is
- A. Javad Zareef
- B. Ayatollah Ali Khamenei
- C. Hassan Rouhani
- D. Ali Tayyebnia

25. The 'Burj Khalifa' is a landmark structure located in
- A. Tehran
- B. Abu Dhabi
- C. Doha
- D. Dubai

SECTION-B

Each question carries 1 mark. Encircle the correct answer.

Directions (Qs. 26-30): *Fill in the blanks with the correct preposition/word from the choices given.*

The history ...26... Ancient Egypt spans the period ...27... the early pre-dynastic settlements of the northern Nile Valley ...28... the Roman conquest in 30 BC. The Pharaonic Period is dated from around 3200 BC, when Lower and Upper Egypt became ...29... unified state, until the country fell ...30... Macedonian rule in 332 BC.

26. A. of   B. about
    C. in   D. for

27. A. between   B. of
    C. from   D. with

28. A. to   B. up to
    C. at   D. until

29. A. a   B. the
    C. one   D. None of the above

30. A. under   B. beneath
    C. for   D. with

Direction (Qs. 31-35): *Select the appropriate word(s) to fill in the blanks.*

31. The Internet serves to _______ people.
    A. contact   B. connect
    C. bind   D. join

32. He _______ asleep while he was driving.
    A. went   B. fell
    C. got   D. left

33. It is a good habit to keep _______ latest developments.
    A. ahead of   B. abreast of
    C. sure of   D. full of

34. That is a story of hardship _______ our own situation into perspective.
    A. that puts   B. and puts
    C. that it puts   D. puts

35. Just go ahead and see what the life _______ for you.
    A. abounds   B. offers
    C. gives   D. has in store

36. The following is a group. Find out which one of the given alternatives will be another member of the group or of that class:
Apple, Grape, Orange
    A. Vegetables   B. Stem
    C. Oats   D. Fruits

37. 'Opthalmia' is related to 'eye' in the same way as 'Rickets' is related to
    A. Kidney   B. Nose
    C. Bone   D. Heart

Directions (Qs. 38-42): *Complete the following by encircling the correct answer.*

38. "To err is human, to forgive is _______"
    A. kind   B. divine
    C. great   D. foolish

39. Early bird catches _______
    A. the fish   B. the prey
    C. the worm   D. the insect

40. Eat humble _______
    A. bread   B. pie
    C. origins   D. biscuits

41. Go the whole _______
    A. square   B. mile
    C. kilometer   D. 9 yards

42. Blood is thicker than _______
    A. oil   B. water
    C. soda   D. liquids

43. Insert the missing number:

16, 33, 65, 131, 261, ...
    A. 523   B. 521
    C. 613   D. 721

44. Find out the alternative which will replace the question mark:

College : Student :: Hospital : ?
    A. Nurse
    B. Doctor
    C. Treatment
    D. Patient

45. In the following pair of words a certain relationship has been shown. Encircle the pair that best illustrates a similar relationship:

Numismatist : Coins
A. Jeweler : Jewels
B. Cartographer : Maps
C. Philatelist : Stamps
D. Geneticist : Chromosomes

46. A statement is given followed by three assumptions numbered I, II and III. You have to consider the statement and the assumptions. Decide which of the assumptions is implicit in the statement and choose your answer accordingly:

Statement: As our business is expanding, we need to appoint more staff. Owner of a company informs his staff.

Assumptions:

   I. The present staff is now competent.

  II. More staff will further expand the business.

 III. Suitable persons to be taken as staff will be available.

A. Only I is implicit
B. Only II is implicit
C. Only III is implicit
D. All are implicit

47. If ROBUST is coded as QNARTS in a certain languages, then which word would be coded as ZXCMP?
A. AWDLQ   B. AYDNQ
C. BZEOR   D. YYBNO

48. Pointing to a man in a photograph, a woman said, "His brother's father is the only son of my grandfather." How is the woman related to the man in the photograph?
A. Sister
B. Aunt
C. Grandmother
D. Daughter

49. In a family there are husband, wife, two sons and two daughters. All the ladies were invited to a dinner. Both the sons went out to play. Husband did not return from office. Who was/ were at home?
A. Only the wife
B. All the ladies
C. Only the sons
D. Nobody

50. Find the odd one out:
A. Gold : Ornaments
B. Cloth : Garments
C. Wood : Furniture
D. Earthen pots : Clay

SECTION-C

Direction (Qs. 51-55): *Read the paragraph carefully and answer briefly the questions that follow.*

"What do students want in exchange for all of the money that they pay for college? Gather any group of college professors in any discipline in any part of the country, and most (if not all) have noticed a mindset affecting many college students in which they seem to value their degree more than their education.

As an example of how this mindset manifests itself, college professors can almost certainly count on the following question being asked most every semester (usually by multiple students):

"What grade do I need to earn on my next assessment in order to have a grade of X in the course?"

As a mathematics professor, this is disturbing for several reasons, not the least of which is that college-level students should possess the mathematical skills needed to determine the answer to the question for themselves. Students enrolled in College Algebra, Statistics, Calculus and above should already know how to use the weights provided in a syllabus together with their known grades in the course to answer their own question.

An even more disturbing consequence of such a question is the eagerness to know the minimum performance necessary to achieve the desired grade. This mentality focuses on how little the student must learn rather than how much the student can learn."

51. Is the author complaining about the education system or the attitude of the students?

52. Do you think the author/teacher is exaggerating the problem?

53. Do you agree with the views of the author/ teacher?

54. In your opinion which is more important, degree or education?

55. Give a suitable title to the above passage.

Direction (Qs. 56-60): *Go through the words of the Language-A and Language-B and answer the question given at the end (Persian and Arabic).*

Language-A	Language-B
I wish	atamanna
To spring	bahar
There are	wujood darand
The colour	laun
Happy journey	rihla saeeda
Season	fasl-e
(For) You	laka
Has arrived	aamade ast

Money	pool
Apple	al-tuffah
In the garden	dar bagh
To buy	baraye khareedane
Is green	akhdar
I don't have	nadram
Books	ketab-haa
Beautiful roses	golhae-zeeba

Direction: *Translate the following using Language-B.*

56. I wish you a happy journey.

57. The spring season has arrived.

58. The colour of apple is green.

59. I don't have money to buy books.

60. There are beautiful roses in the garden.

Direction (Qs. 61-65): *Rearrange the following jumbled sentences.*

61. ship violently the storm rocked the

62. gift free a dad offered him by the was

63. the storm shed damaged the was during

64. parts many coffee popular in world the is very of

65. cave could explore not they torch the without a

SECTION-D

66. Write an essay of 200 words on any one of the following topics:

   A. My Ambition in Life

   B. Value of Education

   C. The City Life and the Village Life

   D. Be with the Time, Time shall not be with you

67. Write a short note on any one of the following:

   A. Rabindranath Tagore

   B. Mirza Ghalib

   C. Avicenna

   D. Mahatma Gandhi

68. Why should you study a foreign language? Explain.

Or

Illustrate the following image:

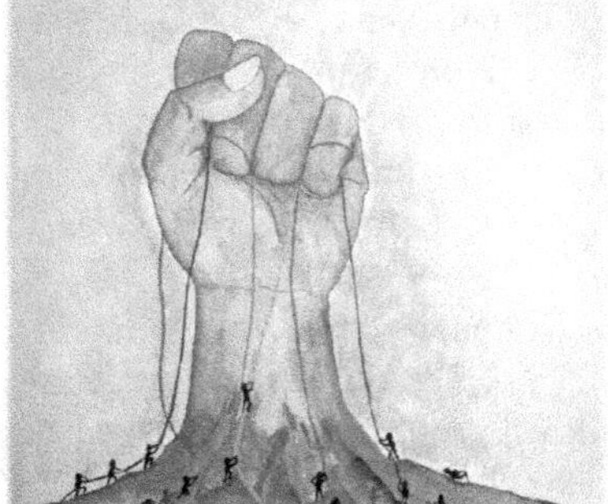

ANSWERS

SECTION-A

1	2	3	4	5	6	7	8	9	10
B	A	B	A	A	B	C	A	C	D

11	12	13	14	15	16	17	18	19	20
B	D	C	C	A	B	B	A	B	C

21	22	23	24	25	26	27	28	29	30
B	C	D	A	D	A	C	A	A	A

31	32	33	34	35	36	37	38	39	40
B	B	B	A	D	C	C	B	C	B

41	42	43	44	45	46	47	48	49	50
D	B	A	D	C	B	B	A	D	D

43.
$$16 \times 2 = 32 + 1 = 33$$
$$33 \times 2 = 66 - 1 = 65$$
$$65 \times 2 = 130 + 1 = 131$$
$$131 \times 2 = 262 - 1 = 261$$
$$261 \times 2 = 522 + 1 = 523$$

47. Since,

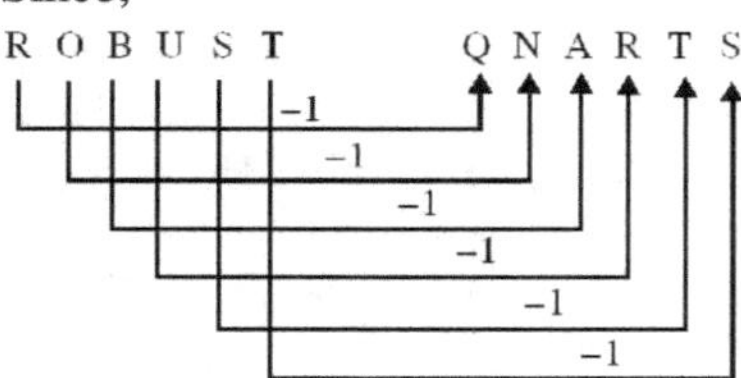

Similarly,

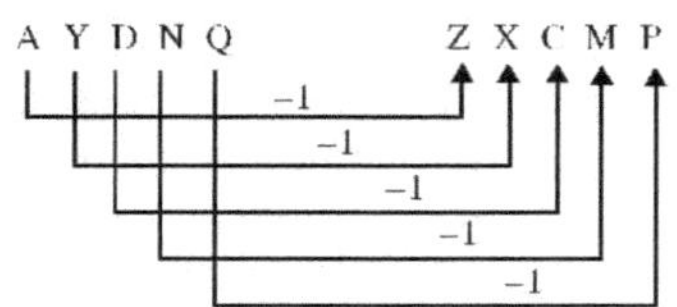

48. Only son of the woman's grandfather = Woman's father

Man's brother's father = Man's father

So, woman is man's sister.

49. In family there are 6 persons.

Out of them 3 are gents and 3 are ladies

All ladies means 3 ladies were invited to dinner. So, remaining persons = 6 – 3 = 3 i.e., 3 gents are remaining.

2 sons went out to play and husband did not return. So, remaining persons = 3 – 3 = 0

Therefore, nobdoy was at home.

SECTION-B

51. The author is complaining about the attitude of the students.

52. The author/teacher is not exaggerating the problem.

53. Yes, I agree with the views of the author/teacher.

54. In my opinion, education is more important than degree.

55. Value the Education Not the Degree.

56. Atamanna laka rihla saeeda.

57. Bahar Fasl-e aamade ast.

58. Laun al-tuffah akhdar.

59. Nadram pool baraye khareedane ketab-haa.

60. Wujood darand golhae-zaeba dar bagh.

61. The storm rocked the ship violently.

62. A free gift was offered him by the dad.

63. The shed was damaged during the storm.

64. Coffee is very popular in many parts of the world.

65. They could not explore the cave without a torch.

66. Choosing a profession is not an easy task. A wrong choice can mar one's career and make one's whole life miserable.

So, the choice of a profession must be made very judiciously and that after long reflection and consultation with elders and other experienced people. In this regard, one's aptitude and bent of mind and general attitude towards life should not be ignored.

After considering all the pros and cons of the matter, I have decided to become a doctor. My main motivation came to me from the noble example set before me by my father.

My father is a renowned doctor of the town. He has a heart of gold as he is filled with milk of human kindness. He pursues the profession of a doctor with a spirit of dedication.

I want to follow in the footsteps of my father. I am a brilliant student. I'm particularly strong in science subjects. Biology is my favourite subject. I have a natural bent of mind for the medical courses. So, I have decided to become a doctor. I belong to a well-to-do family and my parents can easily pay my fees.

My chief aim is to serve humanity. There is so much misery in the world. I want to mitigate it to whatever extent I can. I have decided that I will not charge heavy fees from patients. I'll treat poor patients without charging any fees. May God help me in my venture !

67. Rabindra Nath Tagore was born on 8th May, 1861 in Jorasanku in Calcutta. His father, Maharishi Debendra Nath was a great landlord and was known as 'Thakur', the word which got changed into 'Tagore'. His mother's name was Sharda Devi. He was the youngest of the fourteen children in the family of Debendra Nath and Sharda Devi.

Rabindra Nath Tagore was one of the greatest men of India and he was easily one of the greatest literary personages of the world. He was a versatile genius, being a poet, novelist, playwright, essayist , short story writer, statesman, musician, painter, philosopher, actor, educationist and freedom fighter all rolled into one. He was both a great nationalist and an internationalist and universalist and humanist in equal measure.

He wrote originally in Bengali but later translated his own works into English. His world famous work of lyrics, the Gitanjali, for which he won the Nobel Prize in 1913, was also originally written in Bengali but later translated into English by the poet himself.

He had his education at home, though it was not much of education, since he did not show much interest even in private tuitions at home. The fact is that he was a born poet and writer who was more influenced by nature and human beings. Hence, it is not surprising that we find lofty ideas and descriptions of nature and human beings in his works. Another thing which impressed him was the ancient Indian philosophy. He was by and large a self-taught man who wrote with felicity on almost every conceivable topic of the times such as poetry, literature, drama, criticism, education, novel, religion, politics, music, language and even science. Most of his work was written in Bengali and not all of it was translated into English.

He was a great lover of his country, of humanity and children in particular. He believed in non-violence and rejected traditionalism as much as western chauvinism. The Indian National Anthem 'Jana Gana Mana' was written by him. He also set up the Shantiniketan with the money he got from the Nobel Prize. He gave up the title of 'Sir' as a protest against the Jallianwala Bagh tragedy in 1919. He died on 8th August, 1941.

68. Foreign languages provide a competitive edge in career choices: one is able to communicate in a second language. Foreign language study enhances listening skills and memory. One participates more effectively and responsibly in a multi-cultural world if one knows another language.

Your marketable skills in the global economy are improved if you master another language. Foreign language study offers a sense of the past: culturally and linguistically.

The study of a foreign tongue improves the knowledge of one's own language: English vocabulary skills increase. Foreign languages expand one's view of the world, liberalize one's experiences, and make one more flexible and tolerant.

JAWAHARLAL NEHRU UNIVERSITY [JNU]

First Year of 3-Year B.A. [Hons.] in Foreign Languages

Chinese, French, German, Korean, Japanese, Arabic, Persian, Russian and Spanish

Entrance Examination, 2015

PART–A

All questions carry one mark each. Encircle the correct answer clearly. If more than one option is encircled, the answer will be marked wrong:

1. Who among the following is not a Bharat Ratna?
   (a) Pandit Ravi Shankar
   (b) Rajiv Gandhi
   (c) M.S. Subbulakshmi
   (d) L.K. Advani

2. In collegium system, a judge is:
   (a) appointed by the Lawyers
   (b) appointed by the President of India
   (c) appointed by the Judges
   (d) appointed by the Prime Minister

3. Which of the following days is observed as International Mother Language Day?
   (a) September 5   (b) February 21
   (c) October 2   (d) March 8

4. The G8 member-country which was suspended from G8 in 2014 is:
   (a) Japan   (b) Russia
   (c) France   (d) Germany

5. *Hundred Years of Solitude* is one of the famous novels by:
   (a) Paulo Coelho
   (b) Jorge Amado
   (c) Che Guevara
   (d) Gabriel Garcia Marquez

6. Which one of the following is not a classical language?
   (a) Tamil   (b) Bengali
   (c) Malayalam   (d) Odiya

7. Narendra Modi is India's .... Prime Minister.
   (a) 14th   (b) 16th
   (c) 15th   (d) 13th

8. Who among the following test cricketers is the first to have claimed 10 wickets in a test innings of test cricket?
   (a) Anil Kumble
   (b) Kapil Dev
   (c) Jim Laker
   (d) Muttiah Muralitharan

9. Which among the following planets has got strongest magnetic field?
   (a) Jupiter   (b) Earth
   (c) Mars   (d) Saturn

10. The largest railway network is possessed by:
    (a) India
    (b) China
    (c) United States of America
    (d) Russia

11. Which of the following is the only diamond-producing State in India?
    (a) Gujarat   (b) Maharashtra
    (c) Madhya Pradesh (d) Andhra Pradesh

12. Which of the following countries was not a Member of Allies in the Second World War?
    (a) France   (b) Great Britain
    (c) Russia   (d) Japan

13. Who among the following conducts the Civil Services Examination in India?
    (a) Union Public Service Commission
    (b) University Grant Commission

   (c) Central Board of Secondary Education
   (d) Ministry of Human Resource Development

14. Who among the following is called the father of Indian cinema?
   (a) Satyajit Ray
   (b) G.P. Sippy
   (c) Dada Saheb Phalke
   (d) G. Aravindan

15. Which of the following countries started using paper currency first?
   (a) Greece   (b) Rome
   (c) India   (d) China

16. Which of the following has become India's first Wi-Fi-enabled city?
   (a) New Delhi   (b) Ahmadabad
   (c) Kolkata   (d) Mumbai

17. Linguistics is the:
   (a) study of grammar
   (b) study of language
   (c) study of literature
   (d) study of vocabulary

18. Who among the following holds the record for fastest ODI hundred?
   (a) Shahid Afridi   (b) Corey Anderson
   (c) Chris Gayle   (d) Kumara Sangakara

19. The largest part of India's national income comes from
   (a) agricultural sector
   (b) manufacturing sector
   (c) IT sector
   (d) services sector

20. In which of the following languages did Gautama Buddha preach?

   (a) Pali   (b) Sanskrit
   (c) Hindustani   (d) Prakrit

21. Who among the following is the Metro-man of India?
   (a) Anna Hazare
   (b) E. Sreedharan
   (c) Dr. Verghese Kurien
   (d) Mangu Singh

22. Which among the following is the national fruit of India?
   (a) Apple   (b) Orange
   (c) Banana   (d) Mango

23. Which among the following is the longest railway line?
   (a) Thiruvananthapuram-Jammu Tawi
   (b) Bengaluru-Guwahati
   (c) Chennai-Amritsar
   (d) Mumbai-Kolkata

24. Which among the following is in correct descending chronological order?
   (a) Gupta dynasty → Mauryan empire → Chalukyas → Kushans
   (b) Mauryan empire → Gupta dynasty → Kushans → Chalukyas
   (c) Kushans → Mauryan empire → Chalukyas → Gupta dynasty
   (d) Mauryan empire → Kushans → Gupta dynasty → Chalukyas

25. India is a
   (a) sovereign socialist democratic republic
   (b) sovereign socialist secular democratic republic
   (c) sovereign socialist secular republic
   (d) sovereign democratic republic

PART–B

All questions carry one mark each. Encircle the correct answer clearly. If more than one option is encircled, the answer will be marked wrong:

Directions (Qs. 26 to 30): *Read the following and answer the questions given below:*

There are five persons P, Q, R, S and T. One is a football player, one is a chess player and one is a hockey player. P and S are unmarried ladies and do not participate in any game. None of the ladies plays chess or football. There is a married couple in which T is the husband. Q is the brother of R and is neither a chess player nor a hockey player.

26. Who is the football player?
   (a) P   (b) Q
   (c) R   (d) S
   (e) T

27. Who is the hockey player?
   (a) T   (b) S

(c) R   (d) Q
(e) P

28. Who is the chess player?
(a) S   (b) P
(c) T   (d) R
(e) Q

29. Who is the wife of T?
(a) P   (b) Q
(c) R   (d) S
(e) Data inadequate

30. The three ladies are
(a) P, Q and R   (b) Q, R and S
(c) P, Q and S   (d) P, R and S
(e) None of the above

31. If B says that his mother is the only daughter of A's mother, how is A related to B?
(a) Son   (b) Father
(c) Brother   (d) Grandfather
(e) Uncle

32. A man said to a lady, "Your mother's husband's sister is my aunt." How is the lady related to the man?
(a) Daughter   (b) Granddaughter
(c) Mother   (d) Sister
(e) Aunt

33. C is A's father's nephew. D is A's cousin but not the brother of C. How is D related to C?
(a) Father   (b) Sister
(c) Mother   (d) Aunt
(e) None of the above

34. If X is the brother of the son of Y's son, how is X related to Y?
(a) Son   (b) Brother
(c) Cousin   (d) Grandson
(e) Uncle

35. Q is the brother of R. P is the sister of Q. T is the brother of S. S is the daughter of R. Who are the cousins of Q?
(a) R and P   (b) P and T
(c) Q and T   (d) S and T
(e) None of the above

36. A women introduces a man as the son of the brother of her mother. How is the man related to the woman?
(a) Nephew   (b) Son

(c) Cousin   (d) Uncle
(e) Grandson

37. P is the brother of D. X is the sister of P. A is the brother of F. F is the daughter of D. M is the father of X. Who is the uncle of A?
(a) X   (b) P
(c) F   (d) M
(e) None of the above

38. Lakshmi and Meena are Rohan's sisters. Shalini is Meena's stepdaughter. How is Lakshmi related to Shalini?
(a) Sister   (b) Mother-in-law
(c) Mother   (d) Stepmother
(e) None of the above

Directions (Qs. 39 and 40): *Read the following information carefully and answer the questions given below.*

In a questions paper, there are 12 questions in all, out of which only six are to be answered. Six questions have one alternative each. Each question has four parts, only three of which are to be answered.

39. How many questions (including parts) are there in the question paper?
(a) 24   (b) 48
(c) 72   (d) 96
(e) 36

40. Of these, how many are to be answered?
(a) 6   (b) 12
(c) 15   (d) 18
(e) 24

Directions (Qs. 41 to 50): *Read carefully the following nouns in Zulu language spoken in some African countries, and answer the questions given below.*

Zulu	Gloss	Zulu	Gloss
umfazi	married woman	abafazi	married women
umfani	boy	abafani	boys
umzali	parent	abazali	parents
umfundisi	teacher	abafundisi	teachers
umbazi	carver	ababazi	carvers
umlimi	farmer	abalimi	farmers
umdlali	player	abadlali	players
umfundi	reader	abafundi	readers

41. How is 'singular' marked in Zulu?
(a) aba   (b) um
(c) li

42. How is 'plural' marked in Zulu?
   (*a*) aba   (*b*) urn
   (*c*) li

43. What is the Zulu form meaning 'boy' before singular or plural is marked?
   (*a*) afani   (*b*) mani
   (*c*) fani

44. What is the Zulu form meaning 'parent' before singular or plural is marked?
   (*a*) abaz   (*b*) zali
   (*c*) ali

45. What is the Zulu form meaning 'farmer' before singular or plural is marked?
   (*a*) limi   (*b*) dali
   (*c*) mlali

46. What is the plural word for umpendi (painter)?
   (*a*) abumpende   (*b*) apendi
   (*c*) abapendi

47. What is the plural word for umthengisi (seller)?
   (*a*) umabathengisi   (*b*) abathengisi
   (*c*) abagisi

48. What is the plural word for umipheki (cook)?
   (*a*) abaipheki   (*b*) abapheki
   (*c*) ubapheki

49. What is the plural word for umakhi (builder)?
   (*a*) abakhi   (*b*) abaakhi
   (*c*) abamakhi

50. What is the plural word for umama (mother)?
   (*a*) abamama   (*b*) abama
   (*c*) abaama

PART–C

Directions (Qs. 51 to 60): *Complete the sentence B making it as similar in meaning to A as possible.*

51. A. You will succeed. You must work hard.
   B. Unless ....

52. A. Tagore was a great poet and writer.
   B. Not only ....

53. A. You suggestions will influence his performance.
   B. His performance ....

54. A. Atul is not as intelligent as his sister Arushi.
   B. Arushi ....

55. A. Although Rohan had fractured his wrist, he sat for the exam.
   B. Despite ....

56. A. As soon as the whistle blew, the dogs ran out barking.
   B. No sooner ....

57. A. My ailing grandmother requested me to visit her in Pune.
   B. My ailing grandmother said, ...

58. A. I am sorry I am unable to accompany you.
   B. I regret my ....

59. A. The prices of food grains have increased due to hoarding.
   B. Hoarding has led ....

60. A. The teacher said to us, "Come prepared for the Biology test on Tuesday."
   B. The teacher told ....

Directions (Qs. 61 to 70): *Fill in the blanks.*

61. She will benefit .... his efforts.

62. The writer was lost .... deep thought.

63. Eavesdroppers never hear any good .... themselves.

64. The old lady passed .... in her sleep.

65. Prayer will carry a person .... difficulties.

66. All parents fear .... their children.

67. Our teacher is partial .... the girl students.

68. Anand succeeded .... mobilizing support for the cause.

69. He sat .... the computer all day.

70. The workers called .... the strike after their demands were met.

Directions (Qs. 71 to 80): *Fill in the blanks with the appropriate form of the verbs given in brackets.*

71. Where .... you going? (be)

72. The house that Roshan .... was very large. (buy)

73. Students .... the advice of their teacher. (seek)

74. Avoid .... processed food. (consume)

75. Atif .... regularly when he was in school. (cycle)

76. The soldier .... down his arms upon orders from his superior. (lay)

77. The burglars .... into the house in broad daylight. (break)

78. The joys and sorrows of life .... together. (weave)

79. The government .... three corporations to present their strategy. (ask)

80. The filmmaker .... by local guides who spoke the language. (assist)

Directions (Qs. 81 to 85): *Fill in the blanks with the appropriate word. Write the answers at the space provided below:*

The History of Tea

The history of tea is fascinating (81) offers great insight into the history (82) our world. Since tea was first discovered (83) China, it has travelled the world conquering the thirsts of virtually every country (84) the planet. Tea is the most popular (85) in the world as well as one of the healthiest.

81. ....

82. ....

83. ....

84. ....

85. ....

PART–D

Directions: *Read the passage given below carefully and answer the questions that follow.*

Decades-old training techniques must be ripped up in a microlearning revolution:

The mass attention deficit era

If you struggle to read a book from start to finish or if you start a task only to end up following a maze of different web links instead, you probably suffer from attention deficit. And you'll understand it if you have friends who just can't put their phones down : on all average, we check them 150 times a day, according to Nokia research.

We are living through the first era of mass attention deficit.

It would be tempting to say this is just a millennial phenomenon; that a generation of self-centered 20- and 30-somethings is getting sucked into the screen. But, if you thought this group is bad, just look to the next generation.

The brain is changing

Kids aged 8 to 18 spend twice as much time with screens as they spend in school. Children have fundamentally different cognitive skills nowadays and they are too easily distracted, according to two pieces of research by the Pew Internet Project, in which US teachers said kids need more time away from digital technologies. It has been suggested that children should receive lessons in concentration.

But fighting modern modalities is not the best way to fit the reality of consumption and comprehension today. If brains are evolving to favour constant, short bursts of information, it is unlikely this can be reversed. Even in 1976 a study found that in-lesson concentration ebbed and flowed, topping out at just 10 to 18 minutes.

Schools are adapting

That is why some believe 'microlearning'—in which education is delivered in small, active and frequent snippets rather than big, sit-down monologues-holds the key.

While microlearning has not yet been widely adopted, the individual schools and growing number of district education authorities around the world that have done so are achieving excellent results. In the UK, the digital education initiative Khan Academy is among microlearning's advocates.

Pupils at schools in Galway say they find fun in learning maths through short online video tuition, while schools across the whole of Los Altos, California, are now adopting the techniques. In Australia, standard school lessons are now just 45 minutes. Finnish schools go even further, with most allowing a 15-minute break after each 45-minute lesson. Punctuating scheduled lesson time with 'free-play' break time has seemingly boosted student productivity in Finland.

Word meanings:

Cognitive: of, relating to, being, or involving conscious intellectual activity (as thinking, reasoning or remembering)

Modalities: (modality) a particular mode in which something exists or is experienced or expressed; a particular method or procedure

1. Explain, in your own words, what is meant by 'mass attention deficit'.
2. Make sentences with any *two* of the following words/phrases:
   (*a*) It would be tempting to say ....
   (*b*) consumption
   (*c*) ebbed and flowed
   (*d*) to favour
   (*e*) frequent
3. Do you agree that young people today have similar problems whilst learning? Do you believe that 'microlearning' is a solution?

PART–E

Write a short paragraph of about 300 words on any *one* of the following two pictures:

Grammatical correctness	Clarity of thought	Coherence of structure
3 marks	3 marks	4 marks

Picture—A	Picture—B

ANSWERS

PART-A

1	2	3	4	5	6	7	8	9	10
(*d*)	(*c*)	(*b*)	(*b*)	(*d*)	(*b*)	(*c*)	(*c*)	(*a*)	(*c*)

11	12	13	14	15	16	17	18	19	20
(c)	(d)	(a)	(c)	(d)	(c)	(b)	(a)	(d)	(a)

21	22	23	24	25
(b)	(d)	(a)	(d)	(b)

PART-B

26	27	28	29	30	31	32	33	34	35
(b)	(c)	(c)	(c)	(d)	(e)	(d)	(b)	(d)	(d)
36	37	38	39	40	41	42	43	44	45
(c)	(b)	(c)	(b)	(d)	(b)	(a)	(c)	(b)	(a)

46	47	48	49	50
(c)	(b)	(a)	(b)	(c)

31. As per the given information in the question, B's mother is the only daughter of A's mother. In other words, B is the grandson of A's mother. Hence, A is the uncle of B.

32. Your mother's husband — Your father

Your father's sister — Your aunt

So, the lady's aunt is man's aunt and therefore, lady is man's sister.

33. C is A's father's nephew means C is the son of A's father's brother, therefore, C is the cousin of A. D is also A's cousin. D must be real brother or sister of C. But D is not brother of C. Thus, D must be sister of C.

34. Son of Y's son — Grandson;

Brother of Y's grandson — Y's grandson.

35. T is the brother of S, who is the daughter of R. So, T and S are the children of R. Now, Q is the brother of R. So, T and S are the cousins of Q. Hence, the correct answer is (d).

PART-C

51. Unless you work hard, you will not succeed.

52. Not only was Tagore a great poet but a writer also.

53. His performance will be influenced by your suggestions.

54. Arushi is more intelligent than Atul.

55. Despite his fractured wrist Rohan sat for the exam.

56. No sooner did the whistle blow than the dogs ran out barking.

57. My ailing grandmother said, "Please visit me in Pune."

58. I regret my inability to accompany you.

59. Hoarding has led to increase in the prices of foodgrains.

60. The teacher told us to come prepared for the Biology test on Tuesday.

61. with **62.** in **63.** by **64.** away

65. beyond **66.** for **67.** to **68.** in

69. on **70.** off **71.** are

72. had bought **73.** sought

74. consuming **75.** used to cycle

76. laid **77.** broke

78. are woven **79.** has asked

80. was assisted **81.** and

82. of **83.** in **84.** on **85.** drink

PART-D

1. Mass Attention Deficit

Mass Attention Deficit pertains to the phenomenon of lack of concentration in doing studies and other mental work. It is more common in students and other young people who are active users of mobile and internet socializing sites. They form a habit of checking their call records and status updates every now and then. Whatever they do, be it studies or any other work, they have a frequent urge to check the device they use for the updates and likes. This leads to lack of concentration and disinterest in their work which is known as Mass Attention Deficit.

2. (*a*) It would be tempting to say that you can achieve this target easily but the fact is you really have to work hard for it.

(*b*) If you reduce the consumption of fats you need not worry about your fitness.

(*c*) Many people begin their course in full esteem but very soon their energy is seen to be ebbed and flowed.

(*d*) It is never proper to favour a person who has committed a wrong.

(*e*) There are frequent power cuts in this area now-a-days.

3. I agree that young people today have similar problems. Most of the students find the traditional class-lessons boring and frequently seen yawning, looking out of windows, whispering or making excuses to leave the classrooms. Some even sleep on the back-benches. This all indicates that they lack concentration and some changes should be made in the system of imparting education.

I believe microlearning is a solution to this problem as lengthy lectures on text book lessons are not properly grasped by the students. If these bulky lessons are broken into small informative parts which may be grasped by students easily then the learning will be more effective. If short-free breaks are given to students talk about, discuss and properly absorb the concept then it will definitely effect in quality learning.

PART-E

Picture—A

A scene at a Railway platform can be distressing and boring if one just goes on thinking and grumbling about a late train and it can be thrilling if one rivets one's eyes to observing people and objects all around. I am in the habit of having the latter type of optimistic attitude. Last Sunday, I went to the Railway station to board a train for Delhi. I bought the ticket and went to the platform where I learnt that the train was late by half an hour. As I believe in the dictum of travelling light, I didn't have more than negligible luggage with me. However, I saw people following coolies whose heads were loaded with suitcase, attache-cases and bags. The vendors were crying for their wares like tea, cold drinks and snacks. There was a great hustle and bustle on the platform. People from all parts of the country with their different kinds of dresses could be seen. I was amused to see that some people were grumbling about our late train.

A railway journey is very exhilarating and pleasant if it is comfortable and tension-free. But that is rare. Most often a common man has to experience horrendous moments in trains. This is what happened to me. The first taste of bitterness was at the booking window where I had to stand in a queue for about half an hour to buy the ticket. Then to board the train was a Herculean task as the hostile horde of passengers practically hit me and bit me on every part of my body. I entered the train as a man with a bruised face, crumpled trousers and torn, unbuttoned shirt. As there was no room to sit, I had to stand well-sandwiched between heaving chests and protruded bellies and was all the while compelled to enjoy rancid smells and streams of warm and polluted air from mouths and nostrils besides a good amount of abuses and kicks, jolts and pains due to elbow hits. When the train started, I couldn't much contemplate but hurtling sounds and little sights of moving trees and poles through crevices between heads, assured me that the train was moving indeed. After a nightmarish afternoon, I reached Delhi late at night to thank my stars more than God.

JAWAHARLAL NEHRU UNIVERSITY [JNU]

First Year of 3-Year B.A. [Hons.] in Foreign Languages

Chinese, French, German, Korean, Japanese, Arabic, Persian, Russian and Spanish

Entrance Examination, 2014

PART–A

All questions carry one mark each. Encircle the correct answer clearly. If more than one option is encircled, the answer will be marked wrong.

1. Which of the following is a Francophone region?
   (*a*) Maldives (*b*) Hong Kong
   (*c*) Virgin Islands (*d*) Seychelles

2. Which of the following is not one of the old names of Urdu?
   (*a*) Rekhta (*b*) Hindvi
   (*c*) Dakkani (*d*) Farsi

3. While in India, the Chinese scholar Hiuen Tsang also stayed for a brief period in which one of the following newly discovered universities?
   (*a*) Nalanda (*b*) Vikramshila
   (*c*) Telhara (*d*) Taxila

4. Kimchi is a traditional side dish of
   (*a*) China (*b*) Vietnam
   (*c*) South Korea (*d*) Philippines

5. Who among the following translated *Mahabharata* into Persian?
   (*a*) Mirza Ghalib (*b*) Mulla Badayuni
   (*c*) Akbar (*d*) Amir Khusraw

6. This year marks the .... anniversary of *Panchsheel* between India and China.
   (*a*) 64th (*b*) 60th
   (*c*) 65th (*d*) 55th

7. The notion of 'Chinese dream' has been advocated by which of the following Chinese leaders?

   (*a*) Mao Zedong (*b*) Deng Xiaoping
   (*c*) Jiang Zemin (*d*) Xi Jinping

8. The royal family of Japan recently visited the cities of
   (*a*) New Delhi and Kolkata
   (*b*) New Delhi and Chennai
   (*c*) New Delhi and Mumbai
   (*d*) New Delhi and Bengaluru

9. Which of the following countries won the bid for 2020 Summer Olympics?
   (*a*) Korea (*b*) Canada
   (*c*) Australia (*d*) Japan

10. 'K-Pop' is a popular abbreviation for
    (*a*) South Korean Pop Music
    (*b*) Kazakhstan Popular Arts
    (*c*) Kyrgyzstan Pop Culture
    (*d*) Kenyan Popular Dance and Music

11. Jean-Luc Godard is a French
    (*a*) Poet (*b*) Painter
    (*c*) Film-maker (*d*) Politician

12. The largest Arabic-speaking country in number of speakers is
    (*a*) Saudi Arabia (*b*) Egypt
    (*c*) Algeria (*d*) Syria

13. Rabat is the capital of
    (*a*) Tunisia (*b*) Algeria
    (*c*) Chad (*d*) Morocco

14. Which of the following languages belongs to the Semitic group of languages?

9

(*a*) German   (*b*) French
(*c*) Hebrew   (*d*) Russian

15. Leo Tolstoy was a representative author of
(*a*) romanticism   (*b*) realism
(*c*) natural school   (*d*) symbolism

16. The Mascot for Sochi Winter Olympics, 2014 was
(*a*) Quatchi and Miga
(*b*) Neve and Gliz
(*c*) Powder, Coal and Copper
(*d*) The Hare, the Polar Bear and the Snow Leopard

17. Shakira, the famous singer, is from
(*a*) Peru   (*b*) Mexico
(*c*) Spain   (*d*) Columbia

18. What is the present currency of Spain?
(*a*) Dollar   (*b*) Peseta
(*c*) Euro   (*d*) Spanish dollar

19. In which year was the Project Tiger started in India?
(*a*) 1973   (*b*) 1976
(*c*) 1982   (*d*) 1989

20. Which of the following is not associated with Spain?

(*a*) Flamenco dance
(*b*) Bullfighting
(*c*) Tomatina festival
(*d*) Dia de los muertos

Who wrote the following books?
(for Q. Nos. 21 to 25)

21. *A Brief History of Time*
(*a*) Stephen Hawking
(*b*) Khalil Gibran
(*c*) Jonathan Swift
(*d*) Derrida

22. *Natya-shastra*
(*a*) Narad Muni   (*b*) Bharat Muni
(*c*) Abhinav Gupta   (*d*) Chanakya

23. *Ladies Coupe*
(*a*) Preeti Shenoy   (*b*) Anita Nair
(*c*) Anurag Mathvi   (*d*) Rashmi Bansal

24. *The Inheritance of Loss*
(*a*) Amitava Ghosh   (*b*) R.K. Narayan
(*c*) Arun Tiwari   (*d*) Kiran Desai

25. *The Secret of the Nagas*
(*a*) Shobha Dey   (*b*) Amish Tripathi
(*c*) Arundhati Ray   (*d*) Vikram Seth

PART–B

All questions carry one mark each. Encircle the correct answer clearly. If more than one option is encircled, the answer will be marked wrong (Q. Nos. 26 to 30):

26. Ornithology is the study of
(*a*) bees   (*b*) birds
(*c*) fishes   (*d*) ornamental plants

27. Muga/Mooga is a kind of Indian
(*a*) painting style   (*b*) musical instrument
(*c*) silk   (*d*) None of the above

28. The deepest oceanic trench, Mariana, is located in
(*a*) Atlantic Ocean   (*b*) Pacific Ocean
(*c*) Arctic Ocean   (*d*) Indian Ocean

29. There are deer and peacocks in a zoo. By counting heads, they are 80. The number of their legs is 200. How many peacocks are there?
(*a*) 20   (*b*) 40
(*c*) 60   (*d*) 50

30. Rahul walks northwards. After a while, he turns to his right and a little further to his left. Finally, after walking a distance of one kilometer, he turns to his left again. In which direction is he moving now?
(*a*) East   (*b*) West
(*c*) North   (*d*) South

Select and encircle the most appropriate synonyms of the bracketed words (Q. Nos. 31 to 36):

31. (Placid)
(*a*) Solemn   (*b*) Lazy
(*c*) Devious   (*d*) Calm

32. (Nincompoop)
    (*a*) Sharp and intelligent
    (*b*) Famous person
    (*c*) Foolish person
    (*d*) Cunning

33. (Rudimentary)
    (*a*) Broad   (*b*) Basic
    (*c*) Advanced   (*d*) Sharp

34. (Arboreal)
    (*a*) Jovial   (*b*) Relating to trees
    (*c*) Urban   (*d*) Airy

35. (Shrewd)
    (*a*) Mean   (*b*) Unwise
    (*c*) Astute   (*d*) Kind

36. (Kleptomania)
    (*a*) Sleepwalking
    (*b*) Honesty
    (*c*) Tendency to steal
    (*d*) Modesty

Encircle the correct answer (Q. Nos. 37 to 44):

37. Who defined democracy as government of the people, by the people and for the people?
    (*a*) Napoleon Bonaparte
    (*b*) George Washington
    (*c*) Abraham Lincoln
    (*d*) Winston Churchill

38. Which of the following is not correctly matched?
    (*a*) Syed Kirmani   — Cricketer
    (*b*) Mira Nair   — Film director
    (*c*) Sharan Rani   — Sarod player
    (*d*) Ashapurna Devi — Classical singer

39. According to the Indian mythology, Apsara Menaka married sage
    (*a*) Vashishtha   (*b*) Shaunak
    (*c*) Atri   (*d*) Vishwamitra

40. Priyanka is both the 50th best and the 50th worst student at her school. How many students attend her school?
    (*a*) 98   (*b*) 99
    (*c*) 100   (*d*) 101

41. Who was the winner of 2012 Dada Sahib Phalke Award?
    (*a*) Actor Pran
    (*b*) Singer Manna Dey
    (*c*) Director K. Balachander
    (*d*) Actor Soumitra Chatterjee

42. When light passes from air into glass, it experiences change of
    (*a*) frequency and wavelength
    (*b*) frequency and speed
    (*c*) wavelength and speed
    (*d*) frequency, wavelength and speed

43. What is *Mohiniattam*?
    (*a*) Painting style
    (*b*) Classical dance form
    (*c*) Hindustani classical music raga
    (*d*) Musical instrument of Andhra Pradesh

44. Who is the new CEO of Microsoft?
    (*a*) Satya Nadella
    (*b*) Indira Nooyi
    (*c*) Mark Zuckerberg
    (*d*) Kun Hee Lee

Answer the following questions
(Q. Nos. 45 to 50):

45. Which Indian cricket player wrote the book, *One More Over*?

....

46. Who was the captain of the Indian hockey team, which won the Gold Medal in Tokyo Olympics in 1964?

....

47. Who holds the post of Ex-officio Chairperson of the Planning Commission of India?

....

48. On which date is the International Women's Day celebrated?

....

49. If PENSION is coded as NEISNOP, how is FOLIAGE coded?

....

50. What is the number of already named bones in the human skeleton?

....

PART–C

All questions carry one mark each.

Select appropriate words to fill in the blanks (Q. Nos. 51 to 60):

51. Mrs. Sharma .... rather not invest that money in the stock market.
   (*a*) could (*b*) would
   (*c*) has to (*d*) neither

52. When I graduate from college next June, I .... a student here for five years.
   (*a*) will be (*b*) have been
   (*c*) will have been (*d*) has been

53. The company will upgrade .... computer information systems next month.
   (*a*) their (*b*) its
   (*c*) it's (*d*) own

54. Each of the Olympic athletes .... training for months, even years.
   (*a*) have been (*b*) has been
   (*c*) were (*d*) been

55. I have only a .... Diwali cards left to write.
   (*a*) some (*b*) few
   (*c*) little (*d*) less

56. The police were greatly out-numbered by rioters, ... ran into hundreds.
   (*a*) whose figures
   (*b*) those figures
   (*c*) that its figures
   (*d*) its figures that

57. It is lovely to wake up in the morning and .... birds singing.
   (*a*) hear (*b*) hears
   (*c*) heard (*d*) hearing

58. When Anisha .... her first pay, she bought presents for her parents?
   (*a*) receive (*b*) received
   (*c*) has received (*d*) had received

59. That is a story of hardship .... our own situation into perspective.
   (*a*) puts (*b*) it puts
   (*c*) that it puts (*d*) that puts

60. A : "Have you had enough to eat?"
   B : "I'd like ...., please."
   (*a*) another (*b*) one more
   (*c*) some more (*d*) any more

Fill in the blanks with appropriate prepositions in the following sentences (Q. Nos. 61 to 66):

61. A house .... the sea is where you will find me after retirement.

62. She is .... the other children in her class. Please ensure she studies.

63. I will come back .... two weeks.

64. .... my calculation he must be sixty-three.

65. The picture is .... page 7.

66. .... you and me, I think she is crazy.

Give full form of the following (Q. Nos. 67 to 70):

67. SEBI ....

68. PETA ....

69. BCCI ....

70. ICSSR ....

Rearrange the following words to make meaningful sentences (Q. Nos. 71 to 74):

71. yesterday/at home/you/to visit/were not/I/but/wanted/you

   ....

72. he decided/had seen/to buy/after Ali/the film/the book/ on TV

   ....

73. for you/wait a minute!/this box/I will/carry

   ....

74. for two hours/waiting/girlfriend/I/my/have been/for

   ....

Read carefully the following data from Iselta language:

1. (a) temiban 'I went'
2. (a) amiban 'you went'
3. (a) temiwe 'I am going'
4. mimiaj 'he was going'
5. tewanban 'I came'
6. tewanhi 'I will come'

Answer the following questions (Q. Nos. 75 to 77):

75. How will you say the following in Iselta?

    'He went': ....

76. How will you say the following in Iselta?

    'You will come': ....

77. Translate the following in English:

    'awanban': ....

78. What is missing out of the trio?

    Sine, Cosine and ....

79. If a bag of 30 sweets weighs 20 g, how many sweets would weigh 1 kg?

    ....

80. What is the next number in the following series?

    1, 4, 9, 16, ...

PART–D

Read the passage below and give short answer to the questions that follow. Marks assigned are given against each question:

People moan about poverty as a great evil; and it seems to be an accepted belief that if people only had plenty of money, they would be happy and useful and get more out of life. As a rule, there is more genuine satisfaction in life and more obtained from life in the humble cottage of the poor man than in the palaces of the rich. I always pity the sons and daughters of rich men who are attended by servants and have governesses at a later age; at the same time I am glad to think that they do not know what they have missed.

It is because I know how sweet and happy and pure the home of honest poverty is, how free from perplexing care and from social envies and jealousies—how loving and united its members are in the common interest of supporting the family that I sympathize with the rich man's boy and congratulate the poor man's son. It is for these reasons that from the ranks of the poor so many strong, eminent, self-reliant men have always sprung and always must spring. If you will read the list of the 'Immortals who were not born to die', you will find that most of them have been born poor. It seems, nowadays, a matter of universal desire that poverty should be abolished. We should be quite willing to abolish luxury; but to abolish honest, industrious, self-denying poverty would be to destroy the soil upon which mankind produces the virtues that will enable our race to reach a still higher civilization than it now possesses.

81. Write the summary of the above passage in about one-third of the original length in your own words.

    ....
    ....
    ....
    ....
    ....
    ....
    ....
    ....
    ....
    ....
    ....
    ....
    ....

82. Give a suitable title to the above passage.

    ....

PART–E

Write a brief composition on the following topics in about 400 words each:

83. The tradition or the custom of your region related to daily life that you think should continue.

....

....

....

....

....

....

....

....

84. Foreign language learning (points to be covered—motivation, prospects and relevance in globalization).

....

....

....

....

....

....

....

....

ANSWERS

PART–A

1	2	3	4	5
(d)	(c)	(a)	(c)	(b)
6	7	8	9	10
(b)	(d)	(b)	(d)	(a)
11	12	13	14	15
(c)	(b)	(d)	(c)	(b)
16	17	18	19	20
(d)	(d)	(c)	(a)	(d)
21	22	23	24	25
(a)	(b)	(b)	(d)	(b)

PART–B

26	27	28	29	30
(b)	(c)	(b)	(c)	(b)
31	32	33	34	35
(d)	(c)	(b)	(b)	(c)
36	37	38	39	40
(c)	(c)	(d)	(d)	(b)
41	42	43	44	
(a)	(c)	(b)	(a)	

45. E.A.S. Prasanna

46. Charanjit Singh

47. Prime Minister

48. 8th March

49. EOAILGF

50. 206

PART–C

51	52	53	54	55
(b)	(c)	(b)	(b)	(b)
56	57	58	59	60
(a)	(a)	(d)	(d)	(c)

61. beside

62. behind

63. within

64. To

65. on

66. Between

67. Securities and Exchange Board of India

68. People for the Ethical Treatment of Animals

69. Board of Control for Cricket in India

70. Indian Council of Social Science Research

71. I wanted to visit you yesterday but you were not at home.

72. After Ali had seen the film on TV, he decided to buy the book.

73. Wait a minute, I will carry this box for you.

74. I have been waiting for my girlfriend for two hours.

75. mimiban

76. awanhi

77. you came

78. tangent

79. 1500

80. 25

PART–D

81. It is a common belief that poverty is bad and richness is good for people to have a useful life. But the poor people live with more satisfaction and achieve more in life than the rich. The children of rich always depend upon servants for every work and are spoiled while those of poor grow with more love, unity and responsibility for their families. This makes them strong and self-dependent. Most of the great men were born poor. Those who wish to abolish poverty should wish to abolish luxury instead because poverty nurtures virtues for growth and development of mankind while luxury mars them.

82. Positive Effects of Poverty.

PART–E

83. In our region of India, communities have inherited the rich tradition of love and reverence for nature through ages. Religious preaching, traditions and customs have played a big role in this regard: Indian religions have generally been the advocates of environmentalism. They campaigned for such guidelines to the commoners that ensured an intimate contact and sense of belonging in nature. It came in the form of directives to the believers to perform certain rites and rituals, so that it became a way of their life. Sometimes the messages of environmental protection and conservation are in a veiled form. Today, when the world is undergoing a serious crisis of ecological imbalance and environmental degradation, it is all the more important for us to understand such traditions.

The culture of conservation of nature dates back to the ancient Vedic Period. The four Vedas—Rig-Veda, Sama-Veda, Yajur-Veda and Atharva-Veda—are full of hymns dedicated to the supremacy of various natural entities. The Rigvedic hymns refer to many gods and goddesses identified with sun, moon, thunder, lightening, snow, rain, water, rivers, trees etc. They have been glorified and worshipped as givers of health, wealth and prosperity. The rain–god Indra has the largest number of hymns attached to him.

Sun worship is of vital importance in Vedic worship; the sun was worshipped in the form of gods like Sūrya, Mārtaṇḍa, Uṣa, Pūṣan, Rudra, etc. Today it has been proved that solar energy is the ultimate source of energy that regulates the energy flow through the food-chain, drives various nutrient cycles and thus controls the ecosystem all over the earth, but it was probably well understood and realized by the ancient people as well.

Tress have also been given huge importance the ancient Indian tradition. The four Vedas are full of references to various herbs, trees and flowers and their significance. Trees and plants were considered as animate beings and to harm them was regarded as a sacrilege.

The tradition of sacred groves was also common in the ancient period and is still practised by folk and tribal communities. A sacred grove consists of a bunch of old trees, generally at the outskirts of a village, which were left untouched when the original settlers cleared the forest to establish the village. In many sacred groves, villagers perform sacrifices and offerings to the gods during festivals and other occasions.

Indian traditions, customs and religious beliefs enlighten us about the protection of the flora and fauna. They teach us one fundamental principles of ecology, especially that every living entity of the biosphere has its own important role in the flow of energy and cycle of nutrients which keep the world going.

84. There has always been a growing importance for languages whether native or foreign, especially in today's era were communication has reached its peak and the world has become a smaller place. As globalisation takes a toll on the youth, an increasing number of youngsters are inclined towards learning foreign languages. Learning foreign languages like German, French, Spanish, Japanese and Mandarin gives students an edge.

Today, various institutes and universities are offering a number of courses in languages, among them foreign languages like German, French, Spanish, Japanese and Mandarin are now gaining momentum.

Learning a new language is not only interesting but also increases one's knowledge about the culture and lifestyle of the people of that specific country. Some students also learn languages to make a career in the field of translation and interpretation.

Learning a foreign language gives students an opportunity to appear for international examinations like TOFEL, JLPT and DELE etc. Career options in the field of translation are plenty. Due to growing economic relations between India and various countries of the world, knowing a foreign language gives one the much-needed edge. With various MNCs hiring translators and interpreters, this is a

fast growing field. Being a translator can be an interesting job as you connect with various people of the world and there is an exchange of cultures and ideas from people all across the globe. Besides, many international schools now need teachers who can teach foreign languages to students. Japanese, is gaining importance as a foreign language and can be the next language that will be taught to students in schools after French and German.

With Indian companies emerging as global players and Indian market being eyed by multinational companies, it becomes essential that there is no dearth of professionals who can overcome language barriers and facilitate smooth communication for proper business transactions. Foreign language experts with a good understanding of cultures are in great demand in the corporate world. The scope of foreign languages as career is stupendous and candidates willing to explore it have multitude of job opportunities in various multinational companies and multilateral organisations. Moreover, language skills are essential attribute in most professions and help in the advancement of career.

Whereas Indian MNCs require trained foreign language professionals to open their operations in foreign countries, foreign multinationals require such candidates at cheap salaries from India. The situation is so attractive for Indian foreign language professionals that language experts in Japanese, Chinese and Korean get jobs soon after their five year language course from various institutes. International job opportunities for foreign language experts from India are open in supranational bodies such as United Nations Organization and its other bodies, various projects of India's Foreign Ministry and of course India's spy agencies.

JAWAHARLAL NEHRU UNIVERSITY (JNU)

First Year of 3-Year B.A. (Hons.) in Foreign Languages

Chinese, French, German, Korean, Japanese, Arabic, Persian, Russian and Spanish

Entrance Examination, 2013

PART–A

All questions carry one mark each. Encircle the correct answer clearly. If more than one answers are encircled, the answer will be marked wrong.

1. The first Indian woman to climb the Mount Everest was
   - (*a*) Bachendri Pal
   - (*b*) Junko Tabei
   - (*c*) Anita Sood
   - (*d*) Geetika Jakhar

2. Which of these bodies of water does not border France?
   - (*a*) The Mediterranean
   - (*b*) The English Channel
   - (*c*) The Atlantic
   - (*d*) The Baltic

3. The construction of the Berlin Wall began on
   - (*a*) 9th November, 1989
   - (*b*) 6th March, 1949
   - (*c*) 13th August, 1961
   - (*d*) 20th August, 1947

4. The Korean alphabet is
   - (*a*) Katakana
   - (*b*) Hangul
   - (*c*) Hiragana
   - (*d*) Hanbok

5. Who made 'La Gioconda?
   - (*a*) Leonardo da Vinci
   - (*b*) Tenniel
   - (*c*) Graham Sutherland
   - (*d*) Brighton

6. Isfahan is located in which of the following countries?
   - (*a*) Afghanistan
   - (*b*) Iran
   - (*c*) Uzbekistan
   - (*d*) Tajikistan

7. First Olympiad in Greece was held in
   - (*a*) 10000 BC
   - (*b*) 776 BC
   - (*c*) 58 BC
   - (*d*) 800 BC

8. In which year did terrorists crash aircraft into New York's World Trade Centre?
   - (*a*) 2000
   - (*b*) 2001
   - (*c*) 2003
   - (*d*) 1998

9. The Eiffel Tower was constructed in
   - (*a*) 1789
   - (*b*) 1889
   - (*c*) 1860
   - (*d*) 1887

10. Ravi Shankar is recognized for bringing the Indian classical music tradition to the West. This was done through his association with which of the following?
    - (*a*) John Lennon
    - (*b*) George Harrison
    - (*c*) Oprah Winfrey
    - (*d*) Michael Jackson

Who wrote the following books? (For Q. Nos. 11 to 14):

11. *Untouchables*
    - (*a*) Rudyard Kipling
    - (*b*) Ruskin Bond
    - (*c*) Mulk Raj Anand
    - (*d*) Chetan Bhagat

12. *Paradise Lost*
    - (*a*) John Milton
    - (*b*) John Keats
    - (*c*) D.H. Lawrence
    - (*d*) William Wordsworth

13. *Cancer Ward*
    - (*a*) Maxim Gorky
    - (*b*) Leo Tolstoy
    - (*c*) Alexander Solzhenitsyn
    - (*d*) Boris Pasternak

14. *One Hundred Years of Solitude*
   (*a*) Miguel Ángel Asturias
   (*b*) Jacinto Benavente
   (*c*) Gabriel García Márquez
   (*d*) Jean-Paul Sartre

15. Which aircraft dropped the atomic bomb on Hiroshima?
   (*a*) Enola Gay   (*b*) Samurai Avenger
   (*c*) Aeroflot   (*d*) Kamikaze

16. Which of the following is **not** a public holiday in Japan?
   (*a*) Greenery Day
   (*b*) Respect for the Aged Day
   (*c*) Culture Day
   (*d*) Earthquake Prevention Day

17. 'Tapas' is a word for snacks and the word is originally from
   (*a*) Spanish   (*b*) French
   (*c*) Italian   (*d*) Portuguese

18. Peter the Great moved the capital of Russia to
   (*a*) Moscow   (*b*) St. Petersburg
   (*c*) Kiev   (*d*) Tashkent

19. The Inca Civilization was in
   (*a*) Peru   (*b*) Spain
   (*c*) Brazil   (*d*) France

20. The split between Bolsheviks and Mensheviks happened in
   (*a*) 1917   (*b*) 1924
   (*c*) 1947   (*d*) 1905

21. Former name of Taiwan was
   (*a*) Formosa   (*b*) Canton
   (*c*) Taipei   (*d*) Macau

22. Islands under territorial dispute between Japan and China are
   (*a*) Ryukyu Islands   (*b*) Kurile Islands
   (*c*) Senkaku Islands   (*d*) Takeshima Islands

23. What is known as 'Empty Quarter'?
   (*a*) Homes vacated by Palestinians in Israel
   (*b*) No man's land between Yemen and Saudi Arabia
   (*c*) Sand desert in Saudi Arabia
   (*d*) An area in Tibet

24. Who started the Bauhaus Movement?
   (*a*) Walter Gropius
   (*b*) Ludwig Mies van der Rohe
   (*c*) Daniel Ash
   (*d*) Vassily Kadinsky

25. *Shahnama*, an epic is written in which of the following languages?
   (*a*) Urdu   (*b*) Persian
   (*c*) Arabic   (*d*) Pashto

PART–B

All questions carry one mark each. Encircle the correct answer clearly. If more than one answers are encircled, the answer will be marked wrong (Q. Nos. 26 to 33):

26. Brahmo Samaj was founded by
   (*a*) Vivekananda
   (*b*) Ananda Mohan Bose
   (*c*) Raja Rammohan Roy
   (*d*) Radha Kanta Dev

27. The Jallianwala Bagh Massacre happened in
   (*a*) 1910   (*b*) 1921
   (*c*) 1919   (*d*) 1924

28. Which famous Indian ghazal singer died in 2011?
   (*a*) Begum Akhtar   (*b*) Talat Mehmood
   (*c*) Jagjeet Singh   (*d*) Mohammad Rafi

29. Who was the last Mughal Emperor of India?
   (*a*) Shah Jahan
   (*b*) Akbar
   (*c*) Bahadur Shah Zafar
   (*d*) Aurangzeb

30. Dronacharya Awards are given to
   (*a*) Sports coaches   (*b*) Cricketers
   (*c*) Tennis players   (*d*) Hockey players

31. Which one of the following Indian languages does not have a Dravidian origin?
   (*a*) Kannada   (*b*) Marathi
   (*c*) Malayalam   (*d*) Telugu

32. Sonal Mansingh is associated with
    (*a*) Bharat Natyam   (*b*) Kathak
    (*c*) Kuchipudi   (*d*) Odissi

33. Look at the news items given below. Encircle the correct option to fill in the blank:

Delhi police reported that 15 crates .... by them from three persons in North Delhi.
    (*a*) of illicit liquor were recovered
    (*b*) of illicit liquor was recovered
    (*c*) in illicit liquor was recovered
    (*d*) of illicit liquors were recovered

Rearrange the following words to make meaningful sentences:

34. in the/money/safe/of/there/was/lots

....

35. were queuing/film/a lot of/for the/people

....

Select and encircle the most appropriate synonyms of the bracketed words (Q. Nos. 36 to 41):

36. (Corpulent)
    (*a*) Lean   (*b*) Gaunt
    (*c*) Emaciated   (*d*) Obese

37. (Brief)
    (*a*) Limited   (*b*) Small
    (*c*) Little   (*d*) Short

38. (August)
    (*a*) Common   (*b*) Ridiculous
    (*c*) Dignified   (*d*) Petty

39. (Alert)
    (*a*) Energetic   (*b*) Observant
    (*c*) Intelligent   (*d*) Watchful

40. (Adversity)
    (*a*) Failure   (*b*) Helplessness
    (*c*) Misfortune   (*d*) Crisis

41. (Indict)
    (*a*) Condemn   (*b*) Reprimand
    (*c*) Accuse   (*d*) Allege

Encircle the correct answer :

42. Susan can type 10 pages in 5 minutes. Mary can type 5 pages in 10 minutes. If they are working together, how many pages can they type in 30 minutes?
    (*a*) 20   (*b*) 25
    (*c*) 65   (*d*) 75

43. Consider the following series
    3, 4, 6, 9, 13, ...
What comes next?
    (*a*) 16   (*b*) 17
    (*c*) 18   (*d*) 19

Choose and encircle the pair of words that best completes the sentence (Q. Nos. 44 and 45):

The .... of the timetable caused some ....

44. (*a*) rivision   (*b*) revision
    (*c*) revission   (*d*) revition

45. (*a*) inconvenience (*b*) inconvenince
    (*c*) inconveneince (*d*) inconveniense

46. **Encircle the correct answer:**

The average of ten numbers is 7. If each number is multiplied by 12, then the average of new set of numbers is
    (*a*) 7   (*b*) 19
    (*c*) 82   (*d*) 84

47. Write the missing letter in the following series:
    a c e ? i ....

Encircle the correct answer:

48. Which is the alternative that can replace the question mark (?)?
Mathematics : Pcwjhodvlev :: algebra : ?
    (*a*) dnjgetd   (*b*) cnjgetd
    (*c*) dnjhetd   (*d*) cnjhetc

49. Fear of heights is known as
    (*a*) Arachnophobia
    (*b*) Necrophilia
    (*c*) Acrophobia
    (*d*) Heliophobia

50. Who among the following is a famous scientist?
    (*a*) Stephen Hawking
    (*b*) Steve Jobs
    (*c*) Steven Spielberg
    (*d*) David Cameron

PART–C

All questions carry one mark each. Fill in the blanks with appropriate prepositions in the following sentences:

51. He is standing .... me in the queue.

52. This birthday present is .... your brother.

53. Are there any plants .... your bedroom?

54. All the family members are sitting .... the sofa and talking.

55. You can sit .... the table. Lunch is ready.

Fill in the blanks with appropriate words:

56. The internet serves to .... people all over the world.

57. The wounded soldier was in great .... from the bullet that had hit him.

58. We could not .... the waiter's attention as he was too busy.

59. The painter handled his .... very carefully to add just another touch.

60. I had to climb onto the .... of the house to fix the antenna.

Fill in the blanks with appropriate verbs in the appropriate forms:

61. The Earth .... round the Sun.

62. If you .... at once, you can reach the theatre by 6 o'clock.

63. He usually .... at the back of the class.

64. He .... here for the last five years.

65. My friend .... from cholera since August.

66. If she does not take a taxi, she .... the bus.

67. When I .... the road, I saw a big snake.

68. I .... him before he left India.

69. The journalist .... a new book at present.

70. He .... asleep while he was driving.

Give full forms of the following acronyms/ abbreviations:

71. NATO ....

72. SAARC ....

73. ISRO ....

74. OPEC ....

Encircle the correct answer:

75. In an artificial language the following means
portweagno = mathematical traditions
screnccrue = great mathematicians
goddragno = mathematical formulas

Then what will be the words that translate to international congress of mathematicians?
(a) screntbhjfslkjhagno
(b) goddrtbhjfslkjhagno
(c) screnhjtyrgtlkjbblj
(d) screnccruetylkkhyp

Answer the following:

76. 2013 in Chinese Zodiac is the year of .... (Fill in the blank)

77. Who became the first director to shoot at NASA?

....

78. Who was assigned the task of partitioning India in 1947?

....

79. Which car company launched the new car model Figo?

....

80. Hugo Chavez was the President of .... (Fill in the blank)

PART–D

Read the passage below and give short answers to the following questions. Marks assigned are given against each question:

The hustle and bustle of big cities attracts almost everyone. Big cities are often distinguished from small towns by the skyscrapers, proper means of transport, means of communication and good infrastructure. They say that the city never sleeps. This holds true because every time you look at the roads, you see it full of activity. Like in many cities, problems concerning accommodation is something you should be aware of before you move to a city.

Life in a city seems to be too busy. The start of the day always portrays school buses carrying children to their schools, a long queue of people waiting for the bus to head to their offices, and others who are driving in their own cars. The nights are even more exciting. Different events and occasions add more life to the city.

A city is a mix of people who are good and bad, rich and poor and of different religious backgrounds. Therefore, you will experience nearly all kinds of individuals and all kinds of living standards in a city.

Even though life in a city is considered to bring you more towards a civilized side, providing you with more facilities and higher standards of living, city life is not considered to be good enough for children.

Parents are seen to develop a distance for their children because of their tight schedules and because they get very little time to spend with their children. This might also be the reason of families breaking and impacting a child's mind negatively.

Despite all this, cities generally provide good employment opportunities and high educational standards that will be required to enhance the way of your life. In the end, the advantages outweigh the disadvantages. In order to maintain a good lifestyle one can always improve ambiance in his home and neighbourhood.

81. What do you know about life in a small town? 4

82. Why is city life not good enough for children? 2

83. What are the advantages of city life? 2

84. Between city life and life in a small town which one do you prefer and why? 2

PART–E

Write an essay on the following topic in about 600-700 words

85. My Favourite Advertisement on Television.

Or

The Issue of Safety for Women.

ANSWERS

PART–A

1	2	3	4	5	6	7	8	9	10
(a)	(d)	(c)	(b)	(a)	(b)	(b)	(b)	(d)	(b)
11	12	13	14	15	16	17	18	19	20
(c)	(a)	(c)	(c)	(a)	(d)	(a)	(a)	(a)	(d)
21	22	23	24	25					
(a)	(c)	(c)	(a)	(b)					

PART–B							
26	**27**	**28**	**29**	**30**	**31**	**32**	**33**
(*c*)	(*c*)	(*c*)	(*c*)	(*a*)	(*b*)	(*d*)	(*a*)

34. There was lots of money in the safe.

35. A lot of people were queuing for the film.

36. (*d*)

37. (*d*)

38. (*c*)

39. (*b*)

40. (*c*)

41. (*c*)

42. (*d*)

Susan's 1 min. work $= \dfrac{10}{5} = 2$ pages

Mary's 1 min. work $= \dfrac{5}{10} = \dfrac{1}{2}$ page

(Susan + Mary)'s 1 min. work

$$= 2 + \dfrac{1}{2} = \dfrac{5}{2} \text{ pages}$$

Required no. of pages $= \dfrac{5}{2} \times 30 = 75$ pages

43. (*c*)

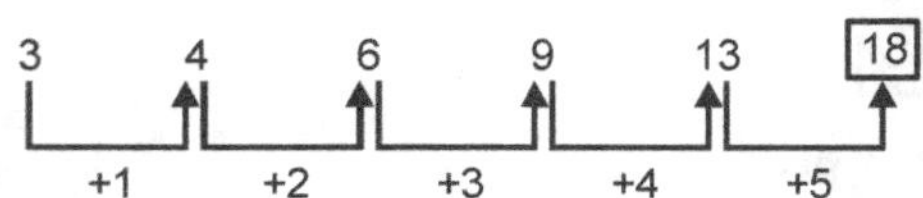

44. (*b*)

45. (*a*)

46. (*d*)
Total no. of 10 numbers $= 10 \times 7 = 70$
Total new no. $= 12 \times 70 = 840$

New average no. $= \dfrac{840}{10} = 84$

47. Missing letter is g.

48. (*a*)

49. (*c*)

50. (*a*)

51. behind

52. for

53. outside

54. in

55. on

56. millions of

57. pain

58. catch

59. work

60. rooftop

61. revolves

62. leave

63. sits

64. has been working

65. has been suffering

66. will miss

67. crossed

68. had met

69. is writing

70. fell

71. NATO—North Atlantic Treaty Organisation

72. SAARC—South Asian Association for Regional Corporation

73. ISRO—Indian Space Research Organisation

74. OPEC—Organisation of Petroleum Exporting Countries

75. (*a*)

76. Snake

77. Ashutosh Gowariker (Swades)

78. Sir Cyril Radcliffe

79. Ford Motor Company

80. Venezuela

PART–D

81. Life in a small town is quite different from life in big cities. There is no such hustle and bustle anywhere, no skyscrapers, no proper means of transport, communication and good infrastructure as in big cities. There is no activity and traffic on the roads at night. In the mornings, there are no long queues for school and office buses and cars. The night life is also dull. People of different religions and classes do not mix properly as in big cities. The life in small towns is less civilized with low standard of living and education but the family bonds are stronger as the people have more time for their families for caring each other and their children. They lack in facilities of a big city but live a peaceful life.

82. Parents in cities are quite busy in their daily routine and work and have lesser time to give each other and their children. There are pressures and many families break away and impact the children's mind and growth negatively making the city life not good enough for children.

83. There are proper means of transport and communication. There are many activities and hustle-bustle in cities. The living and education standards are high. People of all classes and religions mix together. There are good opportunities for employment and higher education available in the cities for the enhancement of life.

84. Between city life and life in a small town, I shall prefer the city life as the this provides better means, standards of life and more opportunities for education and employment which are essential for growth and development in life. Moreover, life in cities is more civilized and all sorts of people mix in cities irrespective of their religions, class or backgrounds that gives a feeling of unity in diversity.

PART–E

The Issue of Safety for Women

In the modern age, whereas on the one hand, we have daily reports of molestation and rapes of women, on the other hand we find them holding high positions in most of the government, public and private departments and concerns.

At the same time we must admit that women need more extra care, protection and rights. They must be given proper education and training which is the latest pertaining to their sphere of work. They must be allowed to express themselves freely and adequately. Sometimes their suggestions can be most useful to the well-being of the concern they work in.

Women need adequate and practical assurance of their safety, security and maintenance of dignity. They must not have to face any gender bias. In the matter of appointment or promotion, they must not be discriminated against. They should be provided proper guards if necessary if they have to work late in the evening. They should be allowed as far as possible, the freedom to have the shifts of their choice. The premises where they work should be absolutely safe and guarded. They should be provided the facility of cabs for pick up and drop at all levels except that at higher level, it may be optional. If the cab is to leave the premises after 8:00 p.m., it must be accompanied by an armed guard. The best way is to avoid shifts in odd hours for women.

Women have a very delicate nature. They must not be harassed. They must be addressed politely. There should be no hitch in granting them expeditiously maternity leave or any other leave which may be essential for them. They must also be provided crèche facility, if necessary. They should not be made to feel lost, harassed, isolated or depressed.

Then there should be a speedy way of redressal of their grievances complaints and problems.

Violence against women is a serious matter and must be taken as such. After all, women constitute one half of mankind.

It is true that domestic violence is not confined just to India. We hear about it in America and European countries also. However, there wife-beating, for instance, is not so common now. In India also it has greatly come down but it is fairly widely prevalent in rural areas and even in urban areas among the people of lower strata of society.

As far as the UK and the USA are concerned, it can be said that because of a flexible culture, there is possibility of a change in thinking. Moreover, as the learned scholar says:

"Besides, the government has special ministries for women and their issues, giving a lot of public funds to deal with issues concerned with gender-mainstreaming. This implies integration of gender concern into all ministries who work keeping these issues in mind. This is needed in India,"

In India, the problem is more serious. It is because the country is very vast and most of the people have a traditional mental make-up. Hence, she says,

"However, the task is much more daunting and challenging in India, the country being large with a past which lays down staunch values. Also, they are largely relying on international funding for help. If the government could be involved in this exercise and funding could come from within as well, the organization would have a greater impact."

It is true that a large number of NGOs are also involved in solving this problem. But all concerned have miles to go before they sleep.

Meanwhile, helplines for women should be set up at police stations and other places to get assistance in case of an emergency. There should also be counselling centres for couples. These should be manned by qualified experts appointed by government or reliable NGOs. Counselling should be provided free of cost. Couples should be all encouraged to get counselling for all kinds of domestic matters.

Already there is a specific clause in the Indian Penal Code allowing women to get their complaints redressed. In case of violence, even a verbal note by a woman is considered enough.

A National Commission for Women is also there, women should be exhorted to approach it in case of need. Women's rights should be protected.

As per apex court orders, women or girls studying in educational institutes, are now to be provided the same sort of protection as is permissible to the working women. Women should be protected not only against rape or molestation but also all kinds of violence such as beating, dragging, pinching, insulting, abusing, etc.

There are suggestions for other remedies also which the girls can apply to defend themselves. Some suggest that girls should be given lessons in Karate. Surprisingly there is a sort of commercialisation even in the matter of rape. Some bright ones are said to have designed handy rapist sprayers which they want to market at offices and educational institutions. Some "helplines" for girls have also been started by some people.

It is wisely suggested that midnight dances, music gathering and orgies should be avoided by girls. Whenever girls or women have to go anywhere after sunset, they should go in groups or have some closely-related or reliable male company. In certain cases, where late nights are unavoidable, women must ensure that they return home only with women companions, especially escorted by some male members.

It is also suggested that a vulnerable area map to concentrate for patrolling should be prepared by the police. Still, it has to be admitted that, so far, no foolproof remedy has been found out.

JAWAHARLAL NEHRU UNIVERSITY [JNU]

First Year of 3-Year B.A. [Hons.] in Foreign Languages

Chinese, French, German, Korean, Japanese, Arabic, Persian, Russian and Spanish

Entrance Examination, 2012

PART–A

All questions carry one mark each. Encircle the correct answer clearly. If more than one answers are encircled, the answer will be marked wrong.

1. What was France known as during the Roman Empire?
   - (*a*) Galles
   - (*b*) Gaulle
   - (*c*) Fransica
   - (*d*) Gayle

2. *Mona Lisa* was created by
   - (*a*) Leonardo da Vinci
   - (*b*) Monet
   - (*c*) Van Gogh
   - (*d*) Rodin

3. Who of the following leaders served in the Imperial Japanese Army and later led China in the Second Sino-Japanese War?
   - (*a*) Sun Yat-sen
   - (*b*) Chiang Kai-shek
   - (*c*) Yuan Shikai
   - (*d*) Jiang Zemin

4. Which of the following is a German port town?
   - (*a*) Frankfurt
   - (*b*) Munich
   - (*c*) Berlin
   - (*d*) Hamburg

5. Machu Picchu belongs to
   - (*a*) Inca civilization
   - (*b*) Maya civilization
   - (*c*) Aztec civilization
   - (*d*) Toltec civilization

6. Which part of Japan was hit by a 9.0 magnitude earthquake that triggered powerful tsunami in March 2011?
   - (*a*) Kanto
   - (*b*) Tohoku
   - (*c*) Kyoto
   - (*d*) Hokkaido

7. Nobel Prize in Literature in 2010 was awarded to
   - (*a*) Gabriel Garcia Marquez
   - (*b*) Octavio Paz
   - (*c*) Mario Vargas Llosa
   - (*d*) Bryce Echenique

8. Which city hosted the G-20 Summit in 2010?
   - (*a*) Seoul
   - (*b*) Kyoto
   - (*c*) Beijing
   - (*d*) Manila

9. Which of the following countries does not have a border with Germany?
   - (*a*) Holland
   - (*b*) France
   - (*c*) Spain
   - (*d*) Austria

10. How many independent emirates constitute the United Arab Emirates?
    - (*a*) 5
    - (*b*) 6
    - (*c*) 7
    - (*d*) 9

11. What is the national costume of Korea?
    - (*a*) Kimono
    - (*b*) Baku
    - (*c*) Yukata
    - (*d*) Hanbok

12. Which automobile company uses the slogan 'Das Auto'?
    - (*a*) Skoda
    - (*b*) Chevrolet
    - (*c*) Audi
    - (*d*) Volkswagen

13. When, after the World War II, did India and Japan sign the Friendship Treaty and establish diplomatic relations?
    - (*a*) 1948
    - (*b*) 1950
    - (*c*) 1952
    - (*d*) 1955

14. Name the Indo-Persian poet who invented *Sitar*.
    - (*a*) Mirza Ghalib
    - (*b*) Amir Khusro
    - (*c*) Faiz Ahmad Faiz
    - (*d*) Majaz

15. Fire temple is the place of worship of which of the following religions?
(*a*) Taoism   (*b*) Judaism
(*c*) Zoroastrianism   (*d*) Shintoism

16. The year 2011 marked the tercentenary of the Russian polymath
(*a*) M.M. Bakhtin   (*b*) V.G. Shukhov
(*c*) M.V. Lomonosov (*d*) A. Borodin

17. Who is the only Arab writer awarded Nobel Prize for Literature?
(*a*) Khalil Gibran   (*b*) Ahmad al-Baradei
(*c*) Ahmed Zewail   (*d*) Naguib Mahfouz

18. Mao Zedong proclaimed the People's Republic of China on
(*a*) August 14, 1945 (*b*) August 14, 1947
(*c*) October 1, 1948 (*d*) October 1, 1949

19. The first direct presidential election in Russian history took place in the year
(*a*) 1980   (*b*) 1985
(*c*) 1990   (*d*) 1991

20. Salvador Dali was a prominent surrealist painter from
(*a*) Spain   (*b*) France
(*c*) Italy   (*d*) Portugal

Note: Who wrote the following books?

21. *The Captain's Daughter*
(*a*) A.P. Chekhov   (*b*) A. Blok
(*c*) L. Tolstoy   (*d*) A. Pushkin

22. *The Reader,* which is also adapted into a popular film
(*a*) Stephen Daldry   (*b*) Ralf Finnes
(*c*) Bernhard Schlink (*d*) Thomas Bernhard

23. Epic of Iran, *Shahnamah*
(*a*) Bijan Najdi   (*b*) Mina Assadi
(*c*) Ferdausi   (*d*) Kahlil Gibran

24. *Strait is the Gate*
(*a*) Henri Bordeaux   (*b*) Andre Gide
(*c*) Marcel Proust   (*d*) Claud Simon

25. *The Tale of Genji,* said to be the world's first novel
(*a*) Chikamatsu Monzaemon
(*b*) Murasaki Shikibu
(*c*) Sei Shonagon
(*d*) Matsuo Basho

PART–B

All questions carry one mark each. Encircle the correct answer clearly. If more than one answers are encircled, the answer will be marked wrong:

26. What is the boundary line demarcating India and Pakistan known as?
(*a*) Radcliffe Line   (*b*) McMahon Line
(*c*) Curzon Line   (*d*) Durand Line

27. Who was also known as the 'Saint of the Gutters'?
(*a*) Baba Amte   (*b*) C.F. Andrews
(*c*) Mother Teresa   (*d*) Jyotirao Phule

28. Which is the longest bone in the human body?
(*a*) Fibula   (*b*) Femur
(*c*) Radius   (*d*) Stapes

29. Gadadhar was the given name of
(*a*) Ramakrishna Paramahansa
(*b*) Chaitanya Mahaprabhu
(*c*) Swami Vivekananda
(*d*) Sathya Sai Baba

30. Which seventh century Indian mathematician was the first in the world to treat 'zero' as a number and show its mathematical operations?
(*a*) Aryabhatta   (*b*) Medhatithi
(*c*) Bhaskaracharya (*d*) Brahmagupta

31. According to the Hindu mythology, who is the Guru of Devas (Gods)?
(*a*) Dhanvantari   (*b*) Shukracharya
(*c*) Brihaspati   (*d*) Vishvakarma

32. Words which are spelled the same in Hindi as in Sanskrit (except for the absence of final case inflections) and have survived without modifications are called
(*a*) Tadbhava   (*b*) Deshaja
(*c*) Prakrit   (*d*) Tatsama

33. According to Puranas, which of the following Yugas is said to have lasted 8,64,000 years?
(*a*) Satyayuga   (*b*) Tretayuga
(*c*) Dwaaparyuga   (*d*) Kaliyuga

34. Which is the alternative that can replace the question mark?

NATION : ANTINO :: HUNGRY : ?
(*a*) UHNGYR   (*b*) HUNGYR
(*c*) RYNGUH   (*d*) UHGNYR

35. At an election, a candidate who gets 84% votes wins by a majority of 476 votes. What is the total number of votes polled?
(*a*) 672   (*b*) 700
(*c*) 800   (*d*) 848

36. Apples cost ₹ 7 each and pears cost ₹ 5 each. If Roma spent ₹ 38 on these fruits, how many apples did she buy?
(*a*) 4   (*b*) 3
(*c*) 2   (*c*) Data is inadequate

37. If South-East becomes 'North', North-East becomes 'West' and so on, what will 'West' become?
(*a*) North-East   (*b*) North-West
(*c*) South-East   (*d*) South-West

38. Today is Varun's birthday. One year from today, he will be twice as old as he was 12 years ago. How old is Varun today?
(*a*) 24 years   (*b*) 25 years
(*c*) 26 years   (*c*) 27 years

39. Sarah bought a puppy and a doghouse for $300. The puppy cost $250 more than the doghouse. How much did the doghouse cost?
(*a*) $50   (*d*) $25
(*c*) $40   (*d*) $20

Note: (a), (b) and (c) are parts of a sentence in the following questions. Encircle the part which is, if any, grammatically incorrect in questions 40-43:

40. (*a*) We discussed about the problem so thoroughly
(*b*) on the eve of the examinations
(*c*) that I found it very easy to work it out.
(*d*) None

41. (*a*) An Indian ship
(*b*) laden with merchandise
(*c*) got drowned in the Pacific Ocean.
(*d*) None

42. (*a*) No sooner did the sun rise
(*b*) when we took a hasty breakfast
(*c*) and resumed our journey.
(*d*) None

43. (*a*) One of my favourite actor
(*b*) is acting
(*c*) in this play also.
(*d*) None

44. A woman came in with a baby who, she said, ... a safety pin. (Fill in the blank with the most appropriate option).
(*a*) was just swallowing
(*b*) swallowed
(*c*) had just swallowed
(*d*) just swallowed

Note: Select the most appropriate synonyms of the bracketed words/idioms:

45. (Lethargy)
(*a*) Sluggishness   (*b*) Boredom
(*c*) Activity   (*d*) Disobedience

46. (Constrict)
(*a*) To freeze   (*b*) To narrow
(*c*) To open   (*d*) To cut

47. (Black sheep)
(*a*) A cheat
(*b*) A good-for-nothing person
(*c*) Victim of a hoax
(*d*) A shy person

48. (Psalm)
(*a*) A devotional song
(*b*) Place of worship
(*c*) Kind of fruit
(*d*) A small amount

49. (Random)
(*a*) Done in a hurry
(*b*) Done without method
(*c*) Unspecific
(*d*) Sketchy

50. (My heart goes out to *A*)
(*a*) I love *A*
(*b*) *A* has won my heart
(*c*) I praise *A*
(*d*) I feel sympathy for *A*

PART–C

All questions carry one mark each.

Fill in the blanks with appropriate prepositions in the following sentences:

As she walked into the hotel, ahead .... (1) her first exhibition in the country, it was difficult to separate the celebrity .... (2) the artist. At 78, her movements were studied, born .... (3) long practice, her head atilt .... (4) an angle as the cameras went off.

The capital of the United States and one federal State are named .... (5) George Washington.

Fill in the blanks with appropriate words:

I saw a .... (6) of sheep in the field.

The grapes are now .... (7) enough to be picked.

"Of course, I won't get lost. I know the city like the back of my .... (8)."

When we reached the office, the work was in .... (9) swing.

It was at about this time .... (10) a Fakir named Govinda Rai arrived there.

Fill in the blanks with appropriate verbs in their appropriate forms:

During election campaigns, people often .... (11) mud at each other.

One night, Hridaya .... (12) up courage and went into the jungle. He found his friend .... (13) in deep meditation under a tree.

If you smuggle goods into the country, they may be .... (14) by the customs authority.

About twenty clerks were .... (15) redundant when the banks introduced computers.

The pilot had been warned about the storm, before he .... (16).

When I heard the name of the winner, I was so shocked you could have .... (17) me down with a feather!

Read carefully some examples from a Polynesian language given below:

1. (a) avaravere 'I will go'
   (b) avaraepa 'I went'
2. (a) avauvere 'You will go'
   (b) avauepa 'You went'
3. (a) avarovere 'He will go'
   (b) avaroepa 'He went'
4. (a) pauravere 'I will sit'
   (b) pauraepa 'I sat'

Now answer the following three questions:

How will you say the following in this language?

18. 'You will sit'

19. 'He sat'

20. In which order do the 'subject', 'verb' and 'auxiliary verb' come in this language?

Answer the following questions:

21. Who was the first cricketer in the world to score 10000 runs in Test Cricket?

22. The price of petrol increases by 10%. By what per cent the consumption must be reduced so that the expenditure remains the same?

23. Jhumpa Lahiri's first novel .... (2003) was adapted into a popular film of the same name.

24. 'Chandrakanta', written by ...., is considered to be the first work of prose in Hindi.

25. The famous philosopher, ... was a disciple of Plato.

26. Who produced the 2007 film, 'Gandhi, my father'?

Give full forms of the following acronyms/ abbreviations:

27. Do, Co and Mo (of DoCoMo Mobile Operators)

28. NREGA

29. VIRUS

30. ZIP (as in ZIP Code)

PART–D

Read the passage below and give short answers to the following questions. Marks assigned are given against each question:

Language, any language, has a dual character: it is both a means of communication and a carrier of culture. Take English. It is spoken in Britain and in Sweden and Denmark. But for Swedish and Danish people, English is only a means of communication with non-Scandinavians. It is not a carrier of their culture. For the British, and particularly the English, it is additionally and inseparably, from its use as a tool of communication, a carrier of their culture and history. Or take Swahili in East and Central Africa. It is widely, used as means of communication across many nationalities. But it is not the carrier of a culture and history of many of those nationalities. However, in parts of Kenya and Tanzania, and particularly in Zanzibar, Swahili is inseparably both a means of communication and a carrier of the culture of those people to whom it is a mother tongue.

Language as communication has three aspects or elements. There is first what Karl Marx once called the language of real life, the element basic to the whole nation of language, its origin and development: that is, the relations people enter into with one another in the labor process, the links they necessarily establish among themselves in the act of people, a community of human beings, producing wealth or means of life like food, clothing, houses...

The second aspect of language as communication is speech and it imitates the language of real life that is communication in production. The verbal signposts both reflect and aid communication or the relations established between human beings in production of their means of life....spoken words mediate between human beings and form the language of speech....

The third aspect is the written signs. The written word imitates the spoken. Where the first two aspects of language as communication through hand and the spoken word historically evolved more or less simultaneously, the written aspect is a much later historical development. Writing is representation of sounds with visual symbols from the simplest knot among shepherds to tell the number in the herd ... to the most complicated and different letter and picture writing systems of the world today.

1. What does the writer mean by language as 'a means of communication' and as 'a carrier of culture'?

2. How is 'language of real life' different from the written language as evident in the extract above?

3. What does the writer mean by 'verbal signposts'?

4. Is English in India either a means of communication or a carrier of culture, or neither or both?

PART–E

Complete the following story in about 600–700 words. Also, give a title to the story:

One morning, Bhola, a villager, stepped out of his hut and saw huge round footmarks in the mud outside his dwelling. "Oh my God!" he shouted. Soon there was a large crowd outside his hut. None of the villagers had ever seen such huge footprints before and they were bewildered by them. They followed.

ANSWERS

PART–A

1	2	3	4	5	6	7	8	9	10
(b)	(a)	(b)	(d)	(a)	(b)	(c)	(a)	(c)	(c)

11	12	13	14	15	16	17	18	19	20
(*d*)	(*d*)	(*c*)	(*b*)	(*c*)	(*c*)	(*d*)	(*d*)	(*d*)	(*a*)

21	22	23	24	25
(*d*)	(*c*)	(*c*)	(*b*)	(*b*)

PART–B

26	27	28	29	30	31	32	33	34	35
(*a*)	(*c*)	(*b*)	(*a*)	(*d*)	(*c*)	(*d*)	(*c*)	(*a*)	(*b*)

36	37	38	39	40	41	42	43	44	45
(*a*)	(*c*)	(*b*)	(*b*)	(*b*)	(*c*)	(*b*)	(*a*)	(*c*)	(*a*)

46	47	48	49	50
(*b*)	(*a*)	(*a*)	(*b*)	(*d*)

PART–C

1. of
2. to
3. of
4. about
5. after
6. herd
7. ripe
8. palm
9. full
10. that
11. fling
12. took
13. immersed
14. confiscated
15. held
16. took off
17. got
18. Pauuvere
19. Pouroepa
20. 'Verb', 'Subject', 'Auxiliary verb'
21. Sunil Gavaskar (India)
22. 9%
23. The Namesake
24. Devki Nandan Khatri
25. Aristotle
26. Bollywood actor Anil Kapoor.
27. Do Communications Over the Mobile network
28. National Rural Employment Guarantee Act
29. Vital Information Resources Under Siege
30. Zone Information Protocol

PART–D

1. When a language is spoken as a mother tongue it becomes a carrier of culture and history alongwith the means of communication. But when the language is spoken between the people to which one it is a mother-tongue while for the other it is not, then it is called only a means of communication between the two.

2. The language of real life is different from written language as it is based on acts of people to earn livelihood while the latter evolved much later through pictures and letters.

3. Verbal signposts are the spoken words and gestures.

4. English in India is both a means of communication and a carrier of culture.

PART–E

The Footmarks

The footprints together forming a large group. Everyone in the group was scared in himself inside. All of them picked either a stick, a spade, a tool and a stone with him so that he may use it in self-defence just in case of danger. Everyone was shaken with unknown danger but as all of them were moving in a group the element of danger and fear was away from them.

They kept moving into the jungle. They were making loud sounds through their mouths and through drumbeats. They also carried with themselves fire-sticks to scare away the wild animals and the unknown, unseen danger. Some of them were discussing about the possible shape and size of the unknown creature. Some suggested it could be a demon or a wild giant.

While the group of villagers kept moving to look out for the unknown danger. Their women and children kept back in the village fear-stricken. They were praying for the well being of their men and for their safe-return from the jungle. They all shut the doors of their dwelling light and kept praying and chanting hymns against the idols of deities at their homes and at village temple. Everyone in the village was full of fear from the unknown danger or demon. The children were clinging to their mothers and refused to eat or sleep until their fathers come back safely.

The group of villagers who had moved to the jungle to look for the unknown monster was now tired and hungry as they had kept on walking the whole day. Some of them suggested to return to the village and give the search for the unknown creature while the others suggested that they should take some food and rest in the jungle and later continue their search. Ultimately it was decided to stay there for food and rest and continue the search after some time.

They found a safe place among big trees. They cleaned the place and sat in the form of a round group. They ignited bonfire in the centre of the group to scare away wild animals. Some of them picked some fruits from the nearby trees and distributed among all to eat. Some of them brought water from a nearby small pond. After eating whatever they could get. They decided to take rest there only as it was dark in the evening and they were quite away from their village. For the time now, neither could return to their village nor could they move ahead in their pursuit. So, it was decided that the youngmen will keep watch in turn while the others were taking rest. Steadily, the night passed in the wild, horrible jungle. The whole night the villagers in the group were shivering with cold in the winter night of December. There were strange sounds of wild animals and other creatures all around. Fortunately none of the wild animals or creatures came near them, because of the bonfire and the guarding youngmen. He kept beating drums also to scare away the animals.

In the morning, as the dawn descended, they woke up by the chirping of birds and the life-giving sunlight. They now felt all their cold, fear, darkness disappearing in the soothing sun rays. They again gathered all their energy and courage and started their pursuit afresh.

As they crossed the jungle, they reached on the banks of a river. There was a beautiful scenary around this place. A number of green trees were lined up along the river bank laden with various types of fruits. There was a waterfall nearby. As they moved towards the waterfall they saw a herd of mammoths bathing in the water and splashing water on each other. The innocent villagers had never seen mammoths before in their lives. They were scared and kept watching from a distance. But very soon they searched that the mammoths, though giant in size, were not at all dangerous to them and their village. As their fear disappeared, they also started bathing in the waterfall and river water and returned to their village after picking the sweet fruits from the river side trees for their children back home.

EXPLANATIONS

35. 84% of x – 16 % of x = 476

$\Rightarrow$ 68% of x = 476

$$x = \frac{476 \times 100}{68} = 700$$

$\therefore$ Total number of votes polled = 700

36. Total spent = ₹ 38

Cost of 4 apples = ₹ 7 × 4 = ₹ 28

Cost of 2 pears = ₹ 5 × 2 = ₹ 10

Hence, she bought 4 apples.

38. Let present age of Varun = x years.

$$2 (x - 12) = x$$

$\Rightarrow$ $x = 24$

Hence, today Varun is 24 years old.

JAWAHARLAL NEHRU UNIVERSITY (JNU)

First Year of 3-Year B.A. (Hons.) in Foreign Languages

Chinese, French, German, Korean, Japanese, Arabic, Persian, Russian and Spanish

Entrance Examination, 2011

PART–A

All questions carry one mark each. Encircle the correct answer clearly. If more than one answer is encircled, the answer will be marked wrong :

1. The words 'Satyameva Jayate' inscribed below the base plate of the emblem of India are taken from
   (a) *Rig-Veda*
   (b) *Satpath Brahmana*
   (c) *Mundak Upanishad*
   (d) *Ramayana*

2. The Parliament of India cannot be regarded as a sovereign body because
   (a) it can legislate only on subjects entrusted to the Centre by the Constitution
   (b) it has to operate within the limits prescribed by the Constitution
   (c) the Supreme Court can declare laws passed by the Parliament as unconstitutional if they contravene the provisions of the Constitution
   (d) All of the above

3. Which of the following is a Human Rights Organization?
   (a) The French Community
   (b) The Organization of African Unity
   (c) The Arab League
   (d) Amnesty International

4. Kemal Ataturk was
   (a) the first President of Independent Kenya
   (b) the founder of modern Turkey
   (c) a revolutionary leader of Soviet Union
   (d) None of the above

5. Philology is the
   (a) study of bones
   (b) study of muscles
   (c) study of architecture
   (d) science of languages

6. R.K. Narayan has his stories centred around which imaginary place?
   (a) Malgudi   (b) Malguri
   (c) Talgudi   (d) Hemkhanakhan

7. Which Academy promotes and develops literature in all the 22 languages of India?
   (a) Sahitya Academy
   (b) Sangeet Natak Academy
   (c) Lalit Kala Academy
   (d) None of the above

8. Kalidasa had written three famous plays, viz., *Abhigyanam Shakuntalam* and *Vikramurvashi*. Name the third play.
   (a) *Kumarasambhava* (b) *Meghadoota*
   (c) *Raghuvansha*   (d) *Malavikagnimitra*

9. What is the Commonwealth of Independent States (CIS)?
   (a) Group of 53 former colonies of Britain
   (b) Group of 12 former republics of dissolved USSR
   (c) Group of 10 Latin American countries
   (d) Group of Islamic countries in Saudi Arabia region

10. The eminent Bengali director Satyajit Ray had made only two films in Hindi. The first is *Satranj ke Khilari* based on the works of Munshi Premchand. Which was the second?
    (a) *Teesri Kasam*   (b) *Maare Gaye Gulfam*
    (c) *Sadgati*   (d) *Junoon*

PART-B

All questions carry one mark each. Encircle the correct answer clearly. If more than one answer is encircled, the answer will be marked wrong :

11. The name of which city was changed to Petrograd and Leningrad?
    (*a*) Moscow   (*b*) Tashkent
    (*c*) Kiev   (*d*) St. Petersburg

12. Which political party was responsible for the Russian October Revolution of 1917?
    (*a*) Bolshevik   (*b*) Provisional Party
    (*c*) Soviet   (*d*) Menshevik

13. Today the primary religion of Iran is Islam but Persia was once very closely associated with another religion. Name it.
    (*a*) Christianity   (*b*) Buddhism
    (*c*) Judaism   (*d*) Zoroastrianism

14. The vast majority of modern Iranian, Persian and Dari text is written in a form of the
    (*a*) Arabic language (*b*) Hebrew alphabet
    (*c*) Arabic alphabet (*d*) Syriac alphabet

15. How is Japanese Emperor's Throne known?
    (*a*) Peacock Throne
    (*b*) Chrysanthemum Throne
    (*c*) Viceregal Throne
    (*d*) White Throne

16. The sacred place of followers of Shintoism is
    (*a*) Central Shrine of Ise
    (*b*) Yasukuni Shrine
    (*c*) Both of the above
    (*d*) None of the above

17. Bastille Day marks the anniversary of the French Revolution. Why did Parisians storm the prison in 1789?
    (*a*) To find the king who was hiding
    (*b*) To look for food
    (*c*) To get powder for muskets
    (*d*) To free prisoners

18. Which French author of the 19th century had the foresight that man would walk on the moon one day?
    (*a*) Victor Hugo   (*b*) Jules Verne
    (*c*) Chateaubriand   (*d*) Mme de Sevigne

19. Which of the following Indian monks is said to have started Shaolin martial art or the 'gongfu' in China?
    (*a*) Kumarajiva   (*b*) Bodhidharma
    (*c*) Dharamratna   (*d*) Bodhiruchi

20. The first ever Chinese National who was conferred 'Padma Bhushan' by the Indian Government for his contribution towards Indology is
    (*a*) Zhou Enlai   (*b*) Ji Xianlin
    (*c*) Tan Chung   (*d*) Tan Yunshan

21. Which Parallel divides North Korea and South Korea?
    (*a*) 23rd   (*b*) 27th
    (*c*) 38th   (*d*) 42nd

22. Which of these is not a Korean company?
    (*a*) Samsung
    (*b*) Hyundai
    (*c*) LG (Luckystar Gold)
    (*d*) Nikon

23. Spanish is the official language of Spain. Which other language has been recognized as co-official by Regional Governments?
    (*a*) Catalan   (*b*) Basque
    (*c*) Galician   (*d*) All of the above

24. Which country borders Spain to the West?
    (*a*) San Marino   (*b*) France
    (*c*) Portugal   (*d*) Gibraltar

25. World War II started in September 1939 with the invasion of
    (*a*) Denmark   (*b*) Belgium
    (*c*) Poland   (*d*) France

26. Which of the German Chancellors received the Nobel Prize for Peace?
    (*a*) Ludwig Erhard   (*b*) Konrad Adenauer
    (*c*) Helmut Schmidt   (*d*) Willy Brandt

27. Which German firm coined the slogan *Vorsprung durch Technik* ('Advancement through Technology')?
    (*a*) Audi   (*b*) BMW
    (*c*) Siemens   (*d*) Bosch

28. Yukio Mishima, Japan's famous post-war novelist committed suicide in 1970 after a failed coup. Which of these methods did he use?

(a) Disemboweled himself with a sword and then ordered his followers to decapitate him

(b) Downed vast quantities of sake before walking into the sea

(c) Hung himself from a tree towards the top of Mt. Fuji

(d) Threw himself under a bullet train during commuter rush hour

29. How many alphabets are there in the Arabic alphabet?
(a) 26   (b) 28
(c) 30   (d) 32

30. Which is the smallest country in the Arab World?
(a) Qatar   (b) Tunis
(c) Bahrain   (d) Kuwait

PART-C

All questions carry one mark each. Encircle the correct answer clearly. If more than one answer is encircled, the answer will be marked wrong :

31. Can I pay by cheque? I don't have any cash on me.
(a) Sorry, we only take hard cash
(b) Sorry, the cheques were stolen
(c) Sorry, that's not fair

32. Do you still feel homesick?
(a) Well, I feel dizzy
(b) Yes, I have problems back home
(c) Well, I am getting over it a little

33. She's .... a snobbish person .... nobody likes to be with her.
(a) such...that
(b) such...as
(c) so...that

34. You'd better take a taxi, ... you'll be late.
(a) consequently   (b) furthermore
(c) otherwise   (d) however

35. Ram wasn't tired, ... he took a nap.
(a) otherwise   (b) hence
(c) nevertheless   (d) furthermore

36. He didn't earn enough money. ...., his wife decided to get a job.
(a) Moreover   (b) Therefore
(c) Although   (c) Otherwise

37. There's some milk in the refrigerator, ...?
(a) isn't there   (b) isn't it
(c) wasn't it   (d) was it

38. The dishes are dirty, ...?
(a) weren't they   (b) isn't they
(c) aren't they   (c) were they

39. It I said that he was a man .... to have the vision of an eagle and the courage of a lion.
(a) who appeared
(d) he appeared
(c) that appears
(d) and appears

40. After the discovery of the abandoned getaway vehicle, ... believed to be hiding in the nearby riverside forest region.
(a) that the bank robber is
(b) the bank robber who
(c) the bank robber is
(d) the bank robber who is

41. .... he was seen to be an aggressive politician, he was a quiet and loving family man at home.
(a) Although   (b) Despite
(c) In spite of   (d) Nevertheless

42. You .... see the doctor if that backache persists.
(a) better   (b) better have
(c) have better   (d) had better

43. How long does it take .... the nearest train station?
(a) get to   (b) to get to
(c) to get   (d) getting

44. She went .... with envy when she saw my new car.
(a) green   (b) blue
(c) black   (d) pink

45. My birthday was a complete surprise. It came completely out of the ....
(a) black   (b) white
(c) red   (d) blue

PART–D

All questions carry one mark each. Some verbs have been removed from the following text. Try to reconstruct the text by putting verbs in the correct form in the blanks provided:

Suresh was born on a farm back in Eastern India. He was happy even though he (46) a harsh life cultivating his field. One day he (47) by a heavy storm at night. When the storm subsided he (48) that his plantation (49). He (50) despondent and felt that he could no longer live on the farm. He (51) to move somewhere else. He left the farm and (52) to the city. The hustle and bustle of the city (53) Suresh a lot, but he refused to go back to his farm. Suresh's life in the city was very difficult. The only person he (54) was Mahesh, a distant relative, who was a very patient and understanding and who tried to help Suresh to get used to (55) in the city.

Fill in the blanks with appropriate articles and put × if it is not required :

56. I'm on .... diet. No .... sugar for me!

57. I'm afraid, I can't remember .... exact date of .... show.

58. I'm afraid .... answer is 'no'. Come back when you can make .... new proposal.

59. You can find .... books you'll need for class at .... Amazon.com.

60. He telephoned .... agent that was listed in .... telephone directory.

Fill in the blanks with correct prepositions :

61. Please carry the box .... the next room.

62. Anil started his current job .... October 10.

63. "Where is the library?"

"It's .... your right".

64. I would like to apply .... for position of sales executive that was advertised in the Sunday newspaper.

65. I came up with a great idea .... I was thinking about the class.

Unscramble the following proverbs and add capital letters and punctuation marks :

66. sow you so as reap you shall

67. book its don't cover a by judge

68. devil's an is workshop idle the brain

What do the underlined idioms mean?

69. Companies producing goods <u>play to the gallery</u> to boost their sales.

70. It was he who <u>put a spoke in my wheel</u>.

Arrange the following sentences in the proper sequence :

S_1 : While crossing a busy road, we should obey the policeman on duty.

P : We should always cross the road at the zebra crossing.

Q : We must look to the signal lights and cross the road only when the road is clear.

R : If there are no signal lights at the crossing, we should look to the right, then to left and again the right before crossing the road.

S : If the road is not clear, we should wait.

S_6 : We should never run while crossing the road.

71. The proper sequence should be
(a) PSRQ   (b) PQRS
(c) RQSP   (d) QRPS

Select the correct answer to complete the sentence :

72. His appearance is unsmiling but ...
(a) his heart is full of compassion for others.
(b) he looks very serious on many occasions.
(c) people are afraid of him.
(d) he is uncompromising on matters of task performance.
(e) he is full of jealousy towards his colleague.

73. The weather outside was extremely pleasant and hence we decided to ...
(a) utilize our time in watching the television.
(b) refrain from going out for a morning walk.
(c) employ this rare opportunity for writing letters.
(d) enjoy a morning ride in the open.
(e) remain seated in our rooms in the bungalow.

Rewrite the sentences as shown in the example :

Ex. They make shoes in that factory.
  Shoes **are made** in that factory.

74. They had finished the preparations by the time the guests had arrived.

75. They are going to perform Beethoven's Fifth Symphony next weekend.

76. Select the correctly punctuated sentence :
  (a) The children's books were all left in the following places : Mrs. Smith's room, Mr. Powell's office and the caretaker's cupboard.
  (b) The children's books were all left in the following places; Mrs. Smith's room, Mr. Powell's office and the caretaker's cupboard.
  (c) The childrens books were all left in the following places; Mrs. Smiths room, Mr. Powells office and the caretakers cupboard.
  (d) The children's books were all left in the following places, Mrs. Smith's room, Mr. Powell's office and the caretaker's cupboard.

Complete the sentences using the underlined word, so that the meaning of the sentence is similar :

77. I find driving on the right in Europe very strange. <u>accustomed</u>
  I .... on the right in Europe.

78. His boss won't tolerate lateness. <u>put</u>
  His boss won't .... lateness.

The following are some words translated from an artificial language :
  Malgauper means peach cobbler
  Malgaport means peach juice
  Moggagrop means apple jelly

79. Which word would mean apple juice?
  (a) Moggaport   (b) Malgaauper
  (c) Gropport   (d) Mogaport

  Gorblflur means fan belt
  Pinxgorbl means ceiling fan
  Arthtusl means tile roof

80. How would you write ceiling tile?
  Ceiling tile ....

PART–E

Read the following passage and answer the questions that follow :

Before the grass has thickened on the roadside verges and leaves have started growing on the trees is a perfect time to look around and see just how dirty Britain has become. The pavements are stained with chewing gum that has been spat out and the gutters are full of discarded fast food cartons. Years ago I remember travelling abroad and being saddened by the plastic bags, discarded bottles and soiled nappies at the edge of every road. Nowadays, Britain seems to look at least as bad. What has gone wrong?

The problem is that the rubbish created by our increasingly mobile lives lasts a lot longer than before. If it is not cleared up and properly thrown away, it stays in the undergrowth for years; a semi-permanent reminder of what a tatty little country we have now.

Firstly, it is estimated that 10 billion plastic bags have been given to shoppers. These will take anything from 100 to 1000 years to rot. However, it is not as if there is no solution to this. A few years ago, the Irish Government introduced a tax on non-recyclable carrier bags and in three months reduced their use by 90%. When he was a minister, Michael Meacher attempted to introduce a similar arrangement in Britain. The plastics industry protested, of course. However, they need not have bothered; the idea was killed before it could draw breath, leaving supermarkets free to give away plastic bags.

What is clearly necessary right now is some sort of combined initiative, both individual and collective, before it is too late. The alternative is to continue sliding downhill until we have a country that looks like a vast municipal rubbish tip. We may well be at the tipping point. Yet we know that people responded to their environment. If things around them are clean and tidy, people behave cleanly and tidily. If they are surrounded by squalor, they behave squalidly. Now, much of Britain looks pretty squalid. What will it look like in five years?

1. Why does the writer say that it is a good time to see Britain before the trees have leaves?

2. What according to the writer has gone wrong with Britain?

3. What did Michael Meacher try to do in order to solve the problem? Was he successful in his efforts?

4. India is also facing similar problems, such as the degradation of the environment. What can you do to bring about a solution to the problem?

PART–F

Select any one of the two pictures and write a short story in about 600-800 words. Give a title to the story?

(*a*)

(*b*)

ANSWERS

PART–A

1	2	3	4	5	6	7	8	9	10
(c)	(d)	(d)	(b)	(d)	(a)	(a)	(d)	(b)	(c)

PART–B

11	12	13	14	15	16	17	18	19	20
(d)	(a)	(d)	(c)	(b)	(c)	(c)	(b)	(b)	(b)
21	22	23	24	25	26	27	28	29	30
(c)	(d)	(d)	(c)	(c)	(d)	(a)	(a)	(b)	(c)

PART–C

31	32	33	34	35	36	37	38	39	40
(a)	(c)	(a)	(c)	(b)	(b)	(a)	(c)	(a)	(c)
41	42	43	44	45					
(a)	(a)	(b)	(c)	(d)					

PART–D

46. lived
47. was hit
48. found
49. had destroyed
50. became
51. decided
52. went
53. disturbed
54. knew
55. life
56. a, ×
57. the, the
58. the, a
59. the, the
60. an, the
61. into
62. on
63. to
64. for
65. upon
66. As you sow, so shall you reap.
67. Don't judge a book by its cover.
68. An idle brain is the devil's workshop.
69. aim to attract popular attention
70. prevented me from doing that
71. (b)
72. (a)
73. (d)
74. The preparations were finished by the time the guests had arrived.
75. Beethoven's Fifth Symphony is going to be performed next weekend.
76. (a)
77. find strange the accustomed driving
78. put up with
79. (a)
80. Pinxarth

PART–E

1. When there are no grass and leaves on the roadside verges, the spit stains, garbage and filth is clearly visible on the pavements and gutters in Britain.

2. According to the writer, the rubbish and garbage created these days decomposes very slowly and if not properly disposed, it takes many years to clear, causing heaps of garbage everywhere in Britain.

3. Michael Meacher tried to impose a tax on using non-recyclable carrier bags as done by Irish Government but he failed to do so because of the protests from the plastics industry. Hence, he was not successful in solving the problem.

4. India is also facing the problem of degradation of the environment unlike Britain and other countries. The Government and NGOs are taking many steps and doing all out efforts to check this but the success is yet minimal. There are laws of imposing penalties on the use of plastic non-recyclable carry bags yet

we find them in every shop and home. The reason being that the law is not exercised and followed by all in its true spirit and force. The solution to this problem lies with ourselves. It we refuse to accept this kind of carrybags from the shops, they will no longer buy them and find alternatives such as paper bags or jute bags, subsequently the manufactures also have to switch over to produce them to survive (in business).

PART–F

(*a*) Long long ago, there was a king in an ancient state of India. The state was prosperous with all its subjects happy and absorbed in their work and families. The king was so keen in the well-being of his subjects that he used to forget his own interests and welfare. He was very popular for his justified and balanced verdicts. Due to his love for his subjects and good administration, there were no fights, thefts or any other crimes in his state. The people were also prosperous.

The king had a very young son, who used to play in the royal garden of the palace whole day. The king loved him so much that he couldn't even think of living a single day without seeing him. He was really fond of him.

The queen of the king was very beautiful. The king loved her not only for her beauty but for her wisdom also. He used to take her advice in all his state related matters and decisions. This way the king, his family and subjects all were happy and prosperous in all ways.

The king was very brave and therefore no other king or neighbouring state could dare to fight him. He had a very strong and well organised army to protect the borders of his state. He had very able ministers with him. Everything was going smoothly in the state. The king, as in those days, thought of going for hunting. He discussed this with the queen and the ministers. The minister agreed and assured him that they will look after the administration of the state in his absence, but the queen insisted on going along with the king for hunting as she had never experienced hunting before that.

The king agreed but he had one great worry, that of his very young son. He was so young and tender that he could not be taken to forests during hunting. As the queen was also accompanying the king for hunting, there was a great concern as to who will look after him. At this juncture the prime minister came forward and took the responsibility of the young prince on himself till the king and queen return from hunting. The king then left for forest along with the queen and few soldiers, leaving the young prince in the care of the prime minister and his family, but with a worried mind.

They kept moving deep into forests in search of a prey, suddenly the queen saw a fawn at some distance around the bush. The fawn was so beautiful that she insisted the king to hunt that fawn first for her. They both started following the fawn in the forest. The soldiers were left behind some where on the way but they kept on moving on horses.

The fawn, though very young and tender, was running very fast and soon it reached its mother and hid behind her. The mother deer saw the king and queen ready to hunt her kid. She shivered with fright but stayed calm. The king asked her to move aside so that he could hunt the fawn. The mother deer gathered all her courage and requested the king to spare her kid. The king was adamant on hunting it. Then she asked the king whether he also had a kid. The king told that he had a lovely prince back at the palace. She then asked the king what would he feel if someone killed his son back at home while he is hunting in the forest. The king and queen both were stunned on this question as both of them could not even imagine living without the prince. Tears rolled from their eyes and they thanked the mother deer for opening their eyes and vowed to never hunt any animal in future.

JAWAHARLAL NEHRU UNIVERSITY [JNU]

First Year of 3-Year B.A. [Hons.] in Foreign Languages

Chinese, French, German, Korean, Japanese, Arabic, Persian, Russian and Spanish

Entrance Examination, 2010

PART–A

All questions carry one mark each. Encircle the correct answer clearly. If more than one option is encircled, the answer will be marked wrong:

1. Which one of the following is essentially a solo dance?
   (*a*) Kuchipudi   (*b*) Kathak
   (*c*) Manipuri   (*d*) Mohiniattam

2. Although fog consists of fine drops of water, we cannot see clearly through it because
   (*a*) the light rays undergo total internal reflection in the drops
   (*b*) fine drops of water in fog polarize the light
   (*c*) the fine drops are opaque to the light
   (*d*) the drops scatter most of the light

3. During the Mughal period, which one of the following were the first to come to India as traders?
   (*a*) Portuguese   (*b*) Dutch
   (*c*) Danish   (*d*) English

4. Who among the following Delhi Sultans is known for introducing market control mechanism?
   (*a*) Iltutmish   (*b*) Balban
   (*c*) Ala-ud-din Khalji (*d*) Feroz Tughluq

5. Which book has been printed in the maximum number of languages and scripts?
   (*a*) *The Bible*   (*b*) *Hiraka Sutra*
   (*c*) *The Super Book* (*d*) *Ramayana*

6. Who of following is the author of *Yashodhara?*
   (*a*) Maithali Sharan Gupt

(*b*) Khushwant Singh
(*c*) Bankimchandra Chatterjee
(*d*) Ramdhari Singh Dinkar

7. Dhayan Chand was
   (*a*) a great hockey player
   (*b*) captained the Indian Hockey Team which won the gold medal in 1936 Berlin Olympics
   (*c*) scored 101 goals at the Olympic Games and 300 goals in International matches
   (*d*) All the statements are correct

8. Which of the following is not an official language of the UN?
   (*a*) English   (*b*) French
   (*c*) Chinese   (*d*) Japanese

9. Which Schedule of Indian Constitution contains languages?
   (*a*) 6th   (*b*) 7th
   (*c*) 8th   (*d*) 9th
   (*e*) 10th

10. With which among the following environment issues is the **Raina Report 2009** related to? (It was recently released by Environment Minister Jairam Ramesh)
   (*a*) Pollution in Ganga
   (*b*) Environmental impacts of Bt Brinjal
   (*c*) CO_2 emission standards
   (*d*) Ozone depletion
   (*e*) Melting glaciers

11. Ants are social insects because
   (*a*) they live in forests

(b) they live in colonies
(c) they have a language
(d) they share food

12. Economic justice has been incorporated in the Constitution of India under
(a) Fundamental Rights
(b) Residuary Powers
(c) Fundamental Duties
(d) Directive Principles of State Policy

13. Numismatics is the study of
(a) coins   (b) numbers
(c) stamps   (d) space

14. Ecology deals with
(a) birds
(b) cell formation
(c) relation between organisms and their environment
(d) tissues

15. The National Calender of India is based on
(a) Gregorian Calender
(b) Hijra Era
(c) Saka Era
(d) None of the above

Directions: *Answer the Following Questions:*

16. In physics, what single-word term normally represents rate of change of position?

17. The symbol ∞ (sideways 8) means what in mathematics?

18. A logophile is a lover of what?

19. Which city hosted the 2009 UN Climate Change Conference?

20. What did NASA claim to have discovered after the LCROSS satellite crashed on the moon?

PART–B

21. Who initiated the policy of open-door and reforms in China?
(a) Mao Zedong   (b) Deng Xiaoping
(c) Jiang Zemin   (d) Hu Jintao

22. What is the status of Hong Kong?
(a) Hong Kong is a republic
(b) Hong Kong is a region of the People's Republic of China
(c) Hong Kong belongs to the UK
(d) Hong Kong is a centrally administered municipality

23. Which country changed allegiances between World War I and World War II?
(a) Russia   (b) Japan
(c) China   (d) Spain

24. The first atom bomb was dropped on Hiroshima on
(a) 6th August, 1945
(b) 9th August, 1945
(c) 9th August, 1946
(d) 6th August, 1942

15. Who of the following lost his position as both the State and party leader of East Germany (GDR) on October 18, 1989?
(a) Walter Ulbricht   (b) Erich Honecker
(c) Egon Krenz   (d) Helmut Kohl

26. The construction of the Berlin Wall began on
(a) November 9, 1989
(b) March 6, 1949
(c) August 13, 1961
(d) June 17, 1953

27. Which country has the largest Japanese population outside Japan?
(a) Brazil   (b) Australia
(c) Peru   (d) Thailand

28. Which one of the following is not a part of Central Asia?
(a) Afghanistan   (b) Tajikistan
(c) Iraq   (d) Uzbekistan

29. Who is known as the 'poet of the East discovered by the West?
(a) Rumi   (b) Hafiz
(c) Iqbal   (d) Khayyam

30. *Crime and Punishment* is a novel by
(a) Leo Tolstoy
(b) Fyodor Dostoyevsky
(c) Aleksander Pushkin
(d) Anton Chekhov

31. Napoleon's army invaded Russia in
    (*a*) 1812   (*b*) 1814
    (*c*) 1816   (*d*) 1818

32. Russian language uses
    (*a*) Roman alphabet (*b*) Glagolitic alphabet
    (*c*) Cyrillic alphabet (*d*) Hebrew alphabet

33. Which Latin dance originated in Andalucia?
    (*a*) Meringue   (*b*) Salsa
    (*c*) Flamenco   (*d*) Sardana

34. Who wrote *Don Quixote de la Mancha?*
    (*a*) Molina   (*b*) Vega
    (*c*) Zorrilla   (*d*) Cervantes

35. Most people in Spain follow which religion?
    (*a*) Judaism   (*b*) Catholicism
    (*c*) Protestantism (*d*) Islam

36. Which French author wrote the book, *Les Miserables,* adapted as a musical in 1980?
    (*a*) Gustave Flaubert
    (*b*) Arthur Rimbaud
    (*c*) Charles Baudelaire
    (*d*) Victor Hugo

37. India has recently signed a Comprehensive Economic Partnership Agreement with which country?
    (*a*) Taiwan   (*b*) Republic of Korea
    (*c*) Sri Lanka   (*d*) Afghanistan

38. What is the official name of North Korea?
    (*a*) Democratic People's Republic of Korea
    (*b*) Socialist Republic of South Korea
    (*c*) Republic of Korea
    (*d*) People's Republic of Democratic Korea

39. Which of the following pairs of countries are not Arab?
    (*a*) Sudan and Somalia
    (*b*) Morocco and Mauritania
    (*c*) Iran and Turkey
    (*d*) Egypt and Jordan

40. How many Arab countries are represented in the League of Arab States?
    (*a*) 2   (*b*) 8
    (*c*) 14   (*d*) 22

PART-C

Directions: *Explain the underlined phrases:*

41. It <u>goes against the grain</u> for me to admit my mistake.

    goes against the grain: ....

42. The party is only <u>paying lip service</u> to women's rights.

    paying lip service: ....

How to use an ATM

Directions: *All verbs have been removed from the following text. Try to reconstruct the text by putting verbs into the blanks:*

(43) your card into the machine and (44) until the instructions (45) on the screen. Then (46) your PIN number. After that you (47) to tell the machine how much money you (48). You (49) that by pushing the correct buttons. Now wait a minute or two while the ATM (50) your account and (51) your money. After that (52) your card and receipt. Finally, take your money out of the money slot and put it in your wallet.

43. _______________________________

44. _______________________________

45. _______________________________

46. _______________________________

47. _______________________________

48. _______________________________

49. _______________________________

50. _______________________________

51. _______________________________

52. _______________________________

Directions: *Unscramble the following proverbs and add capital letters and punctuation marks:*

53. friends known by man a is his

____

54. bread man by live alone cannot

____

55. bird early worm catches the the

____

PART–D

Directions: *Encircle the appropriate word for filling the blanks:*

56. .... his illness, John continued to play rugby.
(*a*) Despite (*b*) Although
(*c*) Even though

57. None of the students .... a car.
(*a*) has (*b*) have
(*c*) have got

58. There has not yet been any decision made .... will represent the country at the Olympics
(*a*) concerned athletes chosen
(*b*) as to which athletes
(*c*) those athletes

Directions: *Encircle the correct answer for filling the blanks:*

59. She held the ..... in her hand.
(*a*) reigns (*b*) rains
(*c*) reins

60. They've got a ..... at the Ritz.
(*a*) suit (*b*) suite
(*c*) sweet

61. Each of the Olympic athletes ..... for months, even years.
(*a*) have been training
(*b*) were training
(*c*) has been training
(*d*) been training

62. Never before ..... as rapidly, as during the last decade.
(*a*) communication have developed
(*b*) have communications developed
(*c*) have developed communications
(*d*) communications developed

63. The company will upgrade .... computer information systems next month.
(*a*) there (*b*) their
(*c*) it's (*d*) its

64. He's a real ..... eyed boy in his office. The boss loves him.
(*a*) green (*b*) grey
(*c*) brown (*d*) blue

65. How can you argue about your salary now? It's there on your contract in .....
(*a*) black (*b*) blue and white
(*c*) black and white (*d*) red and white

Directions: *Encircle the right time preposition for the gaps in each sentence:*

66. We always visit my family ..... Christmas.
(*a*) on (*b*) at
(*c*) in (*d*) by

67. I have been learning English ..... two years.
(*a*) since (*b*) by
(*c*) for (*d*) in

68. My appointment with the doctor is ..... 4 O'clock.
(*a*) on (*b*) at
(*c*) in (*d*) by

69. By the time she arrives, we ..... our homework.
(*a*) finish (*b*) will have finished
(*c*) will finish (*d*) were finished

70. When I stopped .... to Mary, she was picking some flowers in her garden.
(*a*) speaking (*b*) speak
(*c*) to speak (*d*) spoke

71. If I ..... you, I would wait a while to begin investing.
(*a*) was (*b*) am
(*c*) were (*d*) would be

Directions: *One sentence is wrong in each question. Which one?*

72. Capital letters. Which sentence is wrong?
(*a*) We'll see you on Wednesday.
(*b*) I speak Spanish very badly.
(*c*) I like the weather here in the Winter.
(*d*) Paul is a very difficult person to work with.

73. Commas. Which sentence is wrong?
(*a*) On our trip we went to Japan, Thailand, Bali and Australia.
(*b*) It was no surprise, that you failed the exam.

(*c*) My aunt Julie, who often visits us, will be here for Christmas.

(*d*) "I am not happy with your work", he said.

74. Apostrophes. Which sentence is wrong?
    (*a*) He doesn't know the answer, does he?
    (*b*) She has lots of cat's at home.
    (*c*) Joe's sister is in the Himalayas.
    (*d*) The problem with the business is its location.

Directions: *Rewrite the sentence using the phrase given in parenthesis as shown in the example:*

Ex. You must never take your helmet off while you are riding a motorcycle. (at all times) Helmets must be worn at all times when riding a motorcycle.

75. I'm afraid that car is just too expensive. (beyond my means)

____

76. I thought parking was allowed here. (was under the impression)

____

77. A man rode into town on Monday. He stayed for three nights and then left on Monday. How come?

____

78. In the language Bontoc, we find that adjectives can be made into verbs in the following fashion:

fikas strong	**kilad** red	**bato** stone	**fusul** enemy
fumikas he is becoming strong	**kumilad** he is becoming red	**bumato** he is becoming stone	**fumusul** he is becoming an enemy

Make a rule for describing this process.

____

____

____

Consider the following sentence from English. Even while you do not know the meanings of the underlined words, can you identify whether they are nouns or verbs? Give reason for your answer. (Question Nos. 79 & 80).

The disgruntled <u>garfnack twillered</u> across the river in a wooden boat.

79. Garfnack: _______________________________

80. Twillered: _______________________________

PART–E

Directions: *Read the following text and answer the questions that follow:*

Totto-Chan
The Little Girl At The Window
By Tetsuko Kuroyanagi
Translated by Dorothy Britton

The Headmaster

When Mother and Totto-chan went in, the man in the office got up from this chair. His hair was thin on top and he had a few teeth missing, but his face was a healthy color. Although he wasn't very tall, he had solid shoulders and arms and was neatly dressed in a rather shabby black three-piece suit. With a hasty bow, Totto-chan asked him spiritedly, "What are you, a schoolmaster or a stationmaster?" Mother was embarrassed, but before she had time to explain, he laughed and replied, "I'm the headmaster of this school."

Totto-chan was delighted, "Oh, I'm so glad," she said, "because I want to ask you a favor. I'd like to come to your school."

The headmaster offered her a chair and turned to Mother. "You may go home now. I want to talk to Totto-chan."

Totto-chan had a moment's uneasiness, but somehow felt she would get along all right with this man. "Well, then, I'll leave her with you," mother said bravely, and shut the door behind her as she went out.

The headmaster drew over a chair and put it facing Totto-chan, and when they were both sitting down close together, he said, "Now then, tell me all about yourself. Tell me anything at all you want to talk about."

"Anything I like?" Totto-chan had expected him to ask questions she would have to answer. When he said she could talk about anything she wanted, she was so happy she began straight away. It was all a bit higgledy-piggledy, but she talked for all she was worth. She told the headmaster how fast the train went that they had come on; how she had asked the ticket collector but he wouldn't let her keep her ticket; how pretty her homeroom teacher was at the other school; about the swallows' nest; about their brown dog, Rocky, who could do all sorts of tricks; how she used to go snip-snip with the scissors inside her mouth at kindergarten and the teacher said she mustn't do that because she might cut her tongue off, but she did it anyway; how she always blew her nose because mother scolded her if it was runny; what a good swimmer Daddy was, and how he could dive as well. She went on and on. The headmaster would laugh, nod, and say, "And then?" And Totto-chan was so happy she kept right on talking. But finally she ran out of things to say. She sat with her mouth closed trying hard to think of something. "Haven't you anything more you can tell me?", asked the headmaster. What a shame to stop now, Totto-chan thought. It was such a wonderful chance. Wasn't there anything else she could talk about, she wondered, racking her brains? Then she had an idea.

She could tell him about the dress she was wearing that day. Mother made most of her dresses, but this one came from a shop. Her clothes were always torn when she came home in the late afternoon. Some of the rips were quite bad. Mother never knew how they got that way. Even her white cotton panties were sometimes in shreds. She explained to the headmaster that they got torn when she crossed other people's gardens by crawling under their fences, and when she burrowed under the barbed wire around vacant lots. So this morning, she said, when she was getting dressed to come here, all the nice dresses Mother had made were torn so she had to wear one Mother had bought. It had small dark red and gray check and was made of jersey, and it wasn't bad, but Mother thought the red flowers embroidered on the collar were in bad taste. "Mother doesn't like the collar," said Totto-chan, holding it up for the headmaster to see.

After that, she could think of nothing more to say no matter how hard she tried. It made her rather sad. But just then the headmaster got up, placed his large, warm hand on her head, and said, "Well, now you're a pupil of this school."

Those were his very words. And at that moment Totto-chan felt she had met someone, she really liked for the very first time in her life. You see, up till then, no one had ever listened to her for so long. And all that time the headmaster hadn't yawned once or looked bored, but seemed just as interested in what she had to say as she was.

Totto-chan hadn't learned how to tell time yet, but it did seem like a rather long time. If she had been able to, she would have been astonished, and even more grateful to the headmaster. For, you see, Mother and Totto-chan arrived at the school at eight, and when she had finished talking and the headmaster had told her she was a pupil of the school, he looked at his pocket watch and said, "Ah, it's time for lunch." So the headmaster must have listened to Totto-chan for four solid hours!

Neither before nor since did any grown-up listen to Totto-chan for as long as that. And, besides, it would have amazed Mother and her homeroom teacher to think that a seven-year-old child could find enough to talk about for four hours nonstop. Totto-chan had no idea then, of course, that she had been expelled and that people were at their wit's end to know what to do. Having a naturally sunny disposition and being a bit absent-minded gave her an air of innocence. But deep down she felt she was considered different from other children and slightly strange. The headmaster, however, made her feel safe and warm and happy. She wanted to stay with him forever.

That's how Totto-chan felt about headmaster Sosaku Kobayashi that first day. And, luckily, the headmaster felt the same about her.

The above text is an extract from the book "Totto-chan. The Little Girl at the Window" and was first published in 1981 in Japan. It is about a little girl called Totto-chan who did not fit into the normal school system and so her mother takes her to a school started by Sosaku Kobayashi in six abandoned railroad car in 1937.

1. Why does Totto-chan ask the headmaster whether he was a schoolmaster or a stationmaster?

2. What did Totto-chan and the headmaster talk about?

3. Why did the homeroom teacher in the other school tell Totto-chan not to "go snip-snip with the scissors inside her mouth"? Did Totto-chan obey her?

4. Is this encounter between Totto-chan and the headmaster of her new school different from your experiences at school? In what way?

PART–F

Directions: *The following are newspaper headlines. Write a news report on anyone of them:*

1. Aman ki asha
2. Indian festivals celebrate communal harmony
3. Orphans blocked from departing Haiti

OR

Directions: *Write a paragraph on anyone of the following. The character, setting, time and situation is given:*

1. A recent high school graduate/a celebration party/the night of the high school graduation/someone's pride has been injured.

2. A college student/a college library/the first week of college/something embarrassing has just happened.

3. A homeless child/a city park/late at night/someone has accused someone else of doing something wrong.

ANSWERS

1. (*d*)	**2.** (*d*)	**3.** (*a*)	**4.** (*c*)
5. (*a*)	**6.** (*a*)	**7.** (*d*)	**8.** (*d*)
9. (*c*)	**10.** (*e*)	**11.** (*b*)	**12.** (*d*)
13. (*a*)	**14.** (*c*)	**15.** (*c*)	**16.** Velocity
17. Infinity	**16.** Words	**19.** Copenhagen	**20.** Water
21. (*b*)	**22.** (*b*)	**23.** (*b*)	**24.** (*a*)
25. (*b*)	**26.** (*c*)	**27.** (*a*)	**28.** (*c*)
29. (*c*)	**30.** (*b*)	**31.** (*a*)	**32.** (*c*)
33. (*c*)	**34.** (*d*)	**35.** (*b*)	**36.** (*d*)
37. (*b*)	**38.** (*a*)	**39.** (*c*)	**40.** (*d*)

41. It means to do something that you usually do not do or say.

42. Support for something insincerely.	**43.** Insert	**44.** Wait
45. Appear	**46.** Enter	**47.** Have	**48.** Want
49. Do	**50.** Checks	**51.** Debit	**52.** Take

53. A man is known by his friends.

54. Man cannot live by bread alone.

55. The early bird catches the worm.　　　　**56.** (*a*)　　　　**57.** (*c*)

58. (*b*)　　　　**59.** (*a*)　　　　**60.** (*b*)　　　　**61.** (*c*)

62. (*a*)　　　　**63.** (*d*)　　　　**64.** (*d*)　　　　**65.** (*c*)

66. (*a*)　　　　**67.** (*a*)　　　　**68.** (*b*)　　　　**69.** (*c*)

70. (*a*)　　　　**71.** (*a*)　　　　**72.** (*a*)　　　　**73.** (*b*)

74. (*b*)　　　　**75.** The cost of car is beyond my mean.

76. I was under the impression that parking was allowed here.

77. Monday is the name of the vehicle on which he came to into the city.

78. Here, um stands for he is becoming and it comes between the first letter and the rest of the letters of the given word.

79. Nour　　　　**80.** Verb

EXPLANATORY ANSWERS

PART-E

1. The headmaster's look was like stationmaster. He had solid shoulders and arms and was neatly dressed in a black three piece suit. Also the school runs in railroad cars.

2. Totto-chan told him about the train journey, about her other school, about her dog, her family and her days at Kindergarten.

3. Totto-chan used to go snip-snip with the scissors inside her mouth at Kindergarten so the teacher asked her not to do this as this might be harmful. She didn't obeyed him.

4. Yes, the encounter was different, as in normal schools the headmaster seldom gives so much time to listen to his new pupil. Another thing is that during the conversation period he gave his full attention which normal doesn't happen.

PART-F

Aman ki Asha

Aman ki Asha is a campaign jointly started by the two leading media houses The Jang Group in Pakistan and The Time of India in India. The campaign aims for mutual peace and development of the diplomatic and cultural relations between the two nations in South Asia. It started on the 1st of January 2010. The campaign has received warm response from India and Pakistan. Despite this, Bennet & Coleman, the holding company of Times Group has been trying valiantly to keep the campaign afloat through a high decibel media campaign.

Aman ki Asha was inspired by the groundbreaking work of Friends Without Borders, an International NGO, that launched bold, love-based people-to-people campaigns between the children and people of both countries between 2005-2007. The Times of India and the Jang Group both partnered with Friends Without Borders and picked up the efforts after the Dil se Dil Border Concert was canceled in August 2007. "Peace efforts between India and Pakistan are the real need of the hour and only prudence, foresightedness and sincerity can do wonders for both countries. In this people of India communicate with the people of Pakistan."

The campaign has come under severe criticism from a major part of society in both India and Pakistan. Their campaign is rendered as a publicity stunt by these groups who consider the attitude of people of the two nations is beyond any rivalry. Hindu-Muslim agitations in India; decision of Babri Mosque; Hindu persecution in Pakistan and Pakistan's suspected and to a much level proved continued support to Islamic fundamentalists and terrorists in India (see 26/11 Mumbai Attacks) have reignited claims these rival nations find little common ground between themselves. The partition of religions seem far too high a mountain to climb for the nations to have a friendly relation with each other.

JAWAHARLAL NEHRU UNIVERSITY [JNU]

First Year of 3-Year B.A. [Hons.] in Foreign Languages

Chinese, French, German, Korean, Japanese, Arabic, Persian, Russian and Spanish

Entrance Examination, 2009

PART–A

Answer all the following questions. Circle the correct answer clearly. If more than one answer is circled, the answer will be marked wrong:

1. Khalil Gibran is originally from
   (a) Saudi Arabia   (b) Egypt
   (c) Syria   (d) Lebanon

2. Suez Canal was made by
   (a) Egypt   (b) France
   (c) Britain   (d) USA

3. Ural mountains are located in
   (a) China   (b) Serbia
   (c) Russia   (d) Mongolia

4. Russian language belongs to
   (a) Germanic   (b) Roman
   (c) Slavic   (d) Celtic

5. Who is the first woman cosmonaut?
   (a) Kalpana Chawla
   (b) Sunita Williams
   (c) Valentina Tereshkova
   (d) Chiaki Mukai

6. Which is the current currency of Spain?
   (a) Euro   (b) Peso
   (c) Peseta   (d) Spanish Dollar

7. 'Tango' is the dance form which is typical of
   (a) Spain   (b) Argentina
   (c) Brazil   (d) Cuba

8. Which of the following authors is a recipient of the Noble prize for Literature?
   (a) Arundhati Roy
   (b) Jorge Luis Borges
   (c) Gabriel Garcia Marquez
   (d) Miguel Hernandez

9. 'Real Madrid' is a/an
   (a) Oscar winner film   (b) football club
   (c) famous novel   (d) famous wine

10. Who is the present Secretary-General of the UN?
    (a) Ban Ki Moon   (b) Lee Myung Bak
    (c) Han Seung soo   (d) Kin Dae Jung

11. Which city of South Korea will host the 2014 Asian Games?
    (a) Seoul   (b) Busan
    (c) Ulsan   (d) Incheon

12. Which is the only Asian country which is a member of G-8?
    (a) China   (b) Japan
    (c) India   (d) Singapore

13. Which of the Japanese classical performing arts is a world heritage?
    (a) Noh   (b) Kabuki
    (c) Joruri   (d) Bon odori

14. Karate is said to have been derived from
    (a) Kung fu   (b) Tae kwon do
    (c) Kalaripayattu   (d) Judo

15. 'Lacoste' is a/an
    (a) writer   (b) instrument
    (c) brand name   (d) book

16. What is Bordcaux?
    (a) River   (b) City
    (c) Monument   (d) Mountain

17. Which of the following persons has not been the President of France?
   (*a*) Giscard d'Estaing
   (*b*) Nicolas Sarkozy
   (*c*) Jean Marie Le pen
   (*d*) Jacques Chirac

18. Chinese New year is celebrated in the form of
   (*a*) Spring Festival   (*b*) Lantern Festival
   (*c*) Dragon Festival   (*d*) Moon Festival

19. Tian'anmen Square is located in
   (*a*) Shanghai   (*b*) Nanjing
   (*c*) Beijing   (*d*) Kunming

20. The last Emperor of China was called
   (*a*) Li Bai   (*b*) Puyi
   (*c*) Qian long   (*d*) Sun Zhogshan

21. The National Flag of People's Republic of China bas
   (*a*) One big and four small stars
   (*b*) Four small stars
   (*c*) One big star

   (*d*) One big and one small star

22. Sheikh Saadi was a famous poet of
   (*a*) Arabic   (*b*) English
   (*c*) Urdu   (*d*) Persian

23. Who was the founder of Islamic Republic of Iran?
   (*a*) Ayatollah Khamenei
   (*b*) Ayatollah Rafsanjani
   (*c*) Ayatollah Khomeini
   (*d*) Ayatollah Karrubi

24. Who translated the Bible from Latin into German?
   (*a*) William Tyndale
   (*b*) Philipp Melanchthon
   (*c*) Martin Luther
   (*d*) John Calvin

25. Who was the First Chancellor of reunified Germany?
   (*a*) Erich Honecker   (*b*) Angela Merkel
   (*c*) Helmut Kohl   (*d*) Gerhard Schroder

PART–B

A. Circle the correct answer clearly. If more than one answer is circled, the answer will be marked wrong:

26. Which out of the following is not recognized as a classical language by the Government of India?
   (*a*) Sanskrit   (*b*) Tamil
   (*c*) Malayalam   (*d*) Telugu

27. Zoram Nationalist Party is one of the major political parties of
   (*a*) Sikkim   (*b*) Arunachal Pradesh
   (*c*) Mizoram   (*d*) Meghalaya

28. Which Indian state has the lowest male-female ratio?
   (*a*) Punjab   (*b*) Delhi
   (*c*) Bihar   (*d*) Uttar Pradesh

29. Which is the world's highest train route?
   (*a*) Trans Siberian Railways
   (*b*) Konkan Railways
   (*c*) Udhampur-Baramula
   (*d*) Tibet Railways

30. Tata's Nano car factory is being set up in
   (*a*) Gujarat   (*b*) Punjab
   (*c*) Karnataka   (*d*) West Bengal

31. Nepal became a Republic in
   (*a*) 2005   (*b*) 2006
   (*c*) 2007   (*d*) 2008

32. Which of the following is not a SAARC country?
   (*a*) Myanmar   (*b*) Pakistan
   (*c*) Sri Lanka   (*d*) Maldives

33. The Indian historian who won the Kluge Prize for lifetime achievement in 2008 is
   (*a*) Romila Thapar   (*b*) Meera Sanyal
   (*c*) Kumkum Roy   (*d*) Sashi Deshpande

34. Which of the following diseases is caused by virus?
   (*a*) Tuberculosis   (*b*) Typhoid
   (*c*) Influenza   (*d*) Diphtheria

35. The phenomenon of mirage occurs due to
   (*a*) Polarisation of light

(b) Dispersion of light
(c) Diffraction of light
(d) Total internal reflection of light

36. What is the major constituent of biogas?
(a) Carbon dioxide (b) Methane
(c) Hydrogen   (d) Nitrogen oxide

37. The Egyptian *hieroglyphic* is a
(a) Computer language
(b) Pictorial script
(c) Typescript
(d) Musical language

38. The name of the well-known ancient Indian grammarian is
(a) Panini   (b) Shankara
(c) Chaitanya   (d) Aurobindo

39. Maximum number of wickets in One-day International Cricket has been taken by
(a) Kapil Dev
(b) Muttiah Muralitharan
(c) Wasim Akram
(d) Shane Warne

40. Khasi is spoken in the Indian State of
(a) Mizoram
(b) Nagaland
(c) Arunachal Pradesh
(d) Meghalaya

41. Eskimos are inhabitants of

(a) Canada   (b) Japan
(c) Ecuador   (d) Ethiopia

42. Hopis and Mayas are names of people who live in
(a) Africa   (b) Europe
(c) Australia   (d) America

43. The word 'literature' is related to
(a) litter   (b) liter
(c) latter   (d) letter

44. Official language of Morocco is
(a) French   (b) Portuguese
(c) Arabic   (d) Persian

45. The Japanese poem of seventeen syllables is
(a) Haiku   (b) Tanka
(c) Choka   (d) Waka

B. Write the answers in the space given:

46. The only Kashmiri poet to have received Jnanpith Award is ....

47. The stadium where the inaugural ceremony of Beijing Olympics, 2008, was held is known as ....

48. The first Indian Mission to the Moon is called ....

49. The author of the *White Tiger* is ....

50. The mixed doubles in the Australian open championship, 2009, was won by ....

PART–C

A. Give the full forms of the following:

51. CIS

....

52. ASEAN

....

B. Hawaiian is a Polynesian language spoken fluently by about 2000 people. The following Hawaiian sentences, with their English translations, are about a girl named Mele and a boy named Keone:

He has seven elder brothers.	Ehiku ona kaikuaana.
Mele has one brother.	Ekahi o Mele kaikunane.
Keone has one younger brother.	Ekahi o Keon kaikaina.
Mele has no elder sisters.	Aohe o Mele kaikuaana.
Keone has no sisters.	Aohe o Keone kaikuahine.

53. What is the word for 'elder brothers' in Hawaiian?

....

54. What is the word for 'sister' in Hawaiian?

....

55. Is there a word for 'one' in Hawaiian? Circle the correct answer.
(a) Yes
(b) No

C. In the following passage, some words have been omitted. Fill in the blanks with correct words such as:

a, an, the, have, had, in, around

This is true that <u>56</u> picture speaks more than a thousand words. <u>57</u> picture you <u>58</u> sent tells us about the destruction of wildlife. The picture shocked me very much. In the US, some private organizations <u>59</u> saved the largest variety of flora and fauna <u>60</u> the world.

56. ....

57. ....

58. ....

59. ....

60. ....

D. Look at the words given below. Rearrange them to form meaningful sentences. Write your sentences in the space provided:

61. a long / India has / conservation of / history of / forests

....

62. of living beings / conservation of / large mammals / to maintain / will help / the entire web

....

E. Rewrite the sentences following the examples given:

Example 1

Who inspects the machines? the foreman
The machines are inspected by the foreman.

63. Who made the biscuits?

the girls in the factory

....

64. Who dictated that letter?   the manager

....

Example 2

Which button did he push?

It's on the top.

He pushed the button which is on the top.

65. Which machines do you use?

They need electricity.

....

66. Which magazine is he reading?

It was in your office.

....

Example 3

The advertisement - by the personnel manager yesterday afternoon. **Write**

The advertisement **was written** by the personnel manager yesterday afternoon.

67. The job — in the morning paper tomorrow.

....

68. While I was in London I — to the post of general manager. Promote

....

Example 4

We'll advertise the job.

Will the job be advertised?

69. You can send telegrams from here.

....

70. You can buy all kinds of food here.

....

PART–D

A. Circle the correct answer to fill in the blanks:

71. The bag is .... the table
(*a*) on   (*b*) in

72. I came .... bus.
(*a*) on   (*b*) by

73. She likes samosa .... tomato sauce.
(*a*) for   (*b*) with

74. John prefers tea .... coffee.
    (*a*) to   (*b*) than

B. Fill in the blanks with the correct answer:

75. "I wash my hands off the whole incident" means ....
    (*a*) I take full responsibility of the incident
    (*b*) I have nothing to do with the incident

76. I got the better of him. In other words, ...
    (*a*) I got better things from him
    (*b*) I overcame him

77. When I said she seemed out of spirits, I meant ....
    (*a*) she had become a spirit
    (*b*) she appeared sad

78. I was disappointed that he had taken exception to my remark. What I meant was that ....
    (*a*) he had not accepted my remark
    (*b*) he had objected to my remark

79. He knows the ins and outs of the matter. In other words, ...
    (*a*) he knows little about the matter
    (*b*) he knows the matter in detail

C. Complete the sentences with correct word/ words:

80. The coffee tastes a bit .... (musty/mustily)

81. I can't eat this. It tastes .... (awful / awfully)

82. When I returned to my village after 10 years, everything .... (changed/had changed)

D. Circle the correct answer to fill in the blanks:

83. Everyone .... happy about the tour.
    (*a*) is   (*b*) are

84. Ask either .... them.
    (*a*) of   (*b*) to

85. You .... attend the class regularly. It is my advice as your good friend.
    (*a*) would   (*b*) should

86. The horse and carriage .... come.
    (*a*) has   (*b*) have

87. I called .... him at the residence.
    (*a*) up   (*b*) on

88. Akash wants to break .... his engagement.
    (*a*) off   (*b*) up

89. One must not give .... to irrational demands.
    (*a*) up   (*b*) in

90. The landlord wants him to move .... by next week
    (*a*) out   (*b*) away

PART–E

Write five sentences on each topic. Place do not exceed the limit. Each carries five marks:
    (*a*) Barack Obama
    (*b*) Slumdog Millionaire

ANSWERS

1	2	3	4	5	6	7	8	9	10
(*d*)	(*b*)	(*c*)	(*d*)	(*c*)	(*a*)	(*b*)	(*c*)	(*b*)	(*a*)

11	12	13	14	15	16	17	18	19	20
(*d*)	(*b*)	(*b*)	(*a*)	(*c*)	(*b*)	(*c*)	(*a*)	(*c*)	(*b*)

21	22	23	24	25	26	27	28	29	30
(*a*)	(*d*)	(*c*)	(*c*)	(*c*)	(*c*)	(*c*)	(*b*)	(*d*)	(*a*)

31	32	33	34	35	36	37	38	39	40
(*d*)	(*a*)	(*a*)	(*c*)	(*d*)	(*b*)	(*b*)	(*a*)	(*b*)	(*d*)

41	42	43	44	45
(*a*)	(*d*)	(*a*)	(*c*)	(*a*)

46. Rahman Rahi, November 6, 2008.

47. National Stadium.

48. Chandrayaan

49. Arvind Adiga

50. Sania Mirza and Mahesh Bhupati

51. Commonwealth of Independent States

52. Association of South-East Asian Nation

53. Kaikuaana

54. Aohe

55. Yes

56. a

57. the

58. had

59. have

60. around

61. India has a long history of conservation of forest.

62. Conservation of large mammals will help the entire web of living being.

63. The girls in the factory made the biscuits.

64. The manager dictated the letter.

65. You use to machines which need electricity.

66. He is reading the magazine which was in your office.

67. The job advertises in the morning paper tomorrow.

68. While I was in London, I was promoted to the post of General Manager.

69. Can the telegrams be send from here?

70. Can you buy all kinds of food here?

71. (*a*)

72. (*b*)

73. (*b*)

74. (*a*)

75. (*b*)

76. (*b*)

77. (*b*)

78. (*b*)

79. (*b*)

80. musty

81. awful

82. had changed

83. (*a*)

84. (*a*)

85. (*b*)

86. (*b*)

87. (*b*)

88. (*b*)

89. (*a*)

90. (*a*)

PART-E

Barack Hussein Obama: He was born on August 4, 1961. He is the 44th and current President of the United States. He is the first African American to hold the office. Obama previously served as the junior United States Senator from Illinois, from January 2005 until he resigned after his election to the presidency in November 2008. Obama is a graduate of Columbia University and Harvard Law School, where he was the president of the **Harvard Law Review.**

Slumdog Millionaire is a 2008 British film directed by Danny Boyle, screenplay written by Simoon Beaufoy, and co-directed in India by Loveleen Tandan. It is an adaptation of the novel *Q & A* (2005) by Indian author and diplomat Vikas Swarup. **Slumdog Millionaire** was nominated for ten Academy Awards in 2009 and won eight, the most for any film of 2008, including Best Picture, Best Director, and Best Adapted Screenplay. It also won seven BAFTA Awards (including Best Film), five Critics' Choice Awards, and four Golden Globes.

JAWAHARLAL NEHRU UNIVERSITY [JNU]

First Year of 3-Year B.A. [Hons.] in Foreign Languages

Chinese, French, German, Korean, Japanese, Arabic, Persian, Russian and Spanish

Entrance Examination, 2008

PART–A

Answer all the following questions. All questions carry one mark each. Circle the correct answer clearly. If more than one answer is circled, the answer will be marked wrong:

1. The traditional form of drama of Japan which is similar to Yakshagana of India is:
   - (*a*) Bunraku
   - (*b*) Noh
   - (*c*) Gagaku
   - (*d*) Sarugaku

2. The cultural capital of Japan is:
   - (*a*) Nagoya
   - (*b*) Kyoto
   - (*c*) Tokyo
   - (*d*) Osaka

3. The constitutional head of Japan is:
   - (*a*) Prime Minister
   - (*b*) President
   - (*c*) Emperor
   - (*d*) Chancellor

4. Boutros Boutros Ghali, former Secretary-General of UNO belonged to:
   - (*a*) Saudi Arabia
   - (*b*) Kuwait
   - (*c*) UAE
   - (*d*) Egypt

5. The only Arab scientist to have won Nobel Prize is:
   - (*a*) Ahmad Zuwail
   - (*b*) Abdur Rahman Naif
   - (*c*) Munir Ramzi
   - (*d*) Ehsan Khalil

6. *One Hundred Years of Solitude* was written by:
   - (*a*) Vikram Seth
   - (*b*) Dan Brown
   - (*c*) Gabriel Garcia Marqez
   - (*d*) Ayn Rand

7. The term 'Banana Republics' refers to:
   - (*a*) Countries of Africa
   - (*b*) Countries of South-East Asia
   - (*c*) Countries of South America
   - (*d*) Countries of Eastern Europe

8. Which of the following is a Spanish painter?
   - (*a*) Claude Monet
   - (*b*) Leonardo da Vinci
   - (*c*) Paul Klee
   - (*d*) Pablo Picasso

9. In 2007, China's GDP crossed:
   - (*a*) three trillion US dollars
   - (*b*) one trillion US dollars
   - (*c*) four billion US dollars
   - (*d*) six billion US dollars

10. The current President of China is:
    - (*a*) Hu Jintao
    - (*b*) Wa Jiabao
    - (*c*) Jiang Zenia
    - (*d*) Yang Shangkun

11. The 'Tiananmen Square' protests took place in the year:
    - (*a*) 1979
    - (*b*) 1989
    - (*c*) 1999
    - (*d*) None of the above

12. The Berlin Wall collapsed in the year:
    - (*a*) 1960-61
    - (*b*) 1979-80
    - (*c*) 1982-83
    - (*d*) 1989-90

13. The Reformation in Germany is linked with:
    - (*a*) Martin Luther
    - (*b*) Ulrich Zwingli
    - (*c*) Friedrich II
    - (*d*) Otto von Bismarck

14. The official name for Germany is:
    - (*a*) German Democratic Republic
    - (*b*) Federal German Republic

(c) Federal Republic of Germany
(d) Socialist Republic of Germany

15. A Molotov cocktail is:
(a) a drink made of orange juice and vodka
(b) a crude bomb
(c) a special fruit salad
(d) a form of dance

16. Peter the Great belonged to:
(a) the Romanov dynasty
(b) the Rurik dynasty
(c) the Khan dynasty
(d) None of the above

17. The CIS countries refer to:
(a) some of the East-European Countries
(b) some of the South-American Republics
(c) the East-African Block
(d) some of the former Soviet Republics

18. The following President got divorced and remarried during his term in office:
(a) Giscard d'Estaing
(b) Horst Koehler
(c) Nicolas Sarkozy
(d) Boris Yeltsin

19. The following country does not share a border with France:
(a) Germany   *(b)* Greece
(c) Belgium   *(d)* Switzerland

20. The President of France earlier used to be elected for a term of:
(a) four years   *(b)* five years
(c) six years   *(d)* seven years

21. Omar Khayyam was:
(a) a poet   *(b)* a politician
(c) a statesman   *(d)* a warrior

22. Persian has official language status in:
(a) Pakistan   *(b)* Uzbekistan
(c) Afghanistan   *(d)* Iraq

23. Persepolis was the ancient capital of the:
(a) Egyptian Empire
(b) Persian Empire
(c) Byzantine Empire
(d) Ottoman Empire

24. The 38th parallel or Demilitarized Zone is the area that divides:
(a) North and South Korea
(b) China and Tibet
(c) North and South Vietnam
(d) Hong Kong and China

25. Kimchi, Sushi, Bulgogi are:
(a) names of novels
(b) dance forms
(c) language dialects
(d) food items

PART–B

Answer all the following questions. All questions carry one mark each. Circle the correct answer clearly. If more, than one answer is circled, the answer will be marked wrong:

26. The book, *Life Divine,* was written by:
(a) Jawaharlal Nehru
(b) Aurobindo Ghosh
(c) George Bernard Shaw
(d) Rabindranath Tagore

27. *Das Kapital* was written by:
(a) Vladimir Ilyich Lenin
(b) Karl Marx
(c) G.W.F. Hegel
(d) Ludwig Feuerbach

28. The last ruler of the Mughal dynasty was:
(a) Shah Jahan
(b) Aurangzeb
(c) Akbar
(d) Bahadur Shah Zafar

29. The father of the Indian Constitution was:
(a) B.R. Ambedkar
(b) Jawaharlal Nehru
(c) Mohandas Karamchand Gandhi
(d) Bankim Chandra Chatterjee

30. The first Indian actress to have been nominated to the Rajya Sabha was:
(a) Nargis Dutt   *(b)* Hema Malini
(c) Jaya Bachchan   *(d)* Vaijayantimala Bali

31. The chief constituent of 'gobar' gas is:
    (*a*) ethane   (*b*) propane
    (*c*) methane   (*d*) chlorine

32. The first metal used by man was:
    (*a*) iron   (*b*) copper
    (*c*) gold   (*d*) bronze

33. The 'greenhouse effect' refers to:
    (*a*) increasing agricultural yields
    (*b*) gradual warming of the earth surface
    (*c*) buildup of toxic airborne pollutants
    (*d*) reduction in the earth's ozone layer

34. Television in India was introduced in the year:
    (*a*) 1947   (*b*) 1960
    (*c*) 1959   (*d*) 1981

35. The movie 'Tare Zameen Par' deals with:
    (*a*) Dyslexia   (*b*) Paranoia
    (*c*) Schizophrenia   (*d*) Aphasia

36. *Tamasha* is a famous folk form of:
    (*a*) Uttar Pradesh   (*b*) Punjab
    (*c*) Bihar   (*d*) Maharashtra

37. India's first talkie film was:
    (*a*) Shakuntala   (*b*) Indra Sabha
    (*c*) Neel Kamal   (*d*) Alam Ara

38. The UNESCO has declared 2008 as the international year of:
    (*a*) culture
    (*b*) languages
    (*c*) wildlife conservation
    (*d*) heritage restoration

39. Who was appointed the coach of the Indian women's hockey team in 2007?
    (*a*) Herman Kruis
    (*b*) Shah Rukh Khan
    (*c*) Kabir Khan
    (*d*) Mir Ranjan Negi

40. Sania Mirza is the brand ambassador for which soft drink?
    (*a*) Pepsi   (*b*) Coke
    (*c*) Sprite   (*d*) Fanta

41. IPL in cricket stands for:
    (*a*) Indian Professional League
    (*b*) International Players League
    (*c*) Indian Premier League
    (*d*) None of the above

42. The farmers of Singur resisted the State Government's move to acquire land for:
    (*a*) Tata Motors
    (*b*) Maruti Udyog
    (*c*) Infosys
    (*d*) Hindustan Motors

43. The Gir Forests are located in:
    (*a*) Assam (Asom)
    (*b*) Himachal Pradesh
    (*c*) Maharashtra
    (*d*) Gujarat

44. Which of the following pairs is wrong?
    (*a*) Copenhagen – Denmark
    (*b*) Bern   – Sweden
    (*c*) Madrid   – Spain
    (*d*) Prague   – Czech Republic

45. The sea route to India was discovered by:
    (*a*) Columbus   (*b*) Magellan
    (*c*) Vasco da Gama (*d*) Hopkins

46. Mother Teresa was born in:
    (*a*) India   (*b*) Albania
    (*c*) Germany   (*d*) Switzerland

47. Sigmund Freud is associated with:
    (*a*) detective work
    (*b*) leprosy control
    (*c*) birth control
    (*d*) psychology

48. The modern nursing system was started by:
    (*a*) Florence Nightingale
    (*b*) Mother Teresa
    (*c*) Madame Curie
    (*d*) Sharmila Tagore

49. The system of writing and printing for the blind was developed by:
    (*a*) Louis Braille
    (*b*) Robert Wilhelm Bunsen
    (*c*) Sir Humphrey Davy
    (*d*) Marcus Abacus

50. Lumbini is a sacred place of the:
    (*a*) Hindus   (*b*) Christians
    (*c*) Buddhists   (*d*) Jains

PART-C

All questions carry one mark each.

A. Where are the following languages spoken in India? Write the answers in the space given.

51. Konkani _______________________

52. Kurux _______________________

53. Braj _______________________

B. Circle the correct answer.

54. A linguist is a person who knows many languages. [Yes / No]

55. Some languages have no grammar. [Yes / No]

56. All languages have scripts. [Yes / No]

57. Languages that have no script have no grammar. [Yes / No]

58. Languages is inherited, not acquired. [Yes /No]

59. Languages differ in written and spoken forms. [Yes / No]

60. European languages are richer than Indian languages. [Yes / No]

61. In remote past, all human beings spoke only one language. [Yes / No]

C. Following are the words and sentences from Aztec, a language from Mexico. All the words are written without any spaces between them. Read them carefully.

ikalwewe	'his big house'
ikalsolsol	'his old house'
ikalcin	'his little house'
kalmeh	'houses'
petat	'mat'

How would you write the following in this language?

62. his big mats _______________________

63. his little mat _______________________

64. old mat _______________________

65. Suppose A, B, C and D are words in a language which have the possibility of occurring in any order to form a sentence. Also suppose that in this language the minimum length of a sentence is one word and that maximum length is four words. How many sentences can one make from these four words? State only the number of possible sentences.

PART-D

All questions carry one mark each.

A. Fill in the blanks with the correct answer from the choices given below.

66. Instead of ....

   In case of ....

   In spite of ....
   (*a*) his illness he attended the party
   (*b*) driving his car he took a bus
   (*c*) fire, don't use the lift

67. Being late makes him ....

   Ram pushed the door ....

   My job keeps me ....

(*a*) busy   (*b*) open
(*c*) angry

B. Circle the correct answers.

68. I say "I could eat a horse" when I am:
   (*a*) lazy   (*b*) hungry
   (*c*) late

69. I say "I haven't a clue" when I:
   (*a*) am curious
   (*b*) understand nothing
   (*c*) am apologetic

70. I say "You can count on me" when I:
   (*a*) trust someone
   (*b*) dislike someone
   (*c*) support someone

C. Fill in the blanks with the correct answer.

71. Arm is to hand as leg is to ....

72. Beautiful is to beauty as young is to ....

73. I is to 'my' as you is to ....

74. Drive is to drove as eat is to ....

75. One is to two as first is to ....

D. Circle the correct answer.

76. We will visit Udaipur .... Jodhpur during our next vacation.
(*a*) and   (*b*) but
(*c*) so

77. My teeth were hurting .... I made an appointment with the dentist.
(*a*) or   (*b*) so
(*c*) but

78. I wanted to go to the film .... all the tickets were sold out.
(*a*) but   (*b*) so
(*c*) and

79. My brother wanted to buy a novel .... I went to the bookstore after I finished work.
(*a*) or   (*b*) so
(*c*) but

80. After practice, the girls' hockey team said, "We are famished". Famished means
(*a*) tired   (*b*) hungry
(*c*) excited

81. When having a problem it is best to dissect the situation. Dissect means
(*a*) ignore   (*b*) out apart
(*c*) analyze

82. The General tried to instil in his troops the hope of victory. Instil means
(*a*) delay   (*b*) inscribe
(*c*) infuse

83. The scientist was able to evoke powerful emotions from her audience. Evoke means
(*a*) call forth   (*b*) sell
(*c*) calm

84. Do you justify his behaviour .... the function
(*a*) at   (*b*) in

85. Everything in the cupboard .... Ram's.
(*a*) is   (*b*) are

86. No one .... a watch on.
(*a*) have   (*b*) has

87. Each girl brought .... own paper.
(*a*) her   (*b*) their

88. All of the men brought .... wives.
(*a*) his   (*b*) their

89. Everyone of those coats is missing .... buttons.
(*a*) its   (*b*) their

90. None of the children remembered .... lunch.
(*a*) his   (*b*) their

PART–E

Complete the paragraph in 150-200 words. Please do not exceed the word limit.

Learning a foreign language will help me to ....

ANSWERS

1	2	3	4	5	6	7	8	9	10
(*b*)	(*b*)	(*c*)	(*d*)	(*a*)	(*c*)	(*c*)	(*d*)	(*a*)	(*a*)

11	12	13	14	15	16	17	18	19	20
(*b*)	(*d*)	(*d*)	(*c*)	(*b*)	(*a*)	(*d*)	(*c*)	(*b*)	(*d*)

21	22	23	24	25	26	27	28	29	30
(*a*)	(*c*)	(*b*)	(*a*)	(*d*)	(*b*)	(*b*)	(*d*)	(*a*)	(*a*)
31	**32**	**33**	**34**	**35**	**36**	**37**	**38**	**39**	**40**
(*c*)	(*b*)	(*b*)	(*c*)	(*a*)	(*a*)	(*d*)	(*b*)	(*a*)	(*c*)
41	**42**	**43**	**44**	**45**	**46**	**47**	**48**	**49**	**50**
(*d*)	(*a*)	(*d*)	(*b*)	(*c*)	(*b*)	(*d*)	(*a*)	(*a*)	(*c*)

51. Goa

52. Bihar, Jharkhand, Orissa, Madhya Pradesh & Chhattishgarh.

53. Uttar Pradesh.

54. Yes   **55.** No   **56.** No   **57.** No   **58.** No   **59.** Yes

60. No   **61.** No   **62.** ipetatmehwewe   **63.** ipetatcin

64. petatsolsol   **65.** 4! = 24 words   **66.** (*b*) (*c*) (*a*)   **67.** (*c*) (*b*) (*a*)

68	69	70	71	72	73	74	75	76	77
(*b*)	(*b*)	(*c*)	feet	youth	your	ate	second	(*a*)	(*b*)
78	**79**	**80**	**81**	**82**	**83**	**84**	**85**	**86**	**87**
(*a*)	(*b*)	(*a*)	(*c*)	(*c*)	(*a*)	(*a*)	(*a*)	(*a*)	(*a*)
88	**89**	**90**							
(*b*)	(*b*)	(*b*)							

———————

JAWAHARLAL NEHRU UNIVERSITY [JNU]

First Year of 3-Year B.A. [Hons.] in Foreign Languages

Chinese, French, German, Korean, Japanese, Arabic, Persian, Russian and Spanish

Entrance Examination, 2007

PART–A

Answer all the following questions. All questions carry one mark each. Circle the correct answer clearly. If more than one answer is circled, the answer will be marked wrong:

1. The five permanent members of the UN Security Council are:
   (a) Germany, USA, Russia, China, France
   (b) USA, Russia, China, France, UK
   (c) China, France, UK, Russia, Australia
   (d) Germany, Russia, India, USA, China

2. Arrange the following historical events in the correct chronological order starting with the event took place first:
   1. Russian Revolution
   2. French Revolution
   3. Indian Independence
   4. World War II
   (a) 2, 1, 4, 3   (b) 4, 3, 2, 1
   (c) 1, 2, 3, 4   (d) 2, 1, 3, 4

3. Which country occupies almost half the land area of the South American Continent?
   (a) Argentina   (b) Peru
   (c) Brazil   (d) Venezuela

4. Which of these famous leaders was hung to death in 2006?
   (a) Zulfikar Ali Bhutto
   (b) Osama bin Laden
   (c) Saddam Hussain
   (d) Joseph Stalin

5. Which of the following world leaders did *not* attend college in India?
   (a) Zulfikar Ali Bhutto
   (b) Hamid Karzai
   (c) Aung San Suu Kyi
   (d) Benazir Bhutto

6. Which of the following numbers cannot be written in Roman numerals?
   (a) One hundred   (b) Zero
   (c) Five   (d) Thirty-nine

7. During whose reign were the Panchatantra stories written?
   (a) Chandragupta Vikramaditya
   (b) Samudragupta
   (c) Kumaragupta
   (d) Bindusara

8. Kautilya and Panini were the products of which one of the following ancient Indian universities?
   (a) Nalanda   (b) Vikramashila
   (c) Vallabhi   (d) Taxila

9. The official language of the Mughal Court was
   (a) Arabic   (b) Persian
   (c) Urdu   (d) Turkish

10. Which among the following is the oldest Indian language?
    (a) Telugu   (b) Hindi
    (c) Tamil   (d) Punjabi

11. By what name is the river Ganga known in Bangladesh?
    (a) Rupanarayan   (b) Padma
    (c) Bhagirathi   (d) Nubra

12. What is the Booker Prize given for?
    (*a*) Novels   (*b*) Poetry
    (*c*) Art   (*d*) Politics

13. Satish Chandra, Ravi Verma, Anjolie Ela Menon, Arvind Benegal are all:
    (*a*) film directors   (*b*) designers
    (*c*) artists   (*d*) musicians

14. Which of the following is *not* a classical dance form?
    (*a*) Odissi   (*b*) Bharatnatyam
    (*c*) Kuchipudi   (*d*) Ras Leela

15. Which of the following communities celebrates the festival of Navroz in India?
    (*a*) Parsis   (*b*) Coorgis
    (*c*) Khasis   (*d*) Buddhists

16. The Church of Bom Jesus is situated in:
    (*a*) Maharashtra   (*b*) Goa
    (*c*) Kerala   (*d*) Nagaland

17. India's official entry to the Oscars 2007 was:
    (*a*) *Water*
    (*b*) *Lage Raho Munnabhai*
    (*c*) *Rang De Basanti*
    (*d*) *Paheli*

18. The film *Monsoon Wedding* was directed by
    (*a*) Deepa Mehta
    (*b*) Mira Nair
    (*c*) Siddhartha Anand
    (*d*) Aditya Chopra

19. Who was the captain of the Indian Cricket Team when India won the World Cup?
    (*a*) Sunil Gavaskar
    (*b*) Kapil Dev
    (*c*) Mansoor Ali Khan Pataudi
    (*d*) Farooq Engineer

20. How many times has India hosted the Asian Games?
    (*a*) 0   (*b*) 1
    (*c*) 2   (*d*) 3

21. Who was the first Indian to go into space?
    (*a*) Vikram Sarabhai   (*b*) Kalpana Chawla
    (*c*) Sunita Williams   (*d*) Rakesh Sharma

22. India's first atomic reactor is called:
    (*a*) Dhruva   (*b*) Kamini
    (*c*) Purnima I   (*d*) Apsara

23. Who formed the Janata Party and defeated the Congress Party in 1977?
    (*a*) Jayaprakash Narayan
    (*b*) Raj Narain
    (*c*) V.P. Singh
    (*d*) None of the above

24. Which of the following is the main leader of the Narmada Bachao Andolan?
    (*a*) Aamir Khan
    (*b*) Arundhati Roy
    (*c*) Medha Patkar
    (*d*) Sunderlal Bahuguna

25. The Union Budget is presented to the Lok Sabha on:
    (*a*) February 26   (*b*) February 28
    (*c*) March 1   (*d*) March 31

PART–B

Answer all the following questions. All questions carry one mark each. Circle the correct answer clearly. If more than one answer is circled, the answer will be marked wrong:

26. Bach, Schubert, Mahler and Schoneberg were:
    (*a*) writers   (*b*) composers
    (*c*) painters   (*d*) politicians

27. German is not one of the official languages of:
    (*a*) Switzerland   (*b*) Belgium
    (*c*) Austria   (*d*) Liechtenstein

28. Who of the following persons is *not* a German?
    (*a*) Johann Wolfgang V. Goethe
    (*b*) Otto V. Bismarck
    (*c*) Steffi Graf
    (*d*) Philip Roth

29. Which Russian artist has his family house in India?
    (*a*) Andrei Rublev
    (*b*) Nikolai Roerich
    (*c*) Aleksandr Rodchenko
    (*d*) Andrei Sokolov

30. Which Russian leader initiated the Great Purges in which millions of people were executed or exiled?
    (*a*) Lenin
    (*b*) Stalin
    (*c*) Catherine the Great
    (*d*) Nicholas II

31. Who was the first democratically elected President of the Russian Federation?
    (*a*) Mikhail Gorbachov
    (*b*) Vladimir Putin
    (*c*) Boris Yeltsin
    (*d*) Leonid Brezhnev

32. Latin America consists of:
    (*a*) the Caribbean, Mexico, South America
    (*b*) most of South America and the Caribbean
    (*c*) Mexico and South America
    (*d*) most of Central America, South America and the Caribbean

33. Salsa, flamenco and tango are:
    (*a*) musical instruments
    (*b*) dance forms
    (*c*) food items
    (*d*) types of birds

34. What are the official languages of Canada?
    (*a*) Spanish and English
    (*b*) Canadian and Spanish
    (*c*) French and English
    (*d*) Canadian and French

35. The Maghreb countries are:
    (*a*) Algeria, Morocco, Tunisia
    (*b*) Mauritius, Algeria, Egypt
    (*c*) Tunisia, Algeria, Mauritius
    (*d*) Morocco, Egypt, Tunisia

36. Which French writer refused the Nobel Prize for Literature?
    (*a*) Albert Camus
    (*b*) Michel Proust
    (*c*) Jean Paul Sartre
    (*c*) Simone de Beauvoir

37. Which of the following Japanese writers received the Nobel Prize for Literature in 1994?
    (*a*) Asai Ryoi   (*b*) Kazuo Ishiguro
    (*c*) Kensaburo Oe (*d*) Inoue Hisashi

38. The modernisation of Japan began during the rule of
    (*a*) Emperor Taisko (*b*) Emperor Ninko
    (*c*) Emperor Showa   (*c*) Emperor Meiji

39. Who was the Indian Judge who ruled the Japanese Emperor 'not guilty' during the trial of war criminals?
    (*a*) Justice S. Natrajan
    (*d*) Justice Tarun Chatterji
    (*c*) Justice Radha Binod Pal
    (*d*) Justice A. Vardarajan

40. Which was the war that led to the division of Korea into North and South Korea?
    (*a*) World War I
    (*b*) Russo-Japanese War of 1904-05
    (*c*) World War II
    (*d*) None of the above

41. Which of the following is *not* a Korean company?
    (*a*) Sansui   (*b*) Samsung
    (*c*) LG   (*d*) Hyundai

42. The Korean script is called:
    (*a*) Kanji   (*b*) Hangul
    (*c*) Hiragana   (*d*) Katakana

43. The People's Republic of China does *not* include
    (*a*) Mainland China (*b*) Taiwan
    (*c*) Hong Kong   (*d*) Macau

44. Which of the following persons is *not* a Chinese political leader?
    (*a*) Mao Zedong   (*b*) Hu Jintao
    (*c*) Kim II Jong (*d*) Deng Xiaoping

45. Which of the following is *not* a Chinese invention?
    (*a*) Compass   (*b*) Bicycle
    (*c*) Abacus   (*d*) Fireworks

46. Who is the President of Iran?
    (*a*) Mahmud Ahmadi-Nejad
    (*b*) Mogtada Al-Sadr
    (*c*) Nouri Malik
    (*d*) Ahmad Husayn Khudayir as-Samarrai

47. Which of these legendary figures is *not* of Persian origin?

(*a*) Rostam (*b*) Sohraab
(*c*) Zal (*d*) Siegfried

48. Which of the following is **not** a member of the Arab League?
(*a*) Sudan (*b*) Jordan
(*c*) Iraq (*d*) Turkey

49. Which of the following writers from the Arab World won the Nobel Prize for Literature?
(*a*) Naguib Mahfouz
(*b*) Imre Kertesz
(*c*) Wobe Soyinka
(*d*) Jose Saramago

50. Which is the smallest country in the Arab World?
(*a*) Qatar (*b*) Bahrain
(*c*) Kuwait (*d*) Tunisia

PART–C

This part is divided into three Sections. Read the instructions carefully and attempt all the questions. All questions carry one mark each.

Section–I

The questions in this Section are all based on an invented language called Babel. Read each group of examples carefully, paying particular attention to the different forms of words (just as in English there are differences between, e.g., *cat* and *cats* or *call* and *called*). Note also that Babel has no equivalent for the English *the* and *a(n)*, so that, e.g., *King* (in Babel) may be translated as 'the king' or 'a king'. You are advised to work through the questions in the order that they are given.

Example 1:
bats mugs molti 'the king praises the servant'
bats mugans molti 'the king praises the servants'
mugans bats kadonti 'the servant hates kings'
bats totans lubti 'the king likes children'

Translate into English :
51. mugs tots kadti
52. batans totans lubonti

Translate into Babel :
53. The kings praise the servant.

Example 2 :
bats mugans nemolto 'the kings did not praise the servant'
totans gavs pelonto 'the children chased the dog'
tots filans lubto 'the child liked elephants'
filans gavans nelubonti 'elephants do not like dogs'
mugs totans nikto 'the servant washed the children'

Translate into English :
54. gavs fils nepelto
55. bats mugans nemolto

Translate into Babel :
56. The servants did not wash the child.

Section–II

To which languages do the following groups of words belong? Write your answers in the blanks provided:

57. Harakiri Sushi, Sumo, Tsunami:
58. Angst, Ersatz, Kindergarten, Zeppelin:
59. Perestroika, Intelligentsia, Dacha:
60. Laissez faire, Deja vu, Madame:
61. Bazaar, Bungalow, Curry:

Section–III

A. Circle the word which is closest in meaning to the underlined word. If more than one answer is circled, that answer will be marked wrong:

62. The students liked the new teacher because he had an <u>amiable</u> personality.
(*a*) strict (*b*) friendly
(*c*) intelligent (*d*) efficient

63. Many people say that Aishwarya Rai is an <u>ethereal</u> beauty.
(*a*) deadly (*b*) royal
(*c*) heavenly (*d*) unnatural

64. When having a problem, it is best to <u>dissect</u> the situation before taking action.
(*a*) ignore (*b*) analyze
(*c*) define (*d*) postpone

65. The actor was able to <u>evoke</u> powerful emotions from the audience.
   (*a*) call forth   (*b*) disturb
   (*c*) enjoy   (*d*) promote

B. **Circle the correct word from the options given. If more than one answer is circled, that answer will be marked wrong:**

66. Doctor is to patient as lawyer is to:
   (*a*) customer   (*b*) accused
   (*c*) magistrate   (*d*) client

67. Starvation is to nutrition as exhaustion is to:
   (*a*) energy   (*b*) bravery
   (*c*) freshness   (*d*) courage

68. Author is to book as choreographer is to:
   (*a*) drama   (*b*) dance
   (*c*) song   (*d*) painting

69. Bread is to wheat as brick is to:
   (*a*) air   (*b*) fire
   (*c*) clay   (*d*) water

70. Appreciation is to reward as disgrace is to:
   (*a*) allegation   (*b*) crime
   (*c*) guilt   (*d*) punishment

PART–D

Section-I

Fill in the blanks using the correct prepositions. Write your answers in the space provided on the right:

71. The shirt .... the window is very nice.

72. The doctor has been waiting .... the reports.

73. I found the wallet lying .... the drawer.

74. The shop next door .... the bakery is opening tomorrow.

75. I will come and pick you up .... the new car.

76. My mother has invited you all .... dinner.

77. He came home .... many packages.

78. How hard have you studied .... the test?

79. Mother Teresa won the love .... the people.

80. I will have to come .... bus.

Section-II

Insert articles wherever necessary in the following paragraph. Write your answers in the column on the right:

Have you ever heard of Mary Lyon? She was (81) pioneer in (82) education of women. She worked hard so that women could get (83) education to compete with anyone else in the country. She taught in schools in New Hampshire and Massachusetts. In those days, only (84) rich could get (85) good education, especially if they were women. She raised money to open (86) school for middle-class women. In 1837, she opened (87) school in Massachusetts. (88) school was called Mount Holyoke. Today this school has become one of (89) most famous colleges in (90) USA.

Section-III

Read the following passage carefully. Answer the questions given at the end of the passage. Circle the most appropriate option. If more than one option is circled, the answer will be marked wrong:

The Hours That Count in My Life

by Essa Al-Dhaheri

Time is very important in our lives. It organizes our everyday moments. However, time never had any importance in my life untill I received a watch from my father that organized my life and made me more responsible.

It came from Denmark to the UAE jewelry shop in gray box. It weighs 8 oz. It is round in the center with two silver bands that go around my wrist. And all of it is made of silver. This object tells me the importance of time in my life.

I received this gift on a gray-sky day. I had to go to the airport at 9:00 AM to pick up my Uncle Ali and take him to my father's house. However, I was late because I was hanging out with my friends. Later on that day, around 11:00 AM, I remembered my uncle, but I was very late for him. He had left the airport and taken a taxi to my father's house.

I got to my father's house at 2:00 PM on the same day and looked at my angry father's face. I felt ashamed of myself at that moment. After I said hi to my angry father and tired uncle, my father asked me to sit next to him where he handed me this watch which was a gift from him. Then he said, "Essa, did you have fun with your friends today?" I answered, "Yes father and I'm sorry about not picking up my Uncle Ali." He said "What you did was not very nice and you should be sorry for your actions". I was ashamed and said "father I'll never do it again. I promise." He said, "I hope today you learned something important, and this watch will be a reminder for you." He told me to take this watch and use it as an organizer of my life.

I learned a very important lesson from my father: to respect time and never be late to get someone. This watch is important to me, not because of its price, but because of the lesson that I learned from it.

91. When did time become important to Essa?
   (*a*) When he was playing with his friends.
   (*b*) When he lost his watch.
   (*c*) When he received a watch from his father.
   (*d*) When he went to Denmark.
   (*e*) When he met his Uncle Ali.

92. Which of the following is *not* true about Essa's watch?
   (*a*) It came from his father.
   (*b*) It weighed one pound.
   (*c*) It was made of silver.
   (*d*) It will be a reminder to Essa.
   (*e*) It helps to organize his life.

93. Which of the following is true?
   (*a*) Essa was playing with his friends at 2:00 PM
   (*b*) Uncle Ali took a taxi to Essa's father's house.
   (*c*) Essa was supposed to pick up his father at the airport.
   (*d*) Essa never tried to pick up his uncle at the airport.
   (*e*) Essa's uncle had only been on a short trip.

94. What happened last?
   (*a*) Eassa was playing with his friends.
   (*b*) Essa went to meet his Uncle Ali at the airport.
   (*c*) Essa's father talked with him about being on time.
   (*d*) Essa got a watch.
   (*e*) Essa arrived at his father's house.

95. At the end of the story, which was *not* important to Essa?
   (*a*) Pleasing his father
   (*b*) Playing with his friends
   (*c*) The watch
   (*d*) The price of the watch
   (*e*) Being on time and treating people nicely

PART–E

Write a short paragraph (of not more than 150 words) in English or in Hindi on:

I want to learn (the language of your first choice) because.......

(You may discuss the language, the culture, the history of the area where the language of your choice is spoken.)

Please stick to the word limit.

ANSWERS

1	2	3	4	5	6	7	8	9	10
(*b*)	(*a*)	(*c*)	(*c*)	(*d*)	(*b*)	(*d*)	(*d*)	(*b*)	(*c*)

11	12	13	14	15	16	17	18	19	20
(*b*)	(*a*)	(*c*)	(*d*)	(*a*)	(*b*)	(*d*)	(*b*)	(*b*)	(*b*)
21	22	23	24	25	26	27	28	29	30
(*d*)	(*d*)	(*a*)	(*d*)	(*b*)	(*b*)	(*d*)	(*d*)	(*b*)	(*b*)
31	32	33	34	35	36	37	38	39	40
(*c*)	(*d*)	(*b*)	(*c*)	(*a*)	(*d*)	(*c*)	(*d*)	(*c*)	(*c*)
41	42	43	44	45	46	47	48	49	50
(*a*)	(*b*)	(*b*)	(*c*)	(*b*)	(*a*)	(*d*)	(*d*)	(*a*)	(*b*)

51. The servant likes children

52. Kings like the child

53. Batans mug molti

54. Elephant did not care of dogs.

55. The king did not praise the servant.

56. Mugans totans nikolto

57. Japanese

58. German

59. Russian

60. French

61. Hindi

62. Friendly

63	64	65	66	67	68	69	70	71	72
(*c*)	(*b*)	(*a*)	(*d*)	(*a*)	(*b*)	(*c*)	(*c*)	on	for
73	74	75	76	77	78	79	80	81	82
in	to	by	for	with	for	of	by	a	the
83	84	85	86	87	88	89	90	91	92
the	a	a	the	a	the	the	the	(*c*)	(*b*)
93	94	95							
(*b*)	(*d*)	(*e*)							

JAWAHARLAL NEHRU UNIVERSITY (JNU)

First Year of 3-Year B.A. (Hons.) in Foreign Languages

Chinese, French, German, Korean, Japanese, Arabic, Persian, Russian and Spanish

Entrance Examination, 2006

PART–A

Answer the following questions by selecting the most appropriate one from (*a*) to (*d*):

1. Which of the following is not an Arab State?
   - (*a*) Qatar
   - (*b*) Tunisia
   - (*c*) Iran
   - (*d*) Bahrain

2. What was the official language of India till the end of Mughal Rule?
   - (*a*) Urdu
   - (*b*) Farsi
   - (*c*) Arabic
   - (*d*) Hindi

3. Which form of musical worship was popularised by the Indian- born Persian poet, Amir Khusro?
   - (*a*) Kirtan
   - (*b*) Bhakti
   - (*c*) Sufi
   - (*d*) Bhajan

4. Who was the President of the USSR when it disintegrated?
   - (*a*) Vladimir Putin
   - (*b*) Mikhail Gorbachov
   - (*c*) Boris Yeltsin
   - (*d*) Leonid Brezhnev

5. The Latin American country sharing border with the United States is:
   - (*a*) Mexico
   - (*b*) Toronto
   - (*c*) Los Angeles
   - (*d*) Nicaragua

6. The second official language in the United States is:
   - (*a*) Spanish
   - (*b*) French
   - (*c*) German
   - (*d*) Dutch

7. The river Amazon flows through:
   - (*a*) Zambia
   - (*b*) Zimbabwe
   - (*c*) Zurich
   - (*d*) Brazil

8. What was France known as during the Roman Empire?
   - (*a*) Galles
   - (*b*) Gaulle
   - (*c*) Gayle
   - (*d*) Francia

9. Which of these countries does not border Germany?
   - (*a*) Poland
   - (*b*) France
   - (*c*) Italy
   - (*d*) Austria

10. Goa had been colonized by the:
    - (*a*) British
    - (*b*) French
    - (*c*) Americans
    - (*d*) Portuguese

11. The famous cultivated plant which developed in China is:
    - (*a*) tea
    - (*b*) cotton
    - (*c*) coffee
    - (*d*) orange

12. Green revolution is:
    - (*a*) revolution in chemical industry
    - (*b*) revolution in Pakistan
    - (*c*) revolution in Greenland
    - (*d*) revolution in agriculture yield

13. Which one of the following is a form of Japanese theatre?
    - (*a*) Ikebana
    - (*b*) Noh
    - (*c*) Tatani
    - (*d*) Karaoke

14. Which Oscar winning film was based on the life and times of the Asian ruler Pu Yi?
    - (*a*) The Last Samurai
    - (*b*) Dragon King
    - (*c*) King and I
    - (*d*) The Last Emperor

15. What is the name of the Iranian Parliament?
(*a*) Parliman   (*b*) Shura
(*c*) Lilas   (*d*) Majlis

16. Which ruler had inspired Ferdowsi to write *Shahnamah*?
(*a*) Muhammad Ghori
(*b*) Jalaluddin Muhammad Akbar
(*c*) Mahmud Ghaznavi
(*d*) Timur

17. Strasbourg is situated in:
(*a*) Luxemburg   (*b*) France
(*c*) Germany   (*d*) Switzerland

18. Which of these is a kind of popular Latin American dance form?
(*a*) The Break
(*b*) The Tango
(*c*) The Ball
(*d*) The Waltz

19. Who is currently the President of France?
(*a*) Francois Mitterrand
(*b*) Charles de Gaulle
(*c*) Valery Giscard d'Estaing
(*d*) Jacques Chirac

20. Chipko Movement is related to:
(*a*) preventing soil pollution
(*b*) forest conservation
(*c*) preserving threatened species
(*d*) None of the above

PART–B

Directions: (Qs. Nos. 21-30): *In the following passages, certain words have been omitted. Identify the missing words:*

(*a*) Of all the untamed creatures, sparrows seem to love living near the man the most. Wherever **(21)** .... new township springs up, the sparrows follow **(22)** .... no time. They even build **(23)** .... nests inside homes and **(24)** .... they feel sure will not **(25)** .... harmed, they will even come and eat out of your hand.

(*b*) The spread of AIDS in the urban areas has given rise to **(26)** .... number of ethical and legal questions. Should a person who is HIV positive **(27)** .... terminated for services? Should there be **(28)** .... insurance cover for the patients suffering **(29)** .... AIDS? Should **(30)** .... spouse have the right to know that his partner is an AIDS case?

Give short answers to the following questions:

31. Sashimi is a delicacy of which country?

32. When did the Cuban Revolution take place?

33. Who is the author of *Panchatantra*?

34. Which is the national sport of Korea?

35. For which of her novels, later made into a film, did Ruth Prawer Jhabwala win the Booker Prize in 1975?

36. Who is Mona Lisa?

37. What is the significance of 3rd October, 1990 in German history?

38. In the context of Germany, what does 'Holocaust' mean?

39. What is the official name of Germany?

40. What is Maastricht Treaty?

41. To which language family does Persian belong?

42. What was the name of the space shuttle that crashed on February 1, 2003, with astronaut Kalpana Chawla amongst others, on board?

43. Who is Sania Mirza?

44. What do Mikhail Gorbachov, the 14th Dalai Lama and Kofi Annan have in common?

45. Which is the first month of the Indian calendar?

Complete the following sentences:

46. The playwright who wrote *Hayavandane* is ....

47. The Indo-Anglian writer who wrote *Untouchable* is ....

48. The author of *Great Expectations* is ....

49. The capital of Senegal is ....

50. The currency of Portugal is ....

51. The longest river of Europe is ....

52. The portion of the earth and its environment, within which life is manifested is called ....

53. .... defeated Sultan Ibrahim Lodi in the First Battle of Panipat in 1526.

54. India became sovereign democratic republic on ....

55. Mother Teresa was a national of ....

56. Hugo Chavez is the President of ....

57. .... is the highest building in the world.

58. .... is the largest ocean.

59. The invasion of Kuwait by Iraq caused the .... War.

60. The sportsman who fights a bull in Spain is called ....

61. Chess originated in ....

62. The most popular festival of ancient Iran is called ....

63. Mirza Ghalib, a bilingual poet, wrote in Urdu and ....

64. The novel, *The Golden Gate is* written by ....

65. .... is the chief of the Gods in Greek mythology.

66. The architect of the city of Chandigarh is ....

67. The capital of Iraq is ....

68. The largest artificial lake in India is ....

69. Buddha attained enlightenment under .... Tree.

70. The famous philosopher, ... was Plato's disciple.

71. The hardest gemstone is ....

72. Red blood corpuscles are formed in the ....

73. The fastest growing plant in the world is ....

74. The acid turns litmus paper to .... colour.

75. The nearest planet from Sun is ....

76. The Land of the Midnight Sun is ....

77. The Chief Election Commissioner of India is appointed by ....

78. The Finance Commission is constituted after every .... years.

79. .... composed the tune to 'Twinkle twinkle, little star'.

80. The World Health Day is celebrated on ....

PART–C

Give one word each for the following:

81. The study and description of books, or descriptive list of books.

82. The art of map making.

83. One who makes or compiles dictionary.

84. A period of 1000 years.

Expand the following abbreviations:

85. BBC

86. NCERT

87. GATT

Give the meanings of the following idiomatic expressions:

88. In black and white

89. Stone's throw

90. Ins and outs

91. At sixes and sevens

Complete the following sentences:

92. In 1977 .... was the first person to address the UN General Assembly in Hindi?

93. .... was the first writer in English to be awarded the Sahitya Akademi Award in 1961?

94. The last ruler of the Mughal dynasty was ....

95. .... was the founder of Jainism.

96. India's first satellite was launched in the year ....

97. A social practice called .... was abolished by Lord William Bentinck by 'Regulation 17' of 1829.

98. An Air A-India plane called .... exploded on the Irish sea on its flight from Canada to India.

99. *Jataka* tales were written in an ancient language called ....

100. Five boys were climbing up a hill. Jayant was following Hari. Ram was ahead of Govind. Krishna was between Govind and Hari. They were climbing up in a row. Who was the second?

101. The odd one in the series of words—Mercury, Moon, Jupiter, Venus, Pluto is ....

102. If 'air' is called 'water', 'water' is called 'sky' 'sky' is called 'blue', 'blue' is called 'rain', 'rain' is called 'dust' and 'dust' is called 'green', where do the fish live in ....

103. If TOP = 201516; POT = 161520; TAR = 20118; then RAT is ....

104. Which number should come next in this series? 1, 4, 9, 16, 25, ...

105. The brother-in-law of my mother's only brother is closely related to me. Who is he? ....

Go through the languages in Column A and Column B, and answer the questions given at the end:

Column A	Column B
Laulan	I sing
Laulat	You sing
Laulavi	She/He sings
Laulamme	We sing
Yuon	I drink
Yuot	You drink
Yuovi	She/He drinks
Yuovat	They drink

How will you write the following words?

106. I :

107. You :

108. He/She :

109. They sing :

110. We drink :

PART–D

Read the following passage carefully and answer the questions (111 to 115) without repeating the words from the text:

Punctuality is a necessary habit in all public affairs of a civilized society. Without it nothing could ever be brought to a conclusion, everything would be in a state of chaos. Only in a sporsely populated rural community it is possible to disregard it. In ordinary living, there can be some tolerance of unpunctuality. The intellectual, who is working on some abstruse problem has everything, coordinated and organized for the matter in hand. He is therefore forgiven, if late for the dinner party. But people are often reproached for unpunctuality when their only fault is cutting things fine. It is hard for energetic, quick-minded people to waste time, so they are often tempted to finish a job before setting out to keep an appointment. If no accidents occur on the way, like punctured tyres, diversion of traffic, sudden descent of fog, they will be on time, they are often more industrious useful citizens than those who are never late. The over-punctual can as much be a trial to others as the unpunctual. The guest who arrives half an hour too soon is the greatest nuisance. Some friends of my family had this irritating habit. The only thing to do was to ask them to come half an hour later than the other guests. Then they arrived just when we wanted them. If you are catching a train, it is always better to be comfortably early than even a fraction of a minute too late. Although being early may mean wasting a little time, this will be less than if you miss and have to wait an hour or so for the next one. And you avoid the frustration of arriving at the very moment when the train is drawing out of the station and being unable to get on it.

111. Why is punctuality necessary in a civilized society?

112. What are the dangers of leaving the bare minimum of time for appointments?

113. The over-punctual can be as much a trial to others as the unpunctual. Why?

114. Why did the author's family ask some guests to come half an hour later than others?

115. Why, according to the author, is it better to wait on the platform before the train arrives?

Write four sentences each on the following:

116. Sachin Tendulkar

117. The 18th Commonwealth Games

118. Mother Teresa

119. Bird flu

120. Why do you want to learn a foreign language?

Observe the Language A and its translation into English:

Language A	English
TMAN	I buy
AKAN	You wish
MAN	To buy
SLAP	He sleeps
KAN	To wish
KIL	I see
AWAL	You say
IL	To see
LAP	To sleep
JU	He drinks
AL	To say
U	To drink
AWU	You drink
KAL	I say
TLAP	I sleep

Translate the English words given below into the Language A:

English	Language A

121. You

122. I

123. He

124. He wishes

125. You sleep

ANSWERS

1	2	3	4	5	6	7	8	9	10
(c)	(b)	(c)	(b)	(a)	(a)	(d)	(b)	(c)	(d)

11	12	13	14	15	16	17	18	19	20
(a)	(d)	(b)	(d)	(d)	(c)	(b)	(b)	(d)	(b)

21. a **22.** in **23.** their **24.** then **25.** be **26.** a **27.** be **28.** an **29.** from **30.** the

31. Sashimi is a Japanese delicacy.

32. 1959

33. Vishnu Sharma

34. Tae Kwondo

35. Heat and Dust

36. Mona Lisa is a famous painting painted by Leonardo Da Vinci.

37. The five East Germany states officially joined the Federal Republic of Germany on 3rd October 1990.

38. Putting people in gas chamber and killing them.

39. Bundes-republic Deutschland (Federal Republic of Germany).

40. On February 7 the treaty for the creation of European Union was signed in Maastricht.

41. Indo-Europian language family.

42. Columbia.
43. She is flag bearer of India female tennis.
44. Mikhail Gorbachov-1990, the 14th Dalai Lama 1989 and Kofi Annan 2001 all are the winner of Nobel Peace Prize.
45. Chaitra
46. Girish Karnad
47. Mulk Raj Anand
48. Charles Dickens
49. Dakar
50. Escudo
51. Ob
52. Biosphere
53. Babar
54. 26th January 1950
55. Macedonia
56. Venezuela
57. Burj Dubai
58. Pacific ocean
59. Gulf war
60. Bull fighter (Metador)
61. India
62. Happy Yalda Shab ee chelan (night of fortieth).
63. Persian
64. Vikram Seth
65. Zeus
66. Le Corbusier (French)
67. Baghdad
68. Jai Samand Lake in Udaipur
69. Bodhi
70. Aristotle
71. Diamond
72. Bone Marrow
73. Bamboo
74. Blue to red
75. Mercury
76. Norway
77. President of India
78. Five
79. Wolfgand A madeus Mozart
80. 7 April
81. Catalogue
82. Cartography
83. Lexicographer
84. Millenium
85. BBC—British Broadcasting Corporation
86. NCERT—National Council of Education Research and Training
87. GATT—General Agreement on Trade and Tariff
88. In writing
89. too close
90. Inside picture
91. At proper order
92. Atal Behari Vajpayee
93. R.K. Narayan
94. Bahadur Shah Zaffar
95. First Tirthankar Rishabh
96. Aryabhatta on April 19, 1975
97. Sati Pratha
98. Kanishka
99. Pali
100. Govind
101. Moon, all others are planets
102. Sky
103. 18120, as R = 18, A = 1 and T = 20
104. 36, a series is made of square of consectutive numbers
105. Father
106. N
107. T
108. Vi
109. Laulavat

110. Yuomme

111. Punctuality is necessary in a civilized society to avoid chaos in the society. To follow a system and short out the problems this trend must be followed by each and every person.

112. If one is unable to reach in time for an appointment he/she may miss a grand opportunity.

113. They may create nuisance by reaching before time when no one was expecting them.

114. They have an habit of coming half an hour before time.

115. In that case you can't miss the train.

116. **Sachin Tendulkar:** One of the greatest cricketer of this era who can be part of any best team of any time. A legend in his own life having records of maximum runs in ODI and maximum hundreds in both forms (one day/test matches) of cricket. A great entertainer and a person also with a golden arm.

117. The 18th Commonwealth games was held in Melbourne between March 15th and March 26. The site for the opening and closing ceremonies was the Melbourne cricket ground. The mascot for the games was Kork, a red tailed black cock too. For the first time they appointed a goodwill partner, Plan International Australia.

118. **Mother Teresa:** An Albanian by birth was born on August 26, 1910 and died on September 5, 1997. She was a Roman Catholic nun who founded the Missionaries of Charity. She was Nobel Peace Prize winner in 1979 for humanitarian work.

119. **Bird Flu:** It is also known as Avian influenza. It is caused by virus adopted to birds. The virus is known as Influenza. A virus, due to this a large chunck of birds (Hen) were killed in different part of world.

120. I wanted to learn a foreign language to know about the culture, civilisation of that country. It will also provide an employment in different sectors of economy. It will helpful in many more things like intellectual curiosity, travel and secret communication.

121. A

122. T

123. S

124. SKAN

125. ALAP

JAWAHARLAL NEHRU UNIVERSITY [JNU]

First Year of 3-Year B.A. [Hons.] in Foreign Languages

Chinese, French, German, Korean, Japanese, Arabic, Persian, Russian and Spanish

Entrance Examination, 2005

PART–A

Answer the following questions by selecting the most appropriate one from (a) to (d):

1. The South Korean Airlines that flies to Delhi is:
   - (a) Asian Airlines
   - (b) Arirang Airlines
   - (c) Air Korea
   - (d) Korean Airways

2. The author of *Don Quixote* is:
   - (a) Cervantes
   - (b) Shakespeare
   - (c) Gabriel Garcia Marques
   - (d) Tolstoy

3. The expedition of Christopher Columbus was under the royal patronage of:
   - (a) France
   - (b) Italy
   - (c) Portugal
   - (d) Spain

4. Who found the sea route to India?
   - (a) George Luis Broges
   - (b) Salvador Dali
   - (c) Vasco de Gama
   - (d) Afnasii Nikitin

5. Iran is situated in:
   - (a) East Asia
   - (b) West Asia
   - (c) North Asia
   - (d) South Asia

6. Tehran is the capital of:
   - (a) Uzbekistan
   - (b) Tajikistan
   - (c) Iran
   - (d) Afghanistan

7. In which script is Persian written?
   - (a) Arabic
   - (b) Cyrillic
   - (c) Greek
   - (d) Roman

8. Which of these is the highest rank in the Indian Army?
   - (a) Brigadier
   - (b) General
   - (c) Colonel
   - (d) Major General

9. Green, Oolong, Pekoe are different names of :
   - (a) coffee
   - (b) tea
   - (c) cocoa
   - (d) ghee

10. Which of the following is not a primary colour?
    - (a) Red
    - (b) Blue
    - (c) Green
    - (d) Yellow

11. *Dr. Zhivago* was written by:
    - (a) A. Solzhenitsyn
    - (b) B. Pasternak
    - (c) M. Sholokhov
    - (d) A. Chekhov

12. The national animal of China is:
    - (a) the dragon
    - (b) the eagle
    - (c) the giant panda
    - (d) the aligator

13. Who was the first and only Muslim woman ruler who ever presided over the throne of Delhi?
    - (a) Razia Sultan
    - (b) Sardari Begum
    - (c) Shah Bano
    - (d) Noorjehan

14. Algeria, Libya and Tunisia belong to the continent of:
    - (a) Europe
    - (b) Africa
    - (c) Latin America
    - (d) Asia

15. In which Indian hill station was the first ropeway constructed?
    - (a) Ootacamund
    - (b) Matheran
    - (c) Dalhousie
    - (d) Darjeeling

16. The capital of Austria is:
   (*a*) Prague   (*b*) Canberra
   (*c*) Budapest   (*d*) Vienna

17. Who is a famous German philosopher?
   (*a*) Jacques Derrida
   (*b*) Karl Popper
   (*c*) Theodor Fontane
   (*d*) Immanuel Kant

18. Who among the following is a well-known personality of Indian music?
   (*a*) M. F. Husain   (*b*) Shivpujan Sahay
   (*c*) Amartya Sen   (*d*) Bismillah Khan

19. 'Charminar' is situated in:
   (*a*) Chennai   (*b*) Mumbai
   (*c*) Kolkata   (*d*) Hyderabad

20. The official name of North Korea is:
   (*a*) People's Democratic Republic of Korea
   (*b*) Democratic People's Republic of Korea
   (*c*) Republic of Korea
   (*d*) People's Republic of Korea

PART–B

Directions: (Qs. Nos. 21-30): *In the following passage certain words have been omitted. Identify the missing words:*

Education is something **(21)** .... which I am destined **(22)** .... reflect. As a teacher, I **(23)** .... ignore what is happening in the domain **(24)** .... education. **(25)** .... the process of self-reflection, I am required **(26)** .... cope **(27)** .... many pertinent questions: **(28)** .... am I teaching? How do I relate to **(29)** .... students? Is teaching an exercise **(30)** .... power, or is it an art of self-relatedness?

Give short answers to the following questions:

31. Who is the present Chancellor of Germany ?

32. When did Britain hand over Hong Kong to China?

33. Which is the longest river in South America?

34. Which country was known as the 'Hermit Kingdom'?

35. What is a Mascot?

36. What is the Richter scale?

37. What is Flamenco?

38. What is a Tsunami?

39. Who is the President of the Russian Federation?

40. Who discovered Penicillin?

41. Which German music composer was deaf?

42. What is the Western name of Taiwan?

43. Which is the world's biggest dam?

44. What are natural geysers?

45. On whose life is the film 'Aviator' based?

Complete the following sentences :

46. The 2006 Olympics will be held in -----.

47. Clouds float in the atmosphere because of their low ----.

48. The year 2005 is designated by the UN as the International Year of -----.

49. India's first Formula 1 Grand Prix driver is --------.

50. Sania Mirza comes from the city of ----- .

51. In 2010, Delhi will host ---- Games.

52. Arthur Miller was awarded ----- for his book *Death of a Salesman.*

53. Amir Khusro is famous for his compositions and writings in -----.

54. The official language of Afghanistan is ----.

55. Leonardo da Vinci was from ------.

56. The city of Pisa is famous for its ----.

57. The city of Frankfurt is situated on the river -----.

58. Brecht wrote his works in ----.

59. The popular slogan Jai Hind was coined by --------.

60. The indigenous religion of China is -----.

61. The rivers Euphrates and Tigris flow within the territory of ----.

62. The indigenous name of Burma is -----.

63. Tamil was recently accorded the status of -----.

64. The official languages of Canada are -----.

65. Jean Paul Sartre is a ----- philosopher.

66. Garba dance is a dance style from -----.

67. CRY stands for ------.

68. The official language of Tajikistan is -----.

69. The first printing press was invented by ----.

70. Kanchenjunga is a peak in the ------.

71. Kaziranga national park is a ------- reserve.

72. The Indian national calendar was adopted in ----.

73. The first to use artillery in medieval India was -----.

74. The maximum number of World Heritage sites are found in -----.

75. The year 2005 is the ----- for the Chinese.

76. The number that cannot be noted in Roman numerals is -----.

77. *Wings of Fire* is a book written by -----.

78. The Statue of Liberty was gifted to the USA by -----.

79. A numismatist collects -----.

80. South America is known as -----.

PART–C

Give one word each for the following:

81. The study of stars and planets.

82. The study of forces such as heat, light, sound, gravity, etc.

83. Flesh-eating animals.

84. The study of environment.

Expand the following abbreviations:

85. INA

86. UNDP

87. SAARC

Give the meaning of the following idiomatic expressions:

88. To rule the roost

99. To keep track of something

90. To beat about the bush

91. To keep one's word

Complete the following sentences:

92. Tagore won the Nobel Laureate for his work -----.

93. Binary codes used in computer sciences are made up of --------.

94. Booker Prize is given annually to the best work of ---- by a British or Commonwealth writer.

95. The number that comes next in the series 12, 20, 30, 42, 56 is ------.

96. Reggae is an African-Caribbean style of music developed in ------.

97. The book by R. K. Narayan in which R.K. Laxman's cartoons had first appeared is -----.

98. Earthquakes are caused by -----.

99. Mahatma Gandhi largely wrote in ------ language.

100. Eureka in Greek means -----.

101. The odd one in the series of words Rain, Fog, Smoke, Mist is ------.

102. CABIR, the world's first mobile phone virus was born in -------.

103. Mirages are due to ------.

104. Vitamin D is essential for ------.

105. Illegal goods are known as ------.

Go through the sentences of the Language A and Language B, and answer the questions given at the end:

Language A	Language B
I am swimming	RAH KLAM
He is also swimming	TAM KLAM SNE
My friend knows swimming	RAHI GAMI KLAM PRE
My friend knows his brother	RAHI GAMI TAMI DARI PRE
His brother works here	TAMI DARI TRU FOR
I am not working	RAH TRU JON
She knows this work	TAN KAI TRU PRE
I know this poem by heart	RAH KAI BOL IK PRE

We all like this poem	SAH-SAH KAI BOL PLI
We work in the morning	SAH TRU HI
He knows me	TAM PRE RAH
She is reading a poem	TAN BOL KMI

How will you write the following sentences?

Language A	Language B
106. I like swimming	
107. He knows this poem	
108. She works in the morning	
109. I also know this poem	
110. We know all the poems	

PART–D

Read the following passage carefully and answer the questions (111 to 115) given below it:

Catharsis - giving vent to anger is sometimes extolled as a way of handling anger. The popular theory holds that 'it makes you feel better'. But as Zillmann's findings suggest, there is an argument against catharsis. Since the 1950s psychologists started to test the effects of catharsis experimentally and found that giving vent to anger did little or nothing to dispel it. There may be some specific conditions under which lashing out in anger does work : when it is expressed directly to the person who is its target, when it restores a sense of control or rights an injustice. Venting anger is, however, one of the worst ways to cool down: outbursts of rage typically pump up the emotional brain's arousal, leaving people feeling more angry, not less. It is far more effective if people first cool down, and then, in a more constructive or assertive manner, confront the person to settle their dispute.

111. What is catharsis? What does popular theory say about catharsis?

112. What are the conditions under which anger works?

113. Why is the popular theory about catharsis incorrect?

114. Why doesn't anger disappear when it is expressed?

115. What is the best way to deal with anger?

Write four sentences about the following:

116. C. V. Raman

117. B. R. Ambedkar

118. Arundhati Roy

119. Medha Patkar

120. Vinoba Bhave

Go through the words of the Language A and Language B, and answer the questions given at the end:

Language A	Language B
$* + \exists =$	अपना
$\perp = \neq$	काम
$> \forall \supseteq$	रील
$\leq \downarrow > = \perp^\lrcorner$	सुराख
$\perp^\sim \downarrow +^\sim A \approx =$	गुड़िया
$+^\sim \downarrow +^\sim A \approx =$	बुढ़िया
$\leq B \exists = \exists = \approx \perp$	सेनानायक
$> \in \exists =$	रटना
$\oplus = \approx$	चाय
$* \cup \leq >$	अवसर
$+^\lrcorner \supseteq \not\subset^\sim = \approx \perp$	फलदायक
$\neq B \supseteq = \exists \perp^\sim > \forall$	मेलानगरी
$\leq \times \exists =$	सोना

How will you write the following words?

Language B	Language A
121. गिरगिट	
122. धोना	
123. खराब	
124. फुलवारी	
125. जलपान	

ANSWERS

1	2	3	4	5	6	7	8	9	10
(a)	(a)	(d)	(c)	(b)	(c)	(a)	(b)	(b)	(d)

11	12	13	14	15	16	17	18	19	20
(b)	(c)	(a)	(b)	(d)	(d)	(d)	(d)	(d)	(b)

21. in **22.** and **23.** can't **24.** of

25. In **26.** to **27.** with **28.** why

29. the **30.** of

31. Gerhard Schroder

32. June 30, 1997

33. Amazon

34. Korea

35. Mascot is used to represent group with a common public identity.

36. Intensity of Earthquake.

37. Flemenco is a genuine Spanish art which has three things dance, song and music.

38. Tsunami is giant oceanic waves caused by Earthquake or Volcanic eruption.

39. Vladimir Putin

40. Alexander Flemming

41. Beethoven Ludwig Van

42. For masa

43. Itaipu Dam on border of Brazil and Paraguay.

44. These throws up jets of hot water and steam at regular intervals.

45. Howard Hughes

46. Turin, Italy (winter olympics)

47. density

48. Sports and Physical Education

49. Narayan Karthikeyan

50. Hyderabad

51. Commonwealth games

52. Pulitzer Prize

53. Braj Bhasha

54. Poshto

55. Italy

56. Minarat of Pisa

57. Moin

58. German

59. Subhash Chandra Bose

60. Taoism

61. Iraq

62. Myanmar

63. Official Language

64. English and French

65. French

66. Gujarat

67. Children Relief and You

68. Tajik (a variety of person)

69. Johannes Gutenberg

70. Himalayan

71. Biosphere

72. 1957

73. Babar

74. Italy-39 sites

75. Year of Rooster

76. Zero

77. A.P.J. Abdul Kalam

78. France

79. Stamp's (Postal)

80. Latin America

81. Astronomy

82. Mechanics

83. Carnivorous

84. Ecology

85. INA—Indian National Army.

86. UNDP—United Nation Development Programme.
87. SAARC—South Asian Association for Regional Cooperation.
88. Domineer over others
89. Watching very curiously
90. To talk irrelevantly, not coming to point.
91. Fulfilling Promise
92. Gitanjali
93. 0 and 1
94. English
95. 72 as the series increases with 8, 10, 12, 14, 16 and so on.
96. Jamaica
97. Malgudi Days
98. Movement of Plates
99. Hindustani
100. to get
101. Rain
102. 1997
103. refraction of light
104. skin
105. smuggled goods
106. RAH KLAM PLI
107. TAM PRE KAI BOL
108. TAN TRU HI
109. RAH KAI BOL PRE SNE
110. SAH PRE BOL-BOL
111. Catharsis is a way of handling anger. The popular theory holds that it makes you feel better.
112. Anger works when it is expressed directly to the person who is its target, or when it restores a sense of control or rights on injustice.
113. Since 1950s phychologist started to test the effect of catharsis experimentally and found that giving vent to anger did little or nothing to dispel it.

114. When anger is expressed it typically pump up the emotional brains arousal leaving people feeling more angry.
115. The best way of deal with angle is first cool down and then in a more constructor or assertive manner confront the person to settle dispute.
116. **C.V. Raman—** A great Indian Physicist who was awarded Noble Prize in Physics in 1930. He proposed the theory of scattering of light and the effect was named after him, he got knighthood in 1929. He became the director of Raman Research Institute in 1947. The day on which Sir C.V. Raman discovered the Raman effect that is 28th February is observed as National Science Day in India.
117. **B.R. Ambedkar—**(1891-1956) Indian Jurist Social worker, politician, writer, educationist emancipator of the 'untouchables' and crusader for social justice. Drafted the Indian Constitution. Minister in Nehru's Cabinet and awarded Bharat Ratna in 1990.
118. **Arundhati Roy—** (1960) The first Indian author to win Booker Prize (The God of Small Things) Environmentalist winner of Sydney Peace Prize 2004.
119. **Medha Patekar (1956)—**Indian social activist, environmentalist, fire brand leader of Save Narmada Movement, Right Civelihood Award.
120. **Vinoba Bhave—**(1895-1982) Disciple of Mahatma Gandhi, who led the Bhoodan movement, Bharat Ratna 1983, first Magsaysay Award winner.
121. $\perp \tilde{A} > \overparen{\perp A} \in$
122. $B = \exists =$
123. $\perp^{\lrcorner} > = +\sim$
124. $+^{\lrcorner} \downarrow \supseteq = > \forall$
125. $\oplus^{\sim} \supseteq + = \exists$

JAWAHARLAL NEHRU UNIVERSITY (JNU)

First Year of 3-Year B.A. (Hons.) in Foreign Languages

Chinese, French, German, Korean, Japanese, Arabic, Persian, Russian and Spanish

Entrance Examination, 2004

PART–A-1

Answer the following questions by selecting the most appropriate one from (*a*) to (*d*):

1. Lyon is a:
   (*a*) French bread   (*b*) French cheese
   (*c*) French river   (*d*) French city

2. Which language did Buddha preach in?
   (*a*) Pali   (*b*) Apabhramsa
   (*c*) Sauraseni   (*d*) Magadhi

3. With which journal Premchand was associated?
   (*a*) Sahitya   (*b*) Panchjanya
   (*c*) Hans   (*d*) Shiksha

4. Who is hailed as the 'God of Medicine' by practitioners of Ayurveda?
   (*a*) Charaka   (*b*) Susruta
   (*c*) Chyavana   (*d*) Patanjali

5. Who wrote *Gulag Archipelago*?
   (*a*) Tolstoy   (*b*) Navokov
   (*c*) Dostoevsky   (*d*) Solzhenitsyn

6. The only snake in the world that builds nest is found in India. Which one is it?
   (*a*) Viper   (*b*) Python
   (*c*) King Cobra   (*d*) Grass snake

7. The shortest day in Australia will be:
   (*a*) June 21   (*b*) December 22
   (*c*) September 22   (*d*) March 23

8. Which of the following is the oldest atomic power station in India?
   (*a*) Kalpakkam   (*b*) Tarapur
   (*c*) Narora   (*d*) Kota

9. Mixed farming involves:
   (*a*) growing more than one crop on a farm
   (*b*) growing specialised crops
   (*c*) growing crops and keeping livestock
   (*d*) intensive and extensive agriculture

10. The concept of overpopulation is based on the:
   (*a*) availability of food in the area
   (*b*) absolute number of people in an area
   (*c*) density of population in that area
   (*d*) supporting capacity of the land in terms of varied human operations

11. The group of languages spoken by the largest number of people in India is:
   (*a*) Austro-Asiatic   (*b*) Indo-Aryan
   (*c*) Dravidian   (*d*) None of these

12. The Lakshadweep Islands are situated in:
   (*a*) Indian Ocean   (*b*) Arabian Sea
   (*c*) Bay of Bengal   (*d*) None of these

13. Light from the sun reaches us in:
   (*a*) 8 minutes   (*b*) 8 seconds
   (*c*) 8 hours   (*d*) one year

14. The World Trade Organisation is set up to take over the functions of which of the following?
   (*a*) IMF   (*b*) GATT
   (*c*) ECA   (*d*) ECOSOC

15. Ajanta Paintings depict scenes from the:
   (*a*) Ramayana   (*b*) Mahabharata
   (*c*) Jatakas   (*d*) Upanishadas

16. The concept of Third World Countries implies:
  (*a*) the developed countries
  (*b*) the developing countries
  (*c*) block led by USA, UK, etc.
  (*d*) None of these

17. What is depicted in Manipuri dance?
  (*a*) Mahabharata   (*b*) Ramlila
  (*c*) Village Life   (*d*) Raslila

18. What is the household name for sodium bicarbonate?
  (*a*) Salt   (*b*) Soda
  (*c*) Sugar   (*d*) Baking powder

19. What term is used for the study of human races?
  (*a*) Psychology   (*b*) Anthology
  (*c*) Geology   (*d*) Anthropology

20. To which country did 'Aesop's Fables' belong?
  (*a*) Greece   (*b*) Rome
  (*c*) Germany   (*d*) India

21. What transmits typhoid?
  (*a*) Contaminated food or water
  (*b*) Vehicle exhaust
  (*c*) Smoke
  (*d*) Physical touch

22. The capital of Tajikistan is:
  (*a*) Dushanbe   (*b*) Tashkent
  (*c*) Baku   (*d*) Bukhara

23. Who among the following gave a detailed account of Nalanda University?
  (*a*) Hiuen Tsang   (*b*) Fa-hien
  (*c*) Megasthenes   (*d*) Te-tsing

24. Which is the brightest star in the sky?
  (*a*) Proxima Centauri
  (*b*) Nebula
  (*c*) Barnard
  (*d*) None of these

25. Who among the following is a world famous violinist?
  (*a*) Zakir Hussain   (*b*) Bismillah Khan
  (*c*) Pt. Ravishankar   (*d*) Yehudi Menuhin

26. Which of the following Muslim festivals is celebrated on Prophet Mohammed's birthday?
  (*a*) Muharram   (*b*) Id-i-Milad Unnabi
  (*c*) Id-ul-Zuha   (*d*) Id-ul-Fitr

27. What is the removal of top layer of fertile soil called?
  (*a*) Soil erosion   (*b*) Soil conservation
  (*c*) Weathering   (*d*) None of these

PART–A-2

Directions: (Qs. Nos. 28-37): *In the following passage certain words have been omitted. Identify the missing words:*

Another method of sending news was **(28)** --- pigeons. The carrier pigeon **(29)** --- the cat, is extremely attached **(30)** --- its home and if a traveller wanted to send **(31)** --- message back to its starting point, he fixed it **(32)** --- a pigeon **(33)** --- he had taken with him. The bird, once set free, **(34)** --- straight back **(35)** --- its loft, and the message **(36)** --- then be taken from its leg. The invention of **(37)** --- electric telegraph and later, of wireless, speeded up the sending of news.

Give short answers to the following questions:

38. Which Arab country has no river?

39. To which European country did the famous painter Pablo Picasso belong?

40. Which of the four main islands is situated north of Honshu?

41. Which place in Madhya Pradesh is known for its diamond mines?

42. Which Egyptian city was founded by Alexander the Great?

43. Which was the first city destroyed by the atom bomb in the Second World War?

44. What is the instrument used to record earthquake shocks?

45. In which city, Hollywood, the famous centre of film industry, is situated?

46. Who is the only recipient of the Nobel Prize in Arabic Literature?

Complete the following sentences:

47. The fall of Bastille is associated with ------.

48. *Das Capital* was written by -------.

49. The name of the present Chief Election Commissioner is ------.

50. The last SAARC Conference was held in ------.

51. The smallest unit of matter which can take part in a chemical reaction is ------.

52. Amnesty International is an organisation for the protection of ------.

53. Argentina has shifted its capital from Buenos Aires to -------.

54. French speaking countries are called ------.

55. Leningrad is currently known as ------.

56. Goethe is a writer of ------.

57. The author of the book *The Man Eaters of Kumaun* is ------.

58. Sardar Sarovar Project is associated with the river ------.

59. Ramon Magsaysay Award is named after the President of ------.

60. Ulan Bator is the capital of ------.

61. Iranian Parliament is called ------.

62. Turkish is written in ------ script.

63. Kilimanjaro in Africa is a ------.

64. Gir forests are located in the state of ------.

65. The national language of Brazil is ------.

66. The sourness of lemon is caused by ------ acid.

67. The warming of the planet due to accumulation of gases is called ------.

68. The book *Poetics* was written by the ancient Greek Scholar ------.

69. Lhasa is the capital of ------.

70. The capital of North Korea is ------.

71. Linguistics deals with ------.

72. Habib Tanbir is associated with ------.

73. Hamid Karzai is the leader of ------.

74. *Geet Govind* was written by ------.

75. The author of *Captain's Daughter* is ------.

76. Jacques Chirac is the President of ------.

77. Louvre is a world famous ------.

78. A vast collection of stars held together by mutual gravitation is called ------.

79. The currency of Bangladesh is ------.

80. The Elisa test is used to detect ------.

81. *Panchatantra* was written by ------.

82. The religious order established by Mother Teresa is called ------.

83. Kamarupa is the old name of the state of ------.

84. The *Shahnama* was written by ------.

PART–B-1

Expand the following abbreviations:

85. NASA

86. ASEAN

87. WLL

Give one word each for the following:

88. The study of diseases

89. The art of map-making

90. The study of nature and history of universe

Give the meaning of the following idiomatic expressions:

91. A pipe dream

92. To smell a rat

93. To take with a grain of salt

94. To spill the beans

95. To hit below the belt

Complete the following sentences:

96. The world's largest lake is ------.

97. Aryabhatta was a famous ------.

98. The first recipient of Human Rights Award is ------.

99. A colour blind person has difficulty in distinguishing between ------.

100. Camel uses its hump for ------.

101. The original home of the gypsies was ------.

102. As you sow, so ------.

103. Alexander invaded India in ------.

104. Vande Mataram was first published in ------.

105. Kalidasa lived during the reign of ------.

106. The only man-made structure that can be viewed from moon is ----- .

107. The traditional dress of Japanese woman is -----.

108. The word 'Zen' in Zen Buddhism has come from the Indian word ------.

109. Which is the number that comes next in the sequence? 1, 4, 9, 16, 25, 36, 49, ----- ?

110. If 'pen' is called 'pencil', 'pencil' is called 'scale', 'scale' is called 'bag' and 'bag' is called 'book', which is used to carry the books?

111. The boundary between China and India is called ------.

112. Iodination of salt is a public health measure to prevent ------.

Go through the words of the Language A and Language B and answer the question given at the end:

Language A	Language B
$\exists\,\Delta\cap''\approx''$	दरवाजा
$=_+ \forall \perp^+$	खिड़की
$+_=\Delta$	ओर
$\approx \ddot{O}\,\Delta$	ज़हर
$\square''\oplus^+$	पानी
$\geq''+$	चाय
$\square_\wedge \Delta''\,\oplus''$	पुराना
$\times \neq$	बस
$\lrcorner^\wedge \in$	धूल
$\oplus''\cap$	नाव

How will you write the following words?

Language B	Language A
113. और	
114. हरा	
115. सूना	
116. खून	
117. दिन	
118. वर	

PART–B-2

Read the following passage carefully and answer the questions given below it:

Look at any waste garbage dump. In addition to vegetable scraps, paper and broken glass, you will notice a considerable amount of plastic material such as shampoo bottles, bags, worn out slippers and the like. Vegetable scraps and paper are biodegradable, but plastic continues to accumulate and harm the environment. Plastic is often mistaken for food by birds, animals and fish, leading to their death. It also chokes sewer pipes and becomes a trap for living beings in ponds, rivers and oceans.

Investigations have been going on for a long time to produce an environment-friendly plastic in the sense that it decays and becomes a part of the soil like rotting vegetable scraps do. The scientists of Imperial Chemical Industries at London have been able to develop just such a plastic called 'Bipol'. It is manufactured by microbes. Bottles, film and fibres can be made out of it. Fungi and bacteria can eat it and break it down into carbon dioxide and water. This new plastic can also be used to make capsules for slow release in the body of some types of medicines, and of pesticides in the fields.

119. Explain, what you understand by biodegradable substances.

120. How does plastic affects the environment?

121. What is 'Bipol' and what are its advantages?

Write *four* sentences about the following:

122. Martin Luther King

123. Dhirubhai Ambani

124. Amartya Sen

Go through the words of the Language A and Language B and answer the question given at the end:

Language A	*Language B*
a car	en bil
cars	bilar
the cats	kattarna
a cat	en katt
sofas	soffor
the newspapers	tidningarna
the flowers	blommorna
a sofa	en soffa
the sofa	soffan
cats	kattar
flowers	blommor
a lamp	en lampa
in the room	kitonn pana
a room	en kitonn

How would you say the forms of the following words?

	Language A	*Language B*
125.	the sofas	
126.	rooms	
127.	a newspaper	
128.	the lamp	
129.	the cars	
130.	a flower	

ANSWERS

1	2	3	4	5	6	7	8	9	10
(d)	(a)	(c)	(a)	(d)	(c)	(a)	(b)	(c)	(d)

11	12	13	14	15	16	17	18	19	20
(b)	(b)	(a)	(b)	(c)	(b)	(d)	(d)	(d)	(a)

21	22	23	24	25	26	27
(a)	(a)	(a)	(d)	(d)	(d)	(a)

28. by **29.** or **30.** to **31.** a

32. with **33.** that **34.** go **35.** to

36. there **37.** the

38. Oman

39. Italy

40. Hokedo

41. Panna

42. Alexandria

43. Hiroshima August 6, 1945

44. Seismograph

45. Los Angles

46. Naguib Mahfouz

47. French Revolution

48. Karl Marx

49. T.S. Krishna Murthy

50. Sri Lanka

51. atom

52. human right

53. No change in capital

54. Franco phone

55. St. Petersburg

56. Germany

57. Jim Corbett

58. Narmada

59. Philipines

60. Mangolia

61. Majlish

62. Arabic

63. Volcano

64. Gujarat

65. Spanish

66. ascorbic

67. global warming

68. Aristotle

69. Tibet
70. Pyongyang
71. Languages
72. Folk Theatre
73. Afghanistan
74. Jaydev
75. Alexander Puskin
76. France
77. Museum
78. Galaxy
79. Taka
80. AIDS
81. Vishnu Sharma
82. Missionaries of Charity
83. Asom
84. Firdausi
85. NASA—National Aero Space Association.
86. ASEAN—Association of South East Asian Nation.
87. WLL—Wireless in Local Loop.
88. Pathology
89. Cartography
90. Cosmology
91. Distant dream
92. Suspicious about something
93. to accept what some one said with doubt and misgiving.
94. Spoiling another's plan
95. Attack opponent unfairly
96. Caspean sea
97. Astronomer
98. Bob Minton
99. Colour's
100. Water storage
101. India
102. You reap
103. 327 B.C.
104. Anand Math

105. Harsh Vardhan
106. Great wall of China
107. Kimono
108. Dhyana
109. 64, as squares of consecutive numbers
110. book
111. Mac Mahon Line
112. Goitor
113. $+ \, _{=} \, \triangle$ 114. $O\triangle\,"$
115. $\neq \wedge \oplus \,"$ 116. $\forall \wedge \oplus$
117. $\exists_{+} \oplus$ 118. $\cap \triangle$
119. Those substances which can degrade naturally are bio-degradeable substance.
120. Plastic continues to accumulate and doesn't degrade. Animals and birds mistaken it for food and died. It also chokes the sewer line and become a trap for living beings in ponds, river and ocean.
121. Bipole is a plastic developed by Imperial Chemical Industries of London, which is termed as environment friendly as it decays like vegetable scraps.
122. **Martin Luther King Jr. (1929-68):** Black American Clergyman, a non violent civil rights leader and Negro integration leader, Nobel Peace Prize. Associated why we can't wait.
123. **Dhirubhai Ambani:** (Dhiraj Lal Hirachand) (1932-2002) Indian Industrialist Reliance Industries that he set up is India's largest Private Sector Company. Sons: Mukesh Ambani and Anil Ambani now head the Reliance Companies. The latter is Rajya Sabha M.P. since 2004.
124. **Amartya Sen**—(b-1933) Indian Economist, the Professor of Philosophy and Economics at Harvard University, Minister of Trinity college Cambridge, Nobel Prize (1998). Recipient of Bharat Ratna.
125. sofforna   126. kittonnar
127. en tidning   128. lampan
129. bilarna   130. en blomm

JAWAHARLAL NEHRU UNIVERSITY (JNU)

First Year of 3-Year B.A. [Hons.] in Foreign Languages

Chinese, French, German, Korean, Japanese, Arabic, Persian, Russian and Spanish

Entrance Examination, 2003

PART–A-1

Answer the following questions by selecting the most appropriate one from (*a*) to (*d*):

1. In a group of 15, 7 can speak German and 8 can speak Italian while 3 can speak neither. What part of the group can speak both German and Italian?
   (*a*) 1/5
   (*b*) 4/15
   (*c*) 3/5
   (*d*) 1/3

2. Who among the following authors did not receive a Noble Prize in Literature?
   (*a*) M. Gorky
   (*b*) Ivan Bunin
   (*c*) Boris Pasternak
   (*d*) Alexander Solzhenitsyn

3. The author of 'Les Miserable' is:
   (*a*) V. S. Naipaul
   (*b*) Victor Hugo
   (*c*) E. M. Forster
   (*d*) Thomas Hardy

4. If COBRA is written as BOCAR, then how GROUP will be written in that code?
   (*a*) ORPGU
   (*b*) OGRPU
   (*c*) ORUPG
   (*d*) ORGPU

5. If 'water' is called 'food', 'food' is called 'tree', 'tree' is called 'sky', 'sky' is called 'well', on which of the following grows a 'fruit'?
   (*a*) Water
   (*b*) Food
   (*c*) Tree
   (*d*) Sky

6. Occidental culture is associated with:
   (*a*) Asian Society
   (*b*) European Society
   (*c*) African Society
   (*d*) Latin American Society

7. The word 'Hindu' as reference to the people of Hind (India) was first used by:
   (*a*) the Greeks
   (*b*) the Romans
   (*c*) the Chinese
   (*d*) the Arabs

8. Which of the given figures best represents the relationship of Elected body: Member of Parliament and Member of Legislative Assembly?

   (*a*)   (*b*)

   (*c*)   (*d*)

9. Find the missing number in the series 31, 21, 13, ?, 3, 1
   (*a*) 5
   (*b*) 9
   (*c*) 7
   (*d*) 11

10. Mecca is:
    (*a*) A girl's name
    (*b*) Prophet's brother's name
    (*c*) Muslim calendar
    (*d*) Prophet Mohammed birth place

11. Which is not a Gulf country?
    (*a*) Oman
    (*b*) Bahrain
    (*c*) Qatar
    (*d*) Iraq

12. Arrange the following in the right order?
    1. Yarn
    2. Plant

3. Saree   4. Cotton
5. Cloth
(*a*) 2, 4, 5, 1, 3   (*b*) 2, 4, 1, 5, 3
(*c*) 2, 4, 3, 5, 1   (*d*) 2, 4, 5, 3, 1

13. Which of the following provinces of Canada has majority of people speaking French?
(*a*) Ontario
(*b*) Quebec
(*c*) Prince Edward Island
(*d*) Nova Scotia

14. Salvador Dali was a famous?
(*a*) matador   (*b*) painter
(*c*) writer   (*d*) statesman

15. Sancho Panja is a character of the famous Spanish novel:
(*a*) 'Mio 'Cid'
(*b*) The family of Pascal Duarte'
(*c*) Don Quixote'
(*d*) 'Beehive'

16. A street in Delhi was named in March 2003 after an eminent French intellectual, identify the person from the list below:
(*a*) Andre Matraux (*b*) Albert Camus
(*c*) Victor Hugo   (*d*) Andre Gide

17. What was the old name of Japanese capital Tokyo?
(*a*) Meiji   (*b*) Urawa
(*c*) Edo   (*d*) Kyodo

18. Buddhism started spreading from India through which route?
(*a*) China – Japan – Korea
(*b*) China – Korea – Japan
(*c*) Korea – Taiwan – Japan
(*d*) Nepal – Korea – Japan

19. 'Hangul' is a script of which language?
(*a*) Chinese   (*b*) Japanese
(*c*) Korean   (*d*) Malaysian

20. Who wrote 'Natya Shastra'?
(*a*) Kalidas   (*b*) Banabhatta
(*c*) Bharat Muni   (*d*) Jaidev

21. The author of 'Organ of Species' is:
(*a*) Thomas Carlyle (*b*) Charles Darwin
(*c*) Anaicle France (*d*) D. Lawrence

22. Three of the following form a group in some way. Select the one that does not belong to group:
(*a*) Amjad Ali Khan (*b*) Ravi Shankar
(*c*) Ali Akbar Khan (*d*) Shanta Prasad

23. Noble Prizes are awarded annually in:
(*a*) Manila   (*b*) Stockholm
(*c*) Geneva   (*d*) New York

24. Raman Magsaysay Award is named after the former President of:
(*a*) Indonesia   (*b*) Thailand
(*c*) Burma   (*d*) Philippines

25. The novel 'War and Peace' was written by:
(*a*) F. M. Dostoevsky (*b*) L. N. Tolstoy
(*c*) Anton Chekhov   (*d*) Ivan Turgenev

26. Altamira in Spain is known for:
(*a*) a Mosque
(*b*) synagogue
(*c*) bull fighting ring
(*d*) cave of pre-historic art

27. Jaminy Roy was a famous:
(*a*) dancer   (*b*) magician
(*c*) cartoonist   (*d*) painter

28. Which of the following is the major cause of Green Revolution in India?
(*a*) Land reforms
(*b*) Better irrigation facilities
(*c*) Introduction of hybrid seeds fertilisers, etc.
(*d*) Better agricultural marketing

29. Find the odd man out:
(*a*) Amitava Ghose
(*b*) Upamanyu Chatterjee
(*c*) Vikram Seth
(*d*) Jaishankar Prasad

30. Find the odd man out:
(*a*) Sai Paranjape (*b*) Meera Nair
(*c*) Mani Ratnam   (*d*) Om Puri

31. How many squares are there in a chess board?
(*a*) 48   (*b*) 64
(*c*) 36   (*d*) 24

32. The Uruguay round of talks led to the establishment of:

(*a*) NAFTA   (*b*) WTO
(*c*) Group of 77   (*d*) Group of 7

33. What season is there in Australia during Christmas?
(*a*) Spring   (*b*) Autumn
(*c*) Summer   (*d*) Winter

34. Which of the following gives the correct chronological order of the Vedas?
(*a*) Rig, Sama, Atharva, Yajur
(*b*) Rig, Sama, Yajur, Atharva
(*c*) Rig and Sama together, Yajur and Atharva together
(*d*) All simultaneously

35. Which of the following has proved the best source of information for depicting India's ancient history?
(*a*) Religious literature
(*b*) Works of foreign travellers
(*c*) Inscriptions
(*d*) Monuments

36. The Khasi and the Garo tribes belong to:
(*a*) Arunachal Pradesh
(*b*) Sikkim
(*c*) Meghalaya
(*d*) Nagaland

37. The author of 'India Wins Freedom' is:
(*a*) Jawaharlal Nehru
(*b*) Rajendra Prasad
(*c*) Maulana Azad
(*d*) B. C. Roy

38. In an office with 21 workers, 1/3 are men and the rest women. How many women should be hired to obtain a staff in which 1/4 are men?
(*a*) 3   (*b*) 5
(*c*) 6   (*d*) 7

39. Akbar founded his own religion known as Din-i-Ilahi which means:
(*a*) House of worship
(*b*) Universal peace
(*c*) Divine faith
(*d*) None of these

40. In which language did Buddha preach?
(*a*) Pali   (*b*) Prakrit
(*c*) Apabhransha   (*d*) Sanskrit

41. The blood pressure values of four persons are given below:
1.   Mrs. X-90/60
2.   Mr. X-160/120
3.   Mr. Y-120/80
4.   Mrs. Y-140/100

Who among the following has normal blood pressure?
(a) Mrs. Y   (b) Mr. X
(c) Mrs. X   (d) Mr. Y

42. Which of the following is a universal blood donor?
(*a*) A   (*b*) B
(*c*) AB   (*d*) O

43. Red blood corpuscles are formed in:
(*a*) liver   (*b*) small intestine
(*c*) kidney   (*d*) bone marrow

44. Mecca is a holy place for muslims because it houses:
(*a*) Kaaba
(*b*) Prophet's tomb
(*c*) Trade centre
(*d*) Bedouin's abode

45. Pyramids are mostly found in:
(*a*) Jordan   (*b*) Egypt
(*c*) Sudan   (*d*) Morocco

46. Find the odd man out:
(*a*) Leonardo da Vinci
(*b*) Raphael
(*c*) Pablo Picasso
(*d*) Dustin Hoffman

47. The oldest school of Indian Philosophy is believed to be:
(*a*) Nyaya   (*b*) Vaisheshik
(*c*) Sankhya   (*d*) Meemansa

48. What is preserved in a National Park?
(*a*) Only flora
(*b*) Only fauna
(*c*) Both (*a*) and (*b*)
(*d*) None of these

49. Bismillah Khan is associated with:
(*a*) Tabla   (*b*) Sarod
(*c*) Flute   (*d*) Shehnai

50. Renminbi (Yuan) is the currency of:
(*a*) China   (*b*) Cambodia
(*d*) Hongkong   (*d*) Thailand

PART–A-2

Give short answers to the following questions:

51. Which Chinese river is often called as the 'Sorrow of China'?

52. Mahatma Gandhi mostly wrote in which language?

53. Who were the first Europeans who started trade with India?

54. Afanasi Nikitin, who visited India during medieval period, came from which country?

55. The Indian epic 'Mahabharat' was filmed by whom?

56. What subject does 'Charak Samhita' deal with?

57. Who was the first translator of Tagore's Geetanjali' in English?

58. What does 'www' stand for in IT?

59. Which country is called, 'The Land of Morning Calm'?

60. If the word PEARL is written as MBXOI, then how would DIAMOND be written in that code?

61. Find the odd one out of following:
Ravi Shastri, Wasim Akram, Jastin Langer, Gary Sobers, Sunil Gavaskar.

62. The Japanese art of flower arrangement is known as ------.

63. The international boundary between Afghanistan and Pakistan is known as ------.

64. One who compiles a dictionary is known as ------.

65. The word 'Matador' means ------.

66. A stich in time ------.

67. Those who live in glass houses ------.

68. Set of instructions (Programme) that runs a computer's hardware is known as ------.

69. A ball of frozen gas and dust which appears in the sky they say- when great men die or are born, is called ------.

70. The house of Eskimo is called ------.

71. A Francophone is a person who ------.

72. The lower house of the Parliament in Germany is known as ------.

73. Kathak is related to Uttar Pradesh in the same way as Kathakali is related to ------.

74. The longest river in the world is ------.

75. The home for the ancient Sumerian Civilisation was ------.

76. The Chief Guest of this year's Republic day's function was the President of ------.

77. One of the Semitic languages other than Hebrew is ------.

Answer the following questions:

78. If 3 cats can kill 3 rats in 3 minutes, how long it take 100 cats to kill 100 rats?

79. What is warming of the planet due to accumulation of gases called?

80. In a certain code, *Kemp Lamp Tens* means Speak the Truth; *Bis Tim Nak* means Always Seek Knowledge; *Tim Tems Sik* means Knowledge is Truth and *Lik Bis Zap* means Never Seek Violence, then which letter code stands for violence?

81. If BEDI could be given the code number 20, what code number can be given to VISU?

82. Which number replaces the question mark in the following series?
5, 7, 11, ?, 35, 67

83. Who was the first Indian woman to be a Minister at the Centre?

84. What is the other name of the Arabian Gulf?

Directions: (Q. Nos, 85-92): *In the following passage certain words have been omitted. Identify the missing words and write.*

Of all **(85)** --- untamed creatures, sparrows seem to love living near **(86)** --- man the most. Wherever **(87)** --- new township springs up, the sparrows follow **(88)** --- no time. They even build **(89)** --- nests inside homes and **(90)** --- they feel sure they will not **(91)** --- harmed, they will even come and eat out of your hand. That is why they have **(92)** --- called the most human of all birds.

Directions: (Qs. Nos. 93-98): *Fill in the blanks with the most appropriate filler:*

The people of Orissa, where 70% of the cultivable **(93)** --- is rain fed, had no choice but to migrate because of the **(94)** --- of drought. Migration is an annual **(95)** --- in the drought- prone districts of this state. Madhya Pradesh is a favourite destination **(96)** --- Andhra Pradesh, Delhi and even Punjub. A survey **(97)** --- that every year more than 50,000 people **(98)** --- from one district alone.

Fill in the blanks:

99. The term Magic Realism is generally associated with works of ---.

100. The disintegration of Soviet Union took place in ---.

PART–B-1

101. Pointing to a lady, a man said, 'the son of her only brother is the brother of my wife.' How the lady is related to the man?

102. The cricket ball is lighter than the hockey ball and volleyball is lighter than the football. Hockey ball is lighter than the football but heavier than the tennis ball. Which one is the heaviest?

103. Find the odd one from the following series:

3, 5, 7, 9, 11, 13

104. After every 10 metres or so on a railway track a small gap is left. Why is this necessary?

105. Re-arrange the following words to form a meaningful sentence:

a book/Indian/written/and/he/has/leading/on/mythology/by/published/publisher/a reputable

106. A man walks 6 km to the east and then turns to the south and walks 5 km. Again he turns to the east and walks 6 km. Next he turns north-wards and walks 10 km. How far is he now from his starting point?

Directions: (Qs. Nos 107-109): *Read the following passage carefully and answer the questions given below it:*

Hiuen Tsang, the famous Chinese traveller, visited India in the seventh century. He travelled extensively in India. He stayed for some time in Kanauj at the court of the great emperor Harshavardhana. He has left for us graphic descriptions of the pomp and ceremony of the royal regalia and the lavish celebrations of Hindu festivals. During one particular festivity at the confluence of the Ganga and Yamuna, many princes would come to participate in the giving of gifts to the poor and the orphans.

Hiuen Tsang spent a long period at the famed Nalanda, where students by the hundreds flocked from all over India and abroad. It had flourished in the time of Buddha and Mahavira, and now when the Chinese pilgrim visited the place it seemed to have been still full of life and intellectual vigour. For this what the pilgrim notes: "The day is not sufficient for asking and answering profound questions. From morning till night, they engage in discussions; the old and the young mutually help one another. If such is not an ideal place of learning, then what is?

107. Why are the writings of Hiuen Tsang considered very important?

108. Why did Hiuen Tsang spend considerable time at Nalanda?

109. Why did the Princes used to visit the festivity at the confluence of Ganga and Yamuna?

110. Which one is different from the rest three?
(*a*) Jackfruit   (*b*) Apple
(*c*) Guava   (*d*) Watermelon

Directions: (Qs. Nos. 111- 115): *Go through carefully the words given in English and their equivalents in an unknown language 'X' and then give the equivalents of the remaining English words in the language 'X'.*

English	Language 'X'
LIFT	□ ↑ ∀ ⊃
JUMP	○ ⊥ ±
JUNK	○ ⊥ ≥
COLD	>] Γ ↓

GOLD	<] Γ ↓
BRICK	← | ↑ ≥
CRICKET	> | ↑ > ⊂ ⊃
CULT	> ⊥ □ ⊃
LINK	□ ↑ ≥
LIST	□ ↑ ≅ ⊃
CIST	≅ ↑ ≅ ⊃
NO	↔]
TENT	⊃ ⊂ ⊇
PUMP	+ ⊥ ±

111. BEG —
112. CUP —
113. DRINK —
114. PENCIL —
115. JUDGE —

Directions: (Qs. Nos. 116-120): *Go through the words given in two different scripts A and B and then rewrite the words of script A in script B.*

Script A	Script B
बल	∀ ≠
कब	Γ ∀
काल	+ #
जल	0 #
लड़का	# L +
लड़ाई	# 0 ↑
इतना	↑) (
कितना	<) (
मकान	[+ ⊥
इनाम	↑ ([
पास	□ ↓
दूर	⅂ →

116. नाई
117. मत
118. सड़क
119. कल
120. रस

Expand the following abbreviations:

121. HIV
122. ECG
123. LPG
124. STD
125. CRY

Fill in the blanks:

126. The ozone layer in the upper part of the atmosphere protects us from -------.

127. It is easier to swim in a sea than in a river because -------.

128. Burns caused by steam are much more severe than those caused by boiling water -------.

129. The best colours for a sun umbrella will be -------.

130. In the 'Arabian Nights', Aladdin's lamp was a source of wealth and good fortune. What purpose did his ring serve --------?

131. Katyayan, a famous personality of ancient India was primarily a -----.

Directions: (Qs. Nos. 132-134): *Give one word each for the following:*

132. One who cannot be corrected
133. That which cannot be read
134. One who hates mankind

PART–B-2

Directions: (Qs. Nos. 135-139): *Go through carefully the sentences given in English and their equivalents in an unknown language 'Z' and then give the equivalents of the remaining English sentences in the language 'Z'.*

English	Language 'Z'
He is sleeping	NIRWA
She is sleeping	SIRWA
I am not sleeping	KIRWAN
They are sleeping	BIRWA

Are they sleeping?	BIRWAKU?
We are working	HIMLA
He has eaten	NIKWAI
I have eaten	KIKWAI
I have not eaten	KIKWAIN
They are going	BISLA
Are you going today?	WISLA NUKU?
I will sleep outside	KIRWA SIM
I know this place	KILDA TANIM
I know this word	KILDA RWUIM
He will come tomorrow	NIKTA MA

135. He has gone ---------.

136. She is not working -------.

137. Do you know this place ------ ?

138. We are not going today -------.

139. We will go tomorrow ------.

Write four sentences about the following:

140. United Nations

141. Kalpana Chawla

142. A.P.J. Abdul Kalam

ANSWERS

1	2	3	4	5	6	7	8	9	10
(a)	(a)	(b)	(d)	(d)	(b)	(d)	(c)	(c)	(d)
11	12	13	14	15	16	17	18	19	20
(d)	(b)	(b)	(b)	(c)	(c)	(d)	(b)	(c)	(c)
21	22	23	24	25	26	27	28	29	30
(b)	(d)	(b)	(d)	(b)	(d)	(d)	(c)	(b)	(d)
31	32	33	34	35	36	37	38	39	40
(b)	(b)	(c)	(b)	(a)	(c)	(c)	(d)	(c)	(a)
41	42	43	44	45	46	47	48	49	50
(a)	(d)	(d)	(a)	(b)	(d)	(b)	(c)	(d)	(a)

51. Yellow river (Hwang Hu)
52. Hindustani
53. Portugese
54. In 1468 from Russia
55. B.R. Chopra
56. Medicine
57. Tagore himself
58. WWW—World Wide Web
59. Korea
60. AFXJLKA
61. Sunil Gavaskar
62. Ika bena
63. Durand line
64. Lexico-grapher
65. bull fighter
66. Saves nine

67. never throw a stone
68. Software
69. Philosophy
70. Igloo
71. Speaks French
72. Bundestag
73. Kerala
74. Nile
75. Iraq
76. Mauritius, Mr. Cassam Uttem
77. Arabic
78. 3 minutes
79. Global Warmings
80. It can either be lik or zop
81. 71
82. 19

83. Raj Kumari Amrit Kaur (1947, Health minister)

84. Gulf of Persia

85. the

86. the

87. a

88. in

89. their

90. there

91. be

92. also

93. land

94. situation

95. Phenomena

96. above

97. showed

98. migrate

99. magician

100. 1990

101. Mother-in-law

102. Football

103. 9 (all other are prime numbers)

104. So that when the track will expand in summer those will not bend.

105. He has written a book on Indian mythology published by a reputable and leading publisher.

106. 13 km

107. He gave graphic descriptions of pomp, ceremonies and details of the life of the people of the 7th century.

108. Nalanda was a centre of study.

109. To give gift to the poor and orphans

110. (*d*) Watermelon

111. $\leftarrow \subset <$

112. $\cong \perp +$

113. $\downarrow | \uparrow \geq$

114. $+ C \geq \uparrow \square$

115. $O \perp \downarrow < C$

116. $(\uparrow$

117. $[\,)$

118. $\downarrow L +$

119. $[\#$

120. $\rightarrow \downarrow$

121. **HIV:** Human Immuno Deficiency Virus

122. **ECG:** Electro Cardio Gram

123. **LPG:** Liquid Petroleum Gas

124. **STD:** Sexually Transmitted Diseases.

125. **CRY:** Child Relief and You.

126. Ultraviolet radiation.

127. Sea water has more density.

128. Water has more specific heat.

129. White

130. to call the Jinn

131. teacher

132. Incorrigible

133. Unreadable

134. Misanthropist

135. NIKSLAI

136. SIMLAN

137. WILDA TANMU

138. HISLA NUKN

139. HISLA MA

140. **UNITED NATIONS:** UNITED NATION was devised by United States President Franklin D. Roosevelt and was first used in the declaration by United Nation of 2 January 1942 during the second world war when representatives of 26 nation pledge their governments to continue fighting together against the axis powers. Now it consist of 192 members.

141. **KALPANA CHAWLA:** (b-1961-2003) The first Indian American Space Woman. Travelled a board Space Shuttle Columbia in November 1997 and died on her second space voyage on Columbia in February 2003.

142. **A.P.J. ABDUL KALAM:** Abul Pakir Jainul Abdeen Abdul Kalam (b-1931) President of India from 2002 to till date former scientific adviser to Defence minister, the man behind India's missile programme known for his dedication to science, commitment to professional excellence and simplicity of life style, and a Bharat Ratna awardee in 1998.

JAWAHARLAL NEHRU UNIVERSITY (JNU)

First Year of 3-Year B.A. [Hons.] in Foreign Languages

Chinese, French, German, Korean, Japanese, Arabic, Persian, Russian and Spanish

Entrance Examination, 2002

PART–A-1

Answer the following questions by selecting the most appropriate one from (*a*) to (*d*).

1. Bharat II is meant to control:
   - (*a*) AIDS
   - (*b*) Vehicular emission norms
   - (*c*) Water Pollution
   - (*d*) Terrorism

2. Dr. Reddy's Lab is associated with:
   - (*a*) Biotechnology
   - (*b*) Information Technology
   - (*c*) Space Technology
   - (*d*) Fibre Optics

3. In which State is the famous Tirupathi Temple situated?
   - (*a*) Tamil Nadu
   - (*b*) Karnataka
   - (*c*) Andhra Pradesh
   - (*d*) Kerala

4. Which of the following is not a member of SAARC?
   - (*a*) India
   - (*b*) Pakistan
   - (*c*) Sri Lanka
   - (*d*) Afghanistan

5. Raja Ram Mohan Roy's Brahmo Samaj rejected:
   - (*a*) Casteism
   - (*b*) Idolism
   - (*c*) Ritualism
   - (*d*) All of the above

6. Sikh Khalsa was founded by:
   - (*a*) Guru Teg Bahadur
   - (*b*) Guru Nanak
   - (*c*) Guru Govind Singh
   - (*d*) Guru Hargobind

7. Tulsidas was a contemporary of:
   - (*a*) Babar
   - (*b*) Jehangir
   - (*c*) Akbar
   - (*d*) Humayun

8. German attack on Poland was the immediate cause of:
   - (*a*) World War I
   - (*b*) World War II
   - (*c*) West Asian Crisis
   - (*d*) Cold War

9. Source of maximum income to Panchayati Raj Institution is:
   - (*a*) Local Taxes
   - (*b*) Regional Funds
   - (*c*) Government Grants
   - (*d*) Share in Union Government Revenue

10. Kamarupa is the old name of:
    - (*a*) Asom
    - (*b*) Bihar
    - (*c*) Orissa
    - (*d*) Bengal

Select from (a) to (d) the best description common to the three words names on too.

11. Columbus: Megallan : Vasco de Gama:
    - (*a*) They are ancient astronomers
    - (*b*) They are famous explorers
    - (*c*) They discovered some Asian countries
    - (*d*) They were the first to design a ship

12. Sarnath: Kapilvastu: Sanchi
    - (*a*) These are places with massive pillars.
    - (*b*) These are linked with Lord Buddha.
    - (*c*) These are famous for stone carving.
    - (*d*) These are ancient universities.

13. Mandarin: Sinhalese: Tamil:
   (*a*) They are originally Indian languages
   (*b*) They have originated from Sanskrit
   (*c*) They are Asian languages
   (*d*) They have the same type of grammar

14. James Bond : Sherlock Holmes : Hercule Poirot:
   (*a*) They are agents of CBI.
   (*b*) They are the only detective agents with license to kill.
   (*c*) They are private detectives.
   (*d*) They are characters from detective fiction.

15. Green : Violet: Orange:
   (*a*) They are primary colours
   (*b*) They are made by mixing colours
   (*c*) They are not found in butterflies
   (*d*) They occur together in rainbow

Answer the following questions by selecting the most appropriate one from (a) to (d).

16. Bile juice is secreted by
   (*a*) Pancreas   (*b*) Liver
   (*c*) Spleen   (*d*) Gall Bladder

17. Light Year is a unit to measure
   (*a*) speed of light
   (*b*) astronomical distances
   (*c*) speed of rockets
   (*d*) speed of aeroplanes

18. Which of the following is the lightest metal
   (*a*) Mercury   (*b*) Silver
   (*c*) Lithium   (*d*) Lead

19. Which of the following is a universal blood donor
   (*a*) A   (*b*) B
   (*c*) AB   (*d*) O

20. Any foreign particle which stimulates the formation of antibodies is called:
   (*a*) Histone   (*b*) Antigen
   (*c*) Receptor   (*d*) Antibiotic

21. The evolution of human species took place mainly in:
   (*a*) Asia   (*b*) Africa
   (*c*) Europe   (*d*) China

22. Who recast the original single Veda into four Vedas?
   (*a*) Patanjali   (*b*) Vyas
   (*c*) Shankaracharya   (*d*) None of these

23. In Indian Constitution, there is no provision for:
   (*a*) Religious Rights
   (*b*) Political and Social Rights
   (*c*) Educational Rights
   (*d*) Economic Rights

24. The largest Island in the Indian ocean is:
   (*a*) Sri Lanka   (*b*) Maldives
   (*c*) Madagascar   (*d*) Sumatra

25. The first underground railway in India was opened on 1984 in:
   (*a*) Mumbai   (*b*) Chennai
   (*c*) Kolkata   (*d*) Delhi

26. According to Jawaharlal Nehru University (JNU) prospectus, how many centres of examination are there in India for entrance to JNU in 2002?
   (*a*) about 15   (*b*) about 30
   (*c*) about 40   (*d*) about 50

27. The People's Republic of China was founded on:
   (*a*) October 1, 1947
   (*b*) August 10, 1949
   (*c*) October 1, 1949
   (*d*) August 10, 1947

28. Who among the following scholars was the first to visit India?
   (*a*) Hiuen Tsang   (*b*) Ibn Batuta
   (*c*) Marco Polo   (*d*) Fa Hien

29. Sculptures of the Gandhara School reflect the influence of:
   (*a*) Persians   (*b*) Greek
   (*c*) Romans   (*d*) Chinese

30. The largest producer of Uranium in the world is:
   (*a*) U.S.A.   (*b*) France
   (*c*) India   (*d*) Zaire

31. Equator passes through which of the following countries?

(a) Australia   (b) Brazil
(c) China   (d) Saudi Arabia

32. Which continent has the highest density of population?
(a) Asia   (b) Africa
(c) Europe   (d) North America

33. Which planet is known as the Watery Planet?
(a) Venus   (b) Mars
(c) Pluto   (d) Earth

34. The biggest public sector undertaking in India is :
(a) Iron and Steel   (b) Railways
(c) Roadways   (d) Airways

35. Which State has achieved the highest literacy rate in India?
(a) Kerala   (b) Maharashtra
(c) West Bengal   (d) Punjab

36. In a certain code language 526 means 'sky is blue, 24 means 'blue colour' and 436 means 'colour is fun'. Which digit in that language means 'fun'?
(a) 5   (b) 6
(c) 3   (d) 4

37. Which letter in place of '?' will complete the following series?
A C F J ? U B
(a) N   (b) O
(c) P   (d) Q

38. After Vishwanathan Anand, who was the second Indian Chess player to earn the title of Grandmaster?
(a) Subramanyam Raman
(b) Dibyendu Barua
(c) D.V. Prasad
(d) Anupama Abhyankar

39. The 'Shahnama was written by?
(a) Alberuni   (b) Amir Khusro
(c) Abul Fazal   (d) Firdausi

40. Who wrote the famous line 'A thing of beauty is a joy for ever'?
(a) Shelley   (b) Keats
(c) Wordsworth   (d) Shakespeare

41. Kilimanjaro in Africa is a:
(a) Mountain Peak   (b) River
(c) Tribe   (d) Volcano

42. Which is the only Asian country represented in G-7 Group?
(a) India   (b) China
(c) Japan   (d) S. Korea

43. Which of the following Asian languages are official languages of United Nations?
(a) Chinese and Japanese
(b) Chinese and Hindi
(c) Japanese and Arabic
(d) Arabic and Chinese

44. The best colour(s) for a sun umbrella will be :
(a) black
(b) black on top and white inside
(c) white on top and black inside
(d) printed in seven colours of rainbow

45. Hargobind Khurana is credited with the discovery of:
(a) Synthesis of proteins
(b) Synthesis of genes
(c) Insulin
(d) None of these

46. Madhav ranks thirteenth in a class of thirty-one. What is his rank from the last?
(a) 15   (b) 17
(c) 18   (d) None of these

47. Neha says 'Rohan's father is the only son of my father. How is Neha related to Rohan?
(a) Cousin   (b) Aunt
(c) Sister   (d) Daughter

48. Which State of India has the largest coastline?
(a) Kerala   (b) Tamil Nadu
(c) Gujarat   (d) Andhra Pradesh

49. Who was the first Arab writer to receive Nobel Prize in literature?
(a) Yusuf Idris   (b) Yusuf Sibai
(c) Najib Mahfooz   (d) Ahmad Hadrani

50. Who is considered to be the architect of White Revolution?
(a) M.S. Swaminathan
(b) N.E. Borlaug
(c) K.M. Panikkar
(d) V. Kurien

PART–A-2

Complete the names of the following well-known Indian writers.

51. Vidia S.

52. Girish

53. Vikram

54. Bhishm

55. Shivram

56. Indira

Give short answers to the following questions (one or two words only).

57. 'Cleopatra' was the queen of which country?

58. What was added recently to the old well-known slogan 'Jai Jawan, Jai Kisan -------?

59. Which Indian author known internationally, was recently involved with 'Narmada Bachao Andolan'?

60. Which politician and former Union Minister did Amitabh Bachchan defeated in the Lok Sabha Elections of 1984?

61. According to Hindu mythology, which goddess is credited with having invented Sanskrit?

62. The Meiji Restoration in 1868 returned which country to direct imperial rule?

63. What did the Republic of France officially gift to the U.S.A. on the hundredth anniversary of American Independence?

64. Which Indian grammarian is credited with writing 'Ashtadhyayi'?

65. Which post did B.R. Ambedkar hold in independent India's first Cabinet?

66. The autobiography of which woman writer is titled 'Rasidi Ticket?

67. How is Gaul, an ancient country, known today?

68. With what do you associate Pascal and Java languages?

69. Who set *Sare Jahan se Achchha* to music?

70. Which is the first month of the Indian (lunar) calendar?

71. *'Formula Sirf Bharat ke pass hai* refers to which product and brand in a T.V. commercial?

72. In which State of India are Ajanta caves situated?

73. What is Mesopotamia today known as?

74. What was the profession of late Mr. Daniel Pearl?

75. What do you associate Kanjivaram, Chanderi, Patola with?

76. What do you associate Kathakali, Kuchipudi and Odissi with?

77. Who has directed the film 'Lagaan ?

78. Write the name of the singer of the Hindi popular song 'Lift kara de'.

The following words are spelt wrongly. Write the correct spellings for each:

79. vulnarable

80. divertion

81. contension

82. profesion

Directions (83- 92): *Fill in the blanks in the following sentences with appropriate articles/prepositions:*

Some robbers entered **(83)** ------ bank and, pointing guns at **(84)** ------ customers, asked **(85)** -------- cashier **(86)** -------- hand over all **(87)** ------ cash **(88)** ------ them. The cashier put all the money **(89)** ------ a leather bag quietly pushed it **(90)** ---- the counter **(91)** ------ one of **(92)** ----- robbers.

93-96. The English word SINCERELY has nine letters. Using different combinations of these letters make four words (93, 94, 95, 96) of five or more letters each.

97. Select the correct synonym of the word CREDITABLE from the words given below : believable, honest, sincere, praiseworthy

98. Select the correct antonym of the word TRADITIONAL from the words given below: superstitious, secular, modern, futuristic

Each of the following sentences has an error in it. Identify and correct that part of the sentence.

99. You are cordially invited/to a dinner party/ to be held at 7.30 p.m. at Sunday/ in Grand Banquet hall.

100. Many people assembled /to condemn the violent riots/ that had taken place/through many parts of the city.

PART–B

101. What is a Simputer?

102. 38th Parallel divides which two countries in the Far East?

103. Write the full name of the School of JNU which you are seeking admission to?

104. If FRIEND is coded as HUMJTK, how is CANDLE written in this code?

105. In a certain code, 15789 is written as EGKPT and 2346 is written as ALUR how is 23549 written in that code?

106. Samir's rank is tenth from the top in his class. Prabir, who is fifteenth from the end, is lower in rank than Samir by ten. How many students are there in Samir's class?

107. Abhinav walked 2 kms west of his house and then turned south covering 4 kms. Finally, he moved 3 kms towards east and then again 1 km west. How far is he from his initial position?

108. Five persons were playing card game sitting in a circle all facing the center. Mukund was to the left of Rajesh. Vijay was to the right of Anil and between Anil and Nagesh. Who was to the right of Nagesh?

109. Which script(s) do we use to write Hindi and Marathi?

110. What are *apostrophe*, *hyphen*, and *semicolon* part of?

111. Name two Indians other than Rabindra Nath Tagore who have received the Nobel Prize?

112. What are the first two letters in the Greek alphabet?

One in the each of the following groups is different from the other four. Choose the odd one out :

113. ECA—JHF—OMK—TRP—UWY

114. AOT—CPA—REB—TIW—OUD

115. Diamond—Ruby—Topaz—Garnet—Pearl

116. Magadhi—Gujarati—Malayalam—Urdu— Marathi

In the following number series, find out the wrong figure.

117. 10, 26, 74, 218, 654, 1946, 5834

118. 56, 72, 90, 110, 132, 150

Which number can be placed at the sign of the question mark (?) in 119 and 120?

119. 9, 25, 49, 81, 121, ?

120. 17, 19, 23, 29, 31, ?, 41

Answer 121, 122, 123 after reading the following information.

A training college has to conduct a refresher course for teachers of six different subjects— Education, Psychology, Philosophy, Economics, Science and Engineering from 22nd July to 28th July.

(i) The course should start with Psychology.

(ii) 23rd July, being Sunday, should be a holiday.

(iii) Science subject should be on the previous day of the Engineering subject.

(iv) Course should end with Education subject.

(v) Philosophy should be immediately after the holiday.

(vi) There should be a gap of one day between Economics and Engineering.

121. Which subject will be on Tuesday?

122. Which subject precedes Education?

123. How many days' gap is there in between Science and Philosophy?

124. How many of the following blanks can be filled with 'to'?

(*a*) I am grateful ----- you.

(*b*) He is fully contented ----- his life.

(*c*) He is averse -------- hard work.

(*d*) He is not eligible ------- the post of Manager.

Expand the following well-known acronyms:

125. VSNL

126. POTO

127. NDDB

128. Ph.D

129. M.B.A.

130-131. *Write two short sentences (30-31) on the benefits of learning a foreign language?*

132-133 **Write two complete sentences (32, 33) about the medium of instruction in your school and the language you know.**

134-138. Complete 34 and give one-line answers to 35, 36, 37, 38 after reading the following passage:

An electronic mail system is a method of electronically sending messages, mail or documents. It is also known as electronic delivery or electronic document communication. E-mail seeks to replace the old postal and tele-communications system where a person is not sure whether the recipient would receive post through ordinary mail. Studies show that 25-30 per cent of telephone calls go through on the first attempt. Thus on an average, four calls are required to complete one. A few months ago, there was a news report that a person received his letter after 24 years. It sounds funny and interesting but think of him who got the letter after so long.

134. Electronic mail system is also known as ---- (complete the sentence).

135. What does E-mail seek to achieve?

136. What is the risk/ shortcoming in the old postal and tele-communication system?

137. What do studies show about telephone calls?

138. What is the 'funny and interesting' incident mentioned in the passage?

Use the following words in simple sentences of your own:

139. recipient

140. replace

141. documents

142. delivery

The following words are from language X. Look at the words carefully and then translate the sentences that follow (143-147) into English:

rud	= sleep	grish	= warm
rudwa	= slept	nagrish	= cold
sis	= child	ag	= come
ama	= mother	hap	= sit
op	= in/on	tera	= ground/floor
kib	= bed/cot	sisk	= child's
va	= near/ towards	gud	= lap

(ama hapwa op kib = mother sat on bed)

143. sis agwa va ama.

144. ama hapwa op nagrish tera.

145. sis rudwa op grish kib.

146. ama agwa va sisk kib.

147. sis hapwa ama grish gud.

148. Who appoints the Governor of a State in India.

149. How many of the following words are used both as noun and verb?

speech	influence	thought	curl
record	difference	use	trial

150. The coach arrived at the playground at 8.35. Rakesh arrived 45 minutes late and was 15 minutes late for the training. By how much time did the coach come earlier than the scheduled time?

ANSWERS

1	2	3	4	5	6	7	8	9	10
(b)	(a)	(a)	(d)	(d)	(c)	(c)	(b)	(c)	(a)

11	12	13	14	15	16	17	18	19	20
(b)	(b)	(c)	(d)	(d)	(b)	(b)	(c)	(d)	(b)

21	22	23	24	25	26	27	28	29	30
(b)	(d)	(d)	(c)	(c)	(d)	(c)	(d)	(b)	(d)

31	32	33	34	35	36	37	38	39	40
(b)	(c)	(d)	(b)	(a)	(c)	(b)	(b)	(d)	(c)

41	42	43	44	45	46	47	48	49	50
(d)	(c)	(d)	(c)	(b)	(d)	(b)	(c)	(c)	(d)

51. Vidia S. Naipaul
52. Girish Karnad
53. Vikram Seth
54. Bhishm Sahni
55. Shivram Karantha
56. Indira Gandhi/Indira Goswami
57. Rome
58. Jai Vigyan
59. Arundhati Roy
60. Dr. Murli Manohar Joshi
61. Saraswati
62. Japan
63. Statue of Liberty
64. Panini
65. Law minister
66. Amrita Pritam
67. France
68. Computer
69. Ravi Shankar
70. Chaitra
71. Meswak
72. Maharashtra
73. Iraq
74. Journalism
75. Saree

76. Dance
77. Ashutosh Gowarikar
78. Adnan Sami
79. Vulnerable
80. Diversion
81. Contention
82. Profession
83. the
84. the
85. the
86. to
87. the
88. to
89. in
90. to
91. towards
92. the
93. SINCE
94. SINCERE
95. NIECE
96. SCIENCE
97. believable
98. Modern
99. to be held at 7.30 p.m. on Sunday.
100. in many parts of city.

101. Simputer is another form of computer.

102. North and South Korea.

103. School of languages.

104. EDRIRL

105. ALGUT

106. 34 students

107. 4 km

108. MUKUND

109. Devnagri

110. Sentence

111. Dr. C.V. Raman, Dr. Amartya Sen

112. Alpha (α), Beta (β)

113. UWY

114. AOT as all other have two consonents.

115. Garnet (all other are gems where a garnet is used to make gems)

116. Magadhi

117. 654 it should be 650

118. 150

119. 169, square of consecutive prime number

120. 37, next prime number

121. Economics

122. Engineering

123. One

124. (*a*) to (*b*) to (*c*) to (*d*) for

125. VSNL—Videsh Sanchar Nigam Limited.

126. POTO—Prevention of Terrorism Ordinance.

127. NDDB—National Dairy Development Board.

128. Ph.D—Doctor of Philosophy.

129. M.B.A.—Master of Business Administration.

130. To know the culture and civilization of that country.

131. Learning a language is also helpful in getting employment.

132. The medium of instruction in my school was Hindi.

133. I know English and Hindi.

134. e-mail

135. It seeks to replace the old systems of communication.

136. The sender is not sure whether the recipient would receive post through ordinary mail in time and four calls are required to complete one.

137. 25-30% calls go through the 1st attempt.

138. A person received his letter after 24 years.

139. Dr. Amartya Sen is a recipent of Nobel Prize.

140. Suman is replaced by Gurpreet.

141. Mr. Madhav didn't submit his documents.

142. The Pizza boy delivered the Pizza to Aishwarya.

143. Child come towards mother.

144. Mother sat on cold floor.

145. Child slept on warm bed.

146. Mother come near child's bed.

147. Child sat mother warm lap.

148. President of India.

149. Influence, record, use, trail, curl.

150. 30 minutes.

JAWAHARLAL NEHRU UNIVERSITY (JNU)

First Year of 3-Year B.A. (Hons.) in Foreign Languages

Chinese, French, German, Korean, Japanese, Arabic, Persian, Russian and Spanish

Entrance Examination, 2001

PART–A

1. What is called the Fourth Estate?
   (a) Press
   (b) Judiciary
   (c) Police
   (d) Human Rights Commission

2. A country which elects its head of State is known as:
   (a) an oligarchy   (b) a monarchy
   (c) an aristocracy   (d) a republic

3. The term of office of the French President is:
   (a) 5 years
   (b) 7 years
   (c) for life
   (d) Parliament's pleasure

4. Which of these sanctuaries is not found in South India?
   (a) Mudumalai   (b) Mukkurti
   (c) Periyar   (d) Ranthambore

5. The Khumb Mela takes place once in:
   (a) 5 years   (b) 3 century
   (c) a decade   (d) 12 years

6. In India, the census is carried out once in:
   (a) 10 years   (b) 5 years
   (c) 20 years   (d) every year

7. Which for the following zodiac signs is not represented by an animal?
   (a) Libra   (b) Aries
   (c) Cancer   (d) Leo

8. Who founded the Kinnara School of Music in 1967 in Los Angeles?
   (a) George Harrison
   (b) Uday Shankar
   (c) Ravi Shankar
   (d) Amjad Ali Khan

9. Major portion of air is made up of:
   (a) Carbon dioxide
   (b) Oxygen
   (c) Chlorine
   (d) Nitrogen

10. Which Bhakti Saint of 15th century composed "Vaishnava Jana to Tene Kahiye?
    (a) Namdev   (b) Tukaram
    (c) Narsinh Mehta   (d) Meerabai

11. Which of the following French colonies was closest to Kolkata?
    (a) Pondicherry   (b) Mahe
    (c) Karaikal   (d) Chandernagore

Find the odd man out:

12. (a) Birbal   (b) Abul Fazl
    (c) Faiz Ahmad   (d) Tansen

13. (a) Sarod   (b) Sitar
    (c) Veena   (d) Mridangam

14. (a) Saurav Ganguly
    (b) Shahid Afridi
    (c) Mushtaq Mohammad
    (d) Viswanathan Anand

15. (a) Mew   (b) Bark
    (c) Chirp   (d) Roar

16. (a) Hindi   (b) Gurmukhi
    (c) English   (d) Marathi

17. (*a*) Jharkhand—Bihar
    (*b*) Uttaranchal—Uttar Pradesh
    (*c*) Chhattisgarh—Madhya Pradesh
    (*d*) Meghalaya—Manipur

18. Which of the following can also be eaten as a dry fruit?
    (*a*) Grapes   (*b*) Bananas
    (*c*) Apples   (*d*) Oranges

19. Which of the following countries have never played in a World Cup Cricket final?
    (*a*) England   (*b*) South Africa
    (*c*) Pakistan   (*d*) Sri Lanka

Complete the following statements correctly with the most appropriate filler:

20. Unless you work hard ----
    (*a*) you ought to be successful
    (*b*) you be not successful
    (*c*) you are not being successful
    (*d*) you will not be successful

21. She ---- people who are good at music:
    (*a*) supports   (*b*) admires
    (*c*) attracts   (*d*) appeals

22. CRY is an organization dealing with -----:
    (*a*) Environment
    (*b*) Welfare of women
    (*c*) Welfare of neglected children
    (*d*) Community development

23. If book is called watch, watch is called bag, bag is called dictionary and dictionary is called window. Which is used to carry books?
    (*a*) Dictionary   (*b*) Book
    (*c*) Bag   (*d*) Watch

24. A woman introduces a man as the son of the brother of her mother. How is the man related to the woman?
    (*a*) nephew   (*b*) son
    (*c*) cousin   (*d*) uncle

In the number series given in the questions (25 to 27) below one term is missing. Choose the correct number that will continue the same pattern:

25. 5, 10, 13, 26, 29, 58, 61, ----
    (*a*) 122   (*b*) 125
    (*c*) 128   (*d*) 64

26. 12, 32, 72, 152, ----
    (*a*) 312   (*b*) 234
    (*c*) 192   (*d*) 284

27. 64, 32; 16 8; 4, (?)
    (*a*) 0   (*b*) 1
    (*c*) 2   (*d*) 4

28. Who among the following did not invade India?
    (*a*) Alexander   (*b*) Napoleon
    (*c*) Nadir Shah   (*d*) Timur

29. In which country was the music conductor Zubin Mehta bom?
    (*a*) Pakistan   (*b*) India
    (*c*) Israel   (*d*) Kenya

30. In 1876 who assumed the title of Empress of India?
    (*a*) Queen Elizabeth I
    (*b*) Queen Victoria
    (*c*) Mary Queen of Scots
    (*d*) Queen Anne

31. Which country does not share a land border with India?
    (*a*) Nepal   (*b*) Burma
    (*c*) Bhutan   (*d*) Thailand

32. Which of the following places is renowned for its cracker industry?
    (*a*) Kolhapur   (*b*) Sivakasi
    (*c*) Faizabad   (*d*) Dhanbad

33. How many members of the Rajya Sabha retire after every 2 years?
    (*a*) 1/3   (*b*) 3/4
    (*c*) 2/3   (*d*) 1/2

34. If Christmas falls on a Saturday, on which day would the New Year Eve fall?
    (*a*) Sunday   (*b*) Saturday
    (*c*) Monday   (*d*) Tuesday

35. Which of the following rivers flows into the Bay of Bengal?
    (*a*) Tungabhadra   (*b*) Mahanadi
    (*c*) Godavari   (*d*) Narmada

36. Which of the following poets is not from Maharashtra?

(*a*) Gyaneshwar   (*b*) Tukaram
(*c*) Eknath   (*d*) Kabir

37. Which former Prime Minister of India is the author of the novel 'The insider'?
(*a*) V.P. Singh   (*b*) Narasimha Rao
(*c*) Chandra Sekhar (*d*) I. K Gujral

38. Cricket World Cup 2003 will be held at:
(*a*) Johannesburg   (*b*) Melbourne
(*c*) Seoul   (*d*) Mumbai

39. The name of the sheep, which was cloned for the first time, is:
(*a*) Polly   (*b*) Dolly
(*c*) Holly   (*d*) Molly

40. The Shahnama was written by:
(*a*) Al-Beruni   (*b*) Firdausi
(*c*) Amir Khusrao   (*d*) Abul Fazl

Fill in the blank with the most appropriate word:

41. The manager is very competent. He is ----- to the firm.
(*a*) a boon   (*b*) a blessing
(*c*) a credit   (*d*) an asset

42. The earthquake was ------ severe that the entire town and surrounding villages were reduced to a heap of concrete.
(*a*) too   (*b*) so
(*c*) very   (*d*) highly

43. Since you have not been true ----- your word, we shall not entrust you ---- any more work.
(*a*) upon, to   (*b*) of, with
(*c*) to, with   (*d*) by, of

44. Many people ------- whatever leisure they have at their -------
(*a*) misuse, disposal
(*b*) enjoy, time
(*c*) pursue, order
(*d*) utilize, behalf

Each of the following sentences has four parts: (a), (b), (c), (d) . One of the parts may contain an error. Select that part.

45. (*a*) The children/(*b*) were playing/ (*c*) besides the road/ (*d*) in the afternoon.

46. (a) Her bag / (*b*) is definitely / (*c*) more beautiful / (*d*) than your.

47. Which one of the following is not an Internet Service Provider in India?
(*a*) Caltiger
(*b*) Bharat Connect
(*c*) French Connection
(*d*) Satyam

48. India's largest manufacturer of Herbal products is:
(*a*) Dabur
(*b*) Jhandu
(*c*) Ayurvedic Concepts
(*d*) Biotique

49. Which of the following is not a currency that is used anywhere in the world?
(*a*) Cruzeiro   (*b*) Lira
(*c*) Peseta   (*d*) Bhat

50. The Olympic Airlines belongs to:
(*a*) Italy   (*b*) Greece
(*c*) Spain   (*d*) France

51. Which of the following is a cave temple in India?
(*a*) Perli   (*b*) Ajanta
(*c*) Ellora   (*d*) Tuljapur

52. After Kabir's death his tomb was built at:
(*a*) Varanasi   (*b*) Gorakhpur
(*c*) Magahar   (*d*) Basti

53. Which 3 former Soviet Republics form the Baltic States?
(*a*) Estonia, Latvia, Lithuania
(*b*) Uzbekistan, Kazakistan, Mongolia
(*c*) Estonia, Kazakistan, Lithuania
(*d*) Latvia, Uzbekistan, Mongolia

54. Which of the following is an epic poetry in Persian?
(*a*) Jangnama   (*b*) Shahnama
(*c*) Fatahnama   (*d*) Sulahnama

55. The famous history book *Akbarnama* was written by:
(*a*) Faizi
(*b*) Abul Fazl
(*c*) Bairam Khan
(*d*) Abdurrahim Khankhana

56. What is the offspring of an elephant called?
(*a*) Cub   (*b*) Calf
(*c*) Elephantine   (*d*) Kid

57. Film 'Teesari Kasam' was based on a famous story of which writer?
(*a*) Phanishwarnath 'Renu'
(*b*) Munshi Premchand
(*c*) Krishan Chander
(*d*) Rabindra Nath Tagore

58. According to Hindu mythology, who invented the instrument Veena?
(*a*) Saraswati   (*b*) Menaka
(*c*) Narad   (*d*) Indra

59. Which of the following is not a synonym of the word language?
(*a*) Diction   (*b*) Dialect
(*c*) Lingua franca   (*d*) Vernacular

60. Which of the following words is spelt wrongly?
(*a*) Miscellanious   (*b*) Observance
(*c*) Fluorescent   (*d*) Mischievous

61. What is the unit of Korean currency?
(*a*) Yuan   (*b*) Won
(*c*) Yen   (*d*) Bhat

62. What is the group of Korean electronic companies operating in India?
(*a*) Daewoo, Samsung
(*b*) Hyundai, Daewoo
(*c*) L.G., Hyundai
(*d*) Samsung, L.G.

63. The name of Balraj Sahni's 'Do Bigha Jamin' was taken from the name of a poem by a famous poet. Name the poet.
(*a*) Rabindra Nath Tagore
(*b*) Bankim Chandra Chatterjee

(*c*) Sumitra Nandan Pant
(*d*) Ramdhari Singh Dinkar

64. Which European country's official languages are French, Italian, German?
(*a*) Switzerland   (*b*) Italy
(*c*) France   (*d*) Netherlands

65. The hosts of the popular music programme 'Sa Re Ga Ma' on T.V. are the sons of which famous musician?
(*a*) Vilayat Khan
(*b*) Amir Khan
(*c*) Amjad Ali
(*d*) Mallikarjun Mansoor

66. Indonesia is situated in:
(*a*) South-East Asia   (*b*) Far East
(*c*) West Asia   (*d*) Central Asia

Which of the following is NOT correctly matched?

67. (*a*) Sachin Tendulkar   – Cricket
(*b*) Sergio Garcia   – Golf
(*c*) Pele   – Football
(*d*) Ramanathan Krishnan   – Hockey

68. (*a*) Bismillah Khan   – Shehnai
(*b*) L. Subramaniam   – Violin
(*c*) Kadrigopalnath   – Veena
(*d*) Zakir Hussain   – Tabla

69. (*a*) Garba   – Kashmir
(*b*) Bhangra   – Punjab
(*c*) Ghumar   – Rajasthan
(*d*) Kummi   – Tamil Nadu

70. Select the correct synonym of the given word out of the four choices given below
Adept:
(*a*) manage   (*b*) adroit
(*c*) divert   (*d*) suit

PART-B

71. During a Solar eclipse the shadow of what falls on what?
(*a*) Moon on Sun
(*b*) Moon on Earth
(*c*) Earth on Moon
(*d*) Earth on Sun

72. Jim Corbett National Park is in?
(*a*) Uttaranchal   (*b*) Uttar Pradesh
(*c*) Bihar   (*d*) Rajasthan

73. Which is the hardest substance in the human body?

(*a*) Skull bone   (*b*) Tooth enamel
(*c*) Knee cap   (*d*) Finger nail

74. What words were inscribed in the first postage stamp issued in India after independence?
(*a*) Vande Mataram
(*b*) Satyameva Jayate
(*c*) Jai Hind
(*d*) Azad Hind

75. The Elisa test is used to detect:
(*a*) Cancer   (*b*) Tuberculosis
(*c*) AIDS   (*d*) Dengue

76. Who introduced political cartoons in South India?
(*a*) Subramanya Bharathi
(*b*) Kamaraj
(*c*) R.K. Lakshman
(*d*) Moopanar

77. Who was the first External Affairs Minister of Independent India?
(*a*) Abul Kalam Azad
(*b*) Vijaya Lakshmi Pundit
(*c*) Jawaharlal Nehru
(*d*) N.V. Gadgil

78. January 12th is celebrated as National Youth Day in memory of:
(*a*) Jawaharlal Nehru
(*b*) Rajiv Gandhi
(*c*) Radhakrishnan
(*d*) Swami Vivekananda

79. The first satellite launched by India was:
(*a*) Bhaskara   (*b*) Aryabhatta
(*c*) Insat Apple   (*d*) Ariane

80. Which city originally consisted of 7 islands called Heptanasia by the Greeks?
(*a*) Kolkata   (*b*) Mumbai
(*c*) Mangalore   (*d*) Cochin

81. If EXIST is coded as ESIXT, how would PLUTO be coded?
(*a*) PTULO   (*b*) POTUL
(*c*) PLOUT   (*d*) TOPLU

82. If CRICKET is coded as BQHBJDS then FLOWER will be code as:
(*a*) GKPVFC   (*b*) LMWDS
(*c*) GMPVDS   (*d*) EKNVDQ

83. If PENSION is coded as NEISNOP, how is FOLIAGE coded:
(*a*) OFILGAE   (*b*) EGAILOF
(*c*) EOAILGF   (*d*) FILOGAE

84. What is a Geiger counter used to measure?
(*a*) Radioactivity   (*b*) Salinity of water
(*c*) Pressure   (*d*) Seismic waves

85. Who defined democracy as government of the people by the people and for the people?
(*a*) Winston Churchill
(*b*) Abraham Lincoln
(*c*) George Washington
(*d*) Napoleon Bonaparte

86. Which Governor General of British India later become the first Viceroy of India?
(*a*) Lord Dalhousie
(*b*) Lord Canning
(*c*) Lord Wellesley
(*d*) Lord Hastings

87. Who holds the post of the Chairperson of the Planning Commission of India?
(*a*) President
(*b*) Prime Minister
(*c*) Finance Minister
(*d*) Minister of Planning

88. When was the first census held in India?
(*a*) 1872   (*b*) 1945
(*c*) 1790   (*d*) 1848

In each of the following questions select the proper sequence of the parts labelled P, Q, R, S, so as to make a meaningful paragraph.

89. P.   Buildings constructed in reclaimed land were severely affected throughout the state.
Q.   So a new approach to construction is required in order to build a quake resistant Gujarat.
R.   On the other hand, buildings on solid ground saw few casualties and minimal damage.
S.   On January 26th a severe earthquake ravaged the State of Gujarat.
(*a*) SPRQ   (*b*) QPRS
(*c*) RSQP   (*d*) PSRQ

90.
P. Yet paradoxically, man and medicine share an uncertain future on the threshold of the 21st century.
Q. Many a life has been saved, many marvels performed and many have reaped the benefits of this change.
R. Over the last 100 years, science has changed the world and changed medicine with it.
S. This is because mechanisation of medicine has robbed it of its essence, its humanism.
(a) RQPS
(b) PSRQ
(c) QPSR
(d) SRPQ

91.
P. Mount Abu is a part of the Aravalli
Q. about 1685 metres above sea level
R. range in Rajasthan, and
S. its highest peak, the Guru Shikhara, is
(a) PRSQ
(b) PQRS
(c) SPRQ
(d) QPSR

92. Who among the following personalities did not receive the Nobel Peace Prize?
(a) Mikhail Gorbachov
(b) Mahatma Gandhi
(c) Aung San Su Kyi
(d) Yasser Arafat

93. A caddie is found in:
(a) a golf course
(b) zoo
(c) car park
(d) market

94. What does GMT stand for?
(a) Greenland Mean Time
(b) Greenland Mean Temperature
(c) Greenwich Mean Time
(d) Greenwich Mean Temperature

95. Which of these films won a record of 11 Oscars?
(a) Gandhi
(b) Sixth Sense
(c) Jurassic Park
(d) Titanic

96. Which State in the U.S. has been recognized as sister state to Gujarat?
(a) California
(b) Texas
(c) Ohio
(d) Kansas

97. How many rectangles are there in the following figure?

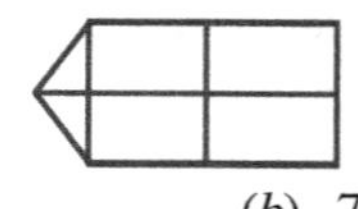

(a) 6
(b) 7
(c) 8
(d) 9

98. How many triangles are there in the following figure?

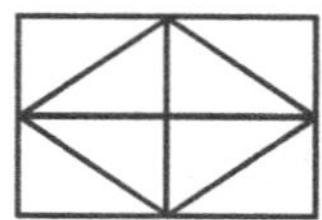

(a) 8
(b) 10
(c) 12
(d) 14

99. The word given below is followed by four other words. Only one of these four words can be formed from the letters used in the given word. Find that word.

CONSTANTINOPLE.
(a) Conscience
(b) Content
(c) Continue
(d) Constance

100. Atul travelled 3 kms Southwards, then turned right and travelled 5 kms. Then again turned right and travelled 7 kms. In which direction was he travelling last?
(a) East
(b) West
(c) North
(d) South

Select the correct meaning of the sentences given below, out of the four responses (a), (b), (c) and (d) which follow each sentence.

101. It is too cold to go out.
(a) It is extremely cold for going out.
(b) It is not cold enough to go out.
(c) It is so cold that one cannot go out.
(d) It is such cold that one cannot go out.

102. This is one of the best novels I have ever read.
(a) Very few novels I have ever read are as good as this.
(b) This is as good as any other novel I have ever read.
(c) This is better than any novel I have ever read.
(d) No other novel I have ever read is as good as this.

103. My sister said to me: "Let us see a film tomorrow":
(*a*) My sister told me to see a film tomorrow.
(*b*) My sister proposed that we see a film the next day.
(*c*) My sister insisted that they should see a film tomorrow.
(*d*) My sister told me that we could see a film tomorrow.

104. Zaikai in Japan are:
(*a*) The elite who control business
(*b*) Akio Morita's successor in Sony
(*c*) Name of an Ikebana School
(*d*) A popular theatre

105. Jehangir minted the words's
(*a*) smallest coins in silver
(*b*) largest coins in gold
(*c*) first diamond-studded coin
(*d*) first ruby-studded coin

106. Hirakud dam is constructed on which river:
(*a*) Kosi   (*b*) Ganga
(*c*) Sutlej   (*d*) Mahanadi

107. The Halley's comet will be seen next in:
(*a*) 2058   (*b*) 2062
(*c*) 2066   (*d*) 2068

108. The + symbol comes from:
(*a*) Latin   (*b*) French
(*c*) Persian   (*d*) Arabic

109. Arabic belongs to which of the following family of languages?
(*a*) Indo-European   (*b*) Indo-Aryan
(*c*) Aryan   (*d*) Semetic

110. At the National Film Festival Awards, for what category is 'Nargis Dutt Award' given?
(*a*) Acting
(*b*) National Integration
(*c*) Direction
(*d*) Patriotism

111. My father was a Hockey Olympian. My mother was a well-known Basketball player. Who am I?
(*a*) Sachin Tendulkar
(*b*) Leander Paes
(*c*) Prakash Padukone
(*d*) Vishwanathan Anand

112. One of the following groups has only adverbs. Which one is it?
(*a*) well, quite, then, fast
(*b*) quite, miserly, along, there
(*c*) therefore, beside, well, quiet
(*d*) well, besides, miserly, along

113. Select the correct meaning of the sentence given below, out of the four responses (*a*), (*b*), (*c*) and (*d*) which follow.
Mr. Ramesh is not so popular as some other employees.
Some employees are ------
(*a*) at least as popular as Mr. Ramesh
(*b*) more popular than Mr. Ramesh
(*c*) less popular than Mr. Ramesh
(*d*) not as popular as Mr. Ramesh

114. Dhanvantari's name is associated with:
(*a*) Sanskrit Grammar
(*b*) Sanskrit Poetry
(*c*) Indian Medicine
(*d*) Classical Music

115. Name the leader who is known as the 'Father of the Chinese Democracy'?
(*a*) Dr. Sun Yat Sen
(*b*) Zhou En Lai
(*c*) Deng Xiaoping
(*d*) Mao Zedong

116. The ancient silk route between India and China, started from Patna (then Pataliputra) in India and went up to the Chinese city:
(*a*) Chengdu
(*b*) Xian
(*c*) Tianjin
(*d*) Kunming

117. The social reformer who founded the Brahmo Samaj in 1828 at Kolkata is:
(*a*) S.P. Mukherjee
(*b*) Rabindranath Tagore

(*c*) Raja Ram Mohan Roy

(*d*) Vidya Sagar

118. Which of the following number cannot be noted in Roman numerals?

(*a*) Zero

(*b*) Fifty

(*c*) Hundred

(*d*) One thousand

In the following questions select the pair of words which has the same relationship as the Italic words.

119. *Numismatist : coins*

(*a*) Philatelist : stamps

(*b*) Jeweller : jewels

(*c*) Cartographer : maps

(*d*) Geneticist : chromosomes

120. *Balance : weigh*

(*a*) Aeroplane : height

(*b*) Radar : detection

(*c*) Satellite : rotation

(*d*) Television : picture

121. Choose from the 4 diagrams given below the one that illustrates the relationship between languages, French and German.

(*a*)

(*b*)

(*c*)

(*d*)

122. Match the words and their synonyms:

(A) Assign   (1) Assume

(B) Fierce   (2) Repair

(C) Presume   (3) Allot

(D) Mend   (4) Violent

(*a*) A3, B2, C1, D4

(*b*) A3, B4, C1, D2

(*c*) A4, B3, C1, D2

(*d*) A3, B4, C2, D1

123. Match the tools with their actions:

(A) Filter   (1) Magnify

(B) Steering   (2) Amplify

(C) Loudspeaker   (3) Drive

(D) Microscope   (4) Purify

                  (5) Observe

(*a*) A3, B4, C5, D2

(*b*) A2, B3, C4, D5

(*c*) A1, B2, C3, D4

(*d*) A4, B3, C2, D1

124. Match the products and raw materials:

(A) Shoes   (1) Latex

(B) Rubber   (2) Jute

(C) Sack   (3) Pulp

(D) Paper   (4) Leather

                  (5) Cotton

(*a*) A4, B3, C2, D5

(*b*) A4, B1, C2, D3

(*c*) A1, B4, C2, D3

(*d*) A1, B4, C5, D2

125. Match the authors with their books (Qs. 125 and 126):

(A) Otakkuzhal   (1) Tara Shankar Bandopadhyaya

(B) Mati Matal   (2) G. Shankar Kurup

(C) Gana Devata   (3) Harivanshrai Bacchan

(D) Madhushala   (4) Gopinath Mohanti

(*a*) A2, B4, C1, D3

(*b*) A2, B1, C4, D3

(*c*) A3, B1, C4, D2

(*d*) A1, B3, C4, D2

126. (A) A Suitable Boy   (1) R.K. Laxman

(B) The Circle of Reason   (2) R.K. Narayan

(C) Man Eaters of Malgudi   (3) Vikram Seth

(D) English August   (4) Upamanyu Chatterjee

                  (5) Amitav Ghosh

(*a*) A3, B2, C5, D4,

(*b*) A2, B3, C5, D4

(*c*) A3, B5, C2, D4

(*d*) A2, B5, C1, D3

127. Match the world leaders with their countries:

(A)	Helmut Kohl	(1)	Indonesia
(B)	Abdurrahman Wahid	(2)	Hellanic Republic
(C)	Constantine Simitis	(3)	Germany
(D)	Abdelaziz Baiteflika	(4)	Iran
		(5)	Algeria

- (a) A3, B1, C4, D2
- (b) A3, B1, C2, D5
- (c) A1, B2, C3, D4
- (d) A2, B4, C5, D1

128. Match the musicians and the instruments:

(A)	Lalgudi G. Jayaraman	(1)	Santoor
(B)	Shivkumar Sharma	(2)	Sarangi
(C)	Amjad Ali Khan	(3)	Violin
(D)	Chitti Babu	(4)	Sarod
		(5)	Veena

- (a) A2, B1, C4, D5
- (b) A5, B2, C1, D3
- (c) A3, B2, C4, D5
- (d) A3, B1, C4, D5

129. Match the following personalities with their specializations:

(A)	Manjit Bawa	(1)	Dance
(B)	Habib Tanvir	(2)	Sports
(C)	Ramanathan Krishnan	(3)	Painting
(D)	Yamini Krishnamurthi	(4)	Theatre

- (a) A3, B4, C2, D1
- (b) A2, B1, C3, D4
- (c) A2, B3, C4, D1
- (d) A1, B4, C2, D3

130. Match the beaches and the States:

(A)	Calangute	(1)	Maharashtra
(B)	Juhu	(2)	Tamil Nadu
(C)	Marina	(3)	Kerala
(D)	Kovalam	(4)	Goa

- (a) A4, B1, C2, D3
- (b) A3, B2, C1, D4
- (c) A4, B1, C3, D2
- (d) A3, B1, C2, D4

131. Match the following dishes with the places they are associated with:

(A)	Dhokla	(1)	Gujarat
(B)	Pongal	(2)	Punjab
(C)	Sarson ka Saag	(3)	Kashmir
(D)	Ghostaba	(4)	Tamil Nadu
		(5)	Andhra Pradesh

- (a) A2, B3, C5, D4
- (b) A3, B4, C1, D2
- (c) A1, B4, C2, D3
- (d) A5, B3, C4, D2

Read the following carefully and answer the questions (132 & 133) that are given below:

sabi	= girl	mogi	= woman
sabe	= girls	koko	= there
ar	= is	aran	= is not
ni	= in	gaku ni	= in the school
yane	= room	osoi	= fat

132. If

Sabe koko ni aar = Girls are there,
How will you say 'Women are in the room'
- (a) Moge aar yane ni
- (b) Mogi aar ni yane
- (c) Mogi yane ni aar
- (d) Moge yane ni aar

133. Girl is not fat:
- (a) Sabi aran osoi
- (b) Sabi osoi aran
- (c) Sabe osoi ar
- (d) Sabi ar osoi

134. In a code language 'mu kay cit' means 'very lucky person' and 'dis hu mu' means 'fortunate and lucky'. Which is the word for lucky in that language?
- (a) mu
- (b) kay
- (c) cit
- (d) hu

135. Which number can be placed at the sign of interrogation?

6	6	8
5	7	5
4	3	?
120	126	320

- (a) 4
- (b) 8
- (c) 12
- (d) 16

ANSWERS

1	2	3	4	5	6	7	8	9	10
(a)	(d)	(b)	(d)	(d)	(a)	(a)	(c)	(d)	(b)

11	12	13	14	15	16	17	18	19	20
(d)	(c)	(d)	(d)	(c)	(b)	(d)	(a)	(b)	(d)

21	22	23	24	25	26	27	28	29	30
(a)	(c)	(a)	(c)	(a)	(a)	(c)	(b)	(b)	(b)

31	32	33	34	35	36	37	38	39	40
(d)	(b)	(a)	(b)	(b)	(d)	(d)	(a)	(b)	(b)

41	42	43	44	45	46	47	48	49	50
(d)	(b)	(c)	(a)	(c)	(d)	(c)	(a)	(a)	(b)

51	52	53	54	55	56	57	58	59	60
(b)	(c)	(a)	(b)	(b)	(a)	(a)	(a)	(b)	(a)

61	62	63	64	65	66	67	68	69	70
(b)	(d)	(d)	(a)	(c)	(a)	(d)	(c)	(a)	(b)

71	72	73	74	75	76	77	78	79	80
(b)	(a)	(b)	(b)	(c)	(c)	(b)	(d)	(b)	(b)

81	82	83	84	85	86	87	88	89	90
(a)	(d)	(c)	(a)	(b)	(b)	(b)	(a)	(a)	(a)

91	92	93	94	95	96	97	98	99	100
(a)	(b)	(a)	(c)	(a)	(a)	(d)	(c)	(b)	(c)

101	102	103	104	105	106	107	108	109	110
(a)	(a)	(b)	(a)	(b)	(d)	(b)	(b)	(d)	(b)

111	112	113	114	115	116	117	118	119	120
(b)	(d)	(b)	(c)	(d)	(b)	(c)	(a)	(a)	(b)

121	122	123	124	125	126	127	128	129	130
(d)	(b)	(d)	(b)	(a)	(c)	(b)	(d)	(a)	(a)

131	132	133	134	135
(c)	(d)	(b)	(a)	(b)

YOUR SPACE